THE HOTTEST WATER

IN CHICAGO

The Hottest Water in Chicago

Notes of a Native Daughter

GAYLE PEMBERTON

Wesleyan University Press
Published by University Press of New England
Hanover and London

Wesleyan University Press
Published by University Press of New England, Hanover, NH 03755
© 1992 by Gayle Pemberton
Originally published in the United States in 1992 by Faber and Faber, Inc.
Wesleyan University Press paperback 1998
Printed in the United States of America   5   4   3   2   1
CIP data appear at the end of the book

Table of Contents

Acknowledgments

Many thanks to Wendy Lesser, Frank Burroughs, Wendy Wipprecht, and Betsy Uhrig for their encouragement, advice, and confidence.

"Do He Have Your Number, Mr. Jeffrey?" first appeared in the *Threepenny Review*.

"I Light Out for the Territory" first appeared in the *Southwest Review*.

"The Hottest Water in Chicago," "On Andrew Wyeth, Checked Suits, Broken Hair, Busted Dreams, and Transcendence," and "The Koan of Nana" first appeared in the *Yale Review* under the title, "None of the Above."

To the memory of my father, Lounneer.

To my mother, Muriel, and my sister, Carolyn, who really have endured.

And to all my fabulous friends, especially Katharine Stall and Jane Eisenhaure O'Brien, who continued to believe in my book and me when I had given up on the both of us.

PART ONE

The Hottest Water
in Chicago

MY FATHER DIED sometime during the wee morning hours of November 12, 1977. He had retired just a few months before and had been ill for longer than that, although none of us really admitted it. He was a "race man"—that is, for almost all of his adult life he worked for an organization that promotes racial equality. Because of the nature of his life, and because he was my father, I had always wanted him to write his memoirs. The whole family thought it a good idea and an exciting project for his retirement. It was agreed, just between my father and me, that I would help him write them.

In the early evening of November 12, 1977, I found three sheets of yellow legal paper on top of the television, sandwiched between a couple of *Good Housekeeping* and *Ebony* magazines. In my father's patented scrawl were the beginnings of his story. It went something like this:

> When I was ten years old I had a job cleaning shit off the boots of black stockyard workers in Clarinda, Iowa. There were three kinds of shit on them: sheep shit, horse shit, and chicken shit. Sheep shit is the worst of all and was nearly impossible to get off.

I haven't researched it myself, but I believe my father, and since reading those pages I have avoided sheep shit like the plague.

He hadn't had a chance to retire. He went from work to the throes of death. He hadn't had a chance to write more than those three pages. I will always wonder whether my reading of his work is correct: that for him, at least, talking about real shit was an appropriate beginning to the story of a life that was steeped in all kinds of it, both real and figurative, and a lot messier than the sheep variety. I will always wonder, too, because I never heard him say the word *shit*.

I cannot help him tell his story. I cannot tell it on my own, either. But I can ghost a tiny part of it now, even though I know of it in only the barest of ways. This part of the story meant a lot to him, and I think my father would okay my version of it, for we had planned to name the entire book after this episode from his working days. It's called "The Hottest Water in Chicago," and, naturally, it is for my father.

The setting is Chicago, of course, in the very early 1950s. Bigger Thomas has been dead for more than ten years; we listen to "Helen Trent" on the radio; we watch "Gang Busters" and "Boston Blackie" on our twelve-inch television — and the fights on Friday night, when my father lifts his portly frame out of his armchair, drops to his knees, and shadowboxes with the flickering images on the screen. We live in a housing project on the South Side, a very nice one as projects go. And when I saw it last, only a few years ago, I thought it had aged very well, weathering generations of youngish black people clinging to the edge of the middle class, the bricks and glass and sidewalks still in place. We lived in Chicago only until I left the first grade. My sister, who later taught in its schools for a number of years, always said it was a good idea we left when we did; otherwise neither of us would have been able to read much now and I certainly would not be able to write this.

I remember being at home with my mother, watching her iron one oxford-cloth shirt after another. She would pull each

4

one out of the refrigerator, already sprinkled and damp from being inside a large plastic bag that had the hint of an odor of mildew. It took about twenty minutes per shirt, and her work was impeccable. Then she would fold them, professional laundry style, and pile them on the dining room table, atop a sheet of newspaper. My father always needed two shirts per day: one for the day's work and a fresh one to wear at night to the interminable community meetings that kept him, throughout his career, away more often than home.

I would do my best to help, which sometimes meant concentrating on a drawing while I sat at a little table in the corner. At other times it meant playing laundry messenger by dropping the shirts onto the kitchen floor. One day — Mother ironing, of course — we were watching "The Bickersons" on TV, with Frances Langford and Don Ameche. At the commercial break, the show went off the air, never to return. Both my mother and I, separately, through the years, have sought corroboration for this major event, and we both have failed.

All in all, I don't recall much about my home life then, probably because things went smoothly. We ate regularly; I got Easter clothes and usually what I'd asked for from Santa. My sister, who is five years older than I am, terrorized me whenever a siren went off, with stories of the earth blowing up. And she tried her best to lose me when my mother would say to her, "Take your sister with you." No, nothing really remarkable. It took several years for me to learn that often my father had no more than a nickel in his pocket, that his paychecks were regularly late, and that my mother all too often had to fend off offensive phone calls from nasty, ill-mannered credit managers.

Most of my recollections of Chicago in those days are images from outside my home, and they are always painted gray. It's a scientific fact, you know, that Chicago is the grayest city on earth. It makes the gray of New York, or San Francisco, or Pittsburgh, or London, or Paris, or Moscow seem positively blue. Another reason I think of gray and Chicago probably has to do with the fact that I was much smaller then, closer to the pavement and the high curbs that seemed like mountains as I approached them. My father, taking my hand, would say, "Jump up!" and I still have a few tiny scars on my knees from those moments when my timing was bad.

The grayness had a sound track too: of sirens, for it seemed as if the whole city was in a perpetual state of burning, a habit formed in 1879. Of the El: we drove across Sixty-third Street on gray Sundays after church, turning onto it from South Parkway, now Martin Luther King, Jr. Drive, and there the El was a noisy, black, frightening umbrella, resembling a Mondrian painting gone out of control. Of streetcars: on State Street they were ready, I was sure, to jump the track as they careened through intersections, on either the left or right set of wheels, with their bells not sonorous but muffled, doing a frenzied *dink-dink-dink-dink-dink-dink-dink-dink-dink*.

There was no Dan Ryan Expressway cutting a tornadic swath through the city. The Loop was a full hour's ride away by streetcar and bus — Mother didn't like the El either — and I remember going there only when someone was coming to town or leaving. My mother, sister, and I would go to California in the summers to visit Nana and Papa, my mother's parents. We'd leave from Dearborn Station if we were riding the Santa Fe, or Union Station if we were taking the Southern Pacific or the Union Pacific. We'd pick up Grandma, my father's mother, from the Illinois Central Station because she came in on the New York Central or the Pennsylvania line from Ohio. I even remember going to the Rock Island Station for friends and relatives from Minnesota who came through Chicago, always on their way to somewhere else. The only other times I went to the Loop were when I was ill, which was often enough. Then, we had to take the El.

Chicago stank. The stockyards sent their bloody odors wafting through the summer evening air. The city dump blew the same smell, at least once a week, I swear, as that of a can of tomato juice that has been sitting in a refrigerator for five days. And there was another smell, one that persists today, after the dump and the stockyards have gone: of burnt potatoes. I have yet to discover its source.

I have other memories of Chicago, too: of being out at 1:00 A.M. with my sister the night Martin Luther King, Jr., was assassinated, and Chicago was burning, riding around in Scotty, her green VW, and seeing National Guard troops riding in jeeps with real live guns mounted on them; and of driving to Midway Airport, on the wrong street, as it were, and passing a building with a huge, white swastika painted on its side; of seeing Sixty-third Street as it looked the last time I saw it, with the street, the buildings, and the El in tatters. Dresden in 1945 looked better.

But those more recent memories are not important for this story. I mention them only to suggest that time passes very slowly and there is much in Chicago that never, ever changes. It is still gray; it still stinks; and it is still largely racially segregated.

But one morning in 1954, the owner of a hotel on Michigan Avenue, just south of the Loop, decided to make a change. The following is my scenario and, at this stage of the story, probably as likely as my father's since he never discovered any intentionality behind the act.

The Supreme Court has just ruled in favor of *Brown*, and this gets our hotel owner—let's call him Sam—to thinking: "Ya know, if they're gonna integrate the schools, I think I'll integrate my hotel. I've been turnin' away these boys, some of them in uniform from Korea, but it don't seem right to keep doin' it. I think I'll integrate this hotel."

It's Tuesday. My sister has chased me down the stairs once again. Mother is yelling at us to stop and to hurry because we're all running late. Daddy is up, drinking his seventh cup of coffee. He hasn't put on his tie yet, and he has the paper napkin folded around the collar of his oxford-cloth, button-down shirt, to keep the egg yolk from ruining one of Mother's

7

masterpieces. I sit down and start consuming milk in large quantities. No one says anything memorable.

Soon Daddy says, "Gotta go."

I say, "Can I come?"

He says, "No. Gotta see a man about a dog." Which is what he always would say to my entreaty. And since I never could go, I at least wanted the dog — but we couldn't get one of them either.

He slips away from the table, grabs his tie, puts it on, puts on his suit jacket, pats my mother on her rear, which causes her to jump and extend his name to eight syllables. He gets in the blue-painted-over-maroon Mercury four-door, and goes to his office, some forty blocks north.

My mother starts a day of ironing.

My sister goes to school.

I plan to help Mother until kindergarten begins; I am on the afternoon shift.

It is a clear, gray day, a little chillier than usual for May 18. A steady breeze is blowing from the east, off the lake, as my father makes his way up Michigan Avenue. He swears at a few drivers, thinks about having to paint the interior walls now that I've been broken of my short-lived wall-drawing habit. He wonders if he'll get paid Friday.

There isn't much on his schedule today. Until eleven he's interviewing job applicants. One of the many things my father's organization does to further the quest for racial equality is to act as a broker for firms willing to hire blacks. Applicants see my father, fill out forms, usually get some comments from him about the importance of promptness, shined shoes, and pressed pants, and then the white firm is contacted. This aspect of the business, I suspect, was not land office, but it kept my father fairly busy.

At 2:00 P.M. his superior, the director, summons him because a call has just come in from a man named Sam Somebody who owns a hotel on Michigan Avenue and who says he wants someone from my father's office to come down and spend the night. It seems the man wants to integrate his hotel. My father is delegated.

Small town Iowa in the teens and early twenties, as I understood it from my father, was a little different from other places. "It was broader in its thinking," he would say. Which meant that, as a young boy, my father met with very little discrimination. He went to grade school and junior high school with all the rest of the children in town. He visited their homes, played baseball, fought, cursed, and learned to spit with them. He shined shoes and became an expert on what could be found on their undersoles. He graduated from high school in Sioux City and then moved to Minnesota to work and to attend the university there.

Minnesota, in the twenties and thirties, was a little different from other places, too. Although the black community there — as everywhere — was kept and did keep to itself, the larger community was "broader in its thinking," he would say, so attending the university was not primarily a matter of breaking down barriers. And employment could be found in some of the farm-support industries in the Twin Cities.

There were, doubtless, many things my father chose not to discuss with his children, or perhaps with anyone. I asked him why we moved so often — four times before I was ten years old — but I never thought to ask him why he hated funerals or what kinds of discrimination he'd faced. He was never in the military; his first visit below the Mason-Dixon line was in 1972. I suspect there are a fair number of black people from my father's generation who will say that Minnesota was devoid of much unpleasantness. But whatever my father faced in Iowa, Minnesota, or anywhere else, I'll never know. I do know that his grandmother, Carrie Roberts, kept a scrapbook with all the newspaper clippings she could find that had any reference to "colored." Most of them detailed lynchings.

Now, at 3:30 P.M., my father calls my mother, making sure there will be another shirt ready. He tells her he needs an early dinner and a change of underwear because he is going downtown to integrate a hotel.

My mother says, "What?"

My father says, "I'm going to integrate a hotel."

My mother says, "What?"

My father asks if she is hard of hearing.

My mother says it sounds pretty stupid to her.

At 7:30 P.M. my father drives up to the address on Michigan Avenue. He looks at the facade of the building: five stories high, about 150 feet wide. Hanging from the third floor level is a large neon sign with the word "Hotel" flashing on and off. The sign is half a chevron, with smaller lighted printing below the horizontal "Hotel." It says, "Rooms To Rent Per Day: No Hourly Rates." A Budweiser beer sign is in the window.

He gets out of his car and walks toward the door, shaking his head slightly, biting his lower lip. Once inside, he notices a dull light shining down from a filthy chandelier coated with the remains of hundreds of insects. To his left is a single walnut counter, the baseboard of which is splintered from too many feet scraping its edge over too many years. From behind the counter a man turns to meet my father, quickly turns away, and then walks toward a tiny office in a corner. He says nothing to my father.

My father waits at the counter, leans against it, pulls out a cigarette, and notices a faint aroma of Raid. At the sixth puff of his cigarette another man appears from behind the counter. He walks around it and out to my father, extends his hand, and announces himself as Sam, the owner of the hotel.

"Are you Mr. Pemberton, from the Urban League?" he asks my father.

"Yes."

"Well good. You're going to integrate my hotel. Please follow me."

My father said the man was about five feet six inches tall,

of a slight frame. He had short, black, very straight hair that was slicked down with a heavy, perfumy pomade. He wore shiny black shoes whose heels were run over on the outsides. And he was dressed in a blue serge suit that had recently been ironed, perhaps for the fifth or sixth time since its last cleaning. There were several spots along the sleeves and a large stain on the lapel.

"Let me show you the rooms," Sam says to my father.

They walk to a single door that opens onto a gated elevator. Smells of urine and alcohol permeate the small space. My father sighs.

Sam takes my father to the third floor. As they get out of the elevator, they are met by a single, dull exit sign, pointing to a stairwell to the left. There are three equally spaced, bare lightbulbs hanging from the ceiling. On either side of the long corridor are cubicles partitioned with chicken wire, each cubicle with a dirty mattress and a rickety nightstand. On each nightstand are aluminum ashtrays, two Dixie cups, a hand towel, and a hotel-sized bar of soap. Unwrapped.

My father coughs slightly, the smell of extermination catching the smoky mucus at the base of his throat.

"I see," he says.

"Every new guest is provided a clean, newly sprayed room," Sam explains. There is an uncomfortable pause as a ragged man passes on his way to the bathroom. The man mutters something inaudible, hawks, prepares to spit, and then suppresses it.

Sam says quickly, "You need anything, you come get me at the desk. Anybody bother you, you let me know. This is a friendly establishment. And, for your information, we have the hottest water in Chicago."

My father said Sam beamed and rose on his toes with that line.

End of story.

Because of the nature of his work, and the opportunity for

it, I like to think that my father did at least one mitzvah each day. He came home tired the morning after he had integrated the hotel; he stayed in the bathroom an hour, and I could hear him talking to himself, occasionally chuckling. He came down to breakfast and surprised us with a line he reserved only for Saturdays: "And how are the sick and the afflicted this morning?"

He worked again on Friday; the paychecks were late. On Saturday we all went to the new shopping center called Evergreen Plaza, where I ate my first soft ice cream cone. And it was now safe, now policy, for a black man in Chicago to register at a particular transient hotel there, and find out whether the water could wash off the flea shit, roach shit, rodent shit, and human shit that was everywhere around him.

Twenty-seven years later I wondered what connection my father would have made between sheep shit and the hottest water in Chicago. I'm still working on that.

Antidisestablishmentarianism

OKAY, SO WHERE'S Gloria Lockerman? I want to know. Gloria Lockerman was partially responsible for ruining my life. I might never have ended up teaching literature if it had not been for her. I don't want to "call her out." I just want to know how things are, what she's doing. Have things gone well, Gloria? How's the family? What's up?

Gloria Lockerman, in case you don't recall, won scads of money on "The $64,000 Question." Gloria Lockerman was a young black child, like me, but she could spell anything. Gloria Lockerman became my nemesis with her ability, her a-n-t-i-d-i-s-e-s-t-a-b-l-i-s-h-m-e-n-t-a-r-i-a-n-i-s-m.

My parents, my sister, and I shared a house in Dayton, Ohio, with my father's mother and her husband, my step-grandfather, during the middle fifties. Sharing is an over-statement. It was my grandmother's house. Our nuclear group ate in a makeshift kitchen in the basement; my sister and I shared a dormer bedroom, and my parents actually had a room on the main floor of the house — several parts of which were off-limits. These were the entire living room, anywhere within three feet of Grandma's African violets, the windows and venetian blinds, anything with a doily on it, the refrigerator, and the irises in the backyard.

It was an arrangement out of necessity, given the unimpressive state of our combined fortunes, and it did not meet with anyone's satisfaction. To make matters worse, we had blockbusted a neighborhood. So, for the first year, I integrated the local elementary school — a thankless and relatively inhuman experience. I remember one day taking the Sunday paper route for a boy up the block who was sick. It was a beautiful spring day, dewy, warm. I walked up the three steps to a particular house and placed the paper on the stoop. Suddenly, a full-grown man, perhaps sixty or so, appeared with a shotgun aimed at me and said that if he ever saw my nigger ass on his porch again he'd blow my head off. I know — typical American grandfather.

Grandma liked spirituals, preferably those sung by Mahalia Jackson. She was not a fan of gospel and I can only imagine what she'd say if she were around to hear what's passing for inspirational music these days. She also was fond of country singers, and any of the members of "The Lawrence Welk Show." ("That Jimmy. Oh, I love the way he sings. He's from Iowa.") She was from Iowa, Jimmy was from Iowa, my father was from Iowa. She was crazy about Jimmy Dean too, and Tennessee Ernie Ford, and "Gunsmoke." She could cook with the finest of them and I wish I could somehow recreate her Parkerhouse rolls, but I lack bread karma. Grandma liked flowers (she could make anything bloom) and she loved her son.

She disliked white people, black people in the aggregate and pretty much individually too, children — particularly female children — her daughter, her husband, my mother, Episcopalianism, Catholicism, Judaism, and Dinah Shore. She had a hot temper and a mean streak. She also suffered from several nagging ailments: high blood pressure, ulcers, an enlarged heart, ill-fitting dentures, arteriosclerosis, and arthritis — enough to make anyone hot tempered and mean,

I'm sure. But to a third grader, such justifications and their subtleties were ultimately beyond me and insufficient, even though I believe I understood in part the relationship between pain and personality. Grandma scared the daylights out of me. I learned to control my nervous stomach enough to keep from getting sick daily. So Grandma plus school plus other family woes and my sister still predicting the end of the world every time the sirens went off — Grandma threatened to send her to a convent — made the experience as a whole something I'd rather forget, but because of the mythic proportions of family, can't.

I often think that it might have been better had I been older, perhaps twenty years older, when I knew Grandma. But I realize that she would have found much more wrong with me nearing thirty than she did when I was eight or nine. When I was a child, she could blame most of my faults on my mother. Grown, she would have had no recourse but to damn me to hell.

Ah, but she is on the gene. Grandma did everything fast. She cooked, washed, cleaned, moved — everything was at lightning speed. She passed this handicap on to me, and I have numerous bruises, cuts, and burns to show for it. Watching me throw pots and pans around in the creation of a meal, my mother occasionally calls me by my grandmother's first name. I smile back, click my teeth to imitate a slipping upper, and say something unpleasant about someone.

Tuesday nights were "$64,000 Question" nights, just as Sundays we watched Ed Sullivan and Saturdays were reserved for Lawrence Welk and "Gunsmoke." We would all gather around the television in what was a small, informal family section between the verboten real living room and the mahogany dining table and chairs, used only three or four times a year. I don't remember where I sat, but it wasn't on the floor since that wasn't allowed either.

As we watched these television programs, once or twice I sat briefly on Grandma's lap. She was the world's toughest critic. No one was considered worthy, apart from the above-mentioned. To her, So-and-So or Whosits could not sing, dance, tell a joke, read a line — nothing. In her hands "Ted Mack's Amateur Hour" would have lasted three minutes. She was willing to forgive only very rarely — usually when someone she liked gave a mediocre performance on one of her favorite shows.

I must admit that Grandma's style of teaching critical thinking worked as well as some others I've encountered. My father had a different approach. Throughout my youth he would play the music of the thirties and forties. His passion was for Billie Holiday, with Ella Fitzgerald, Peggy Lee, Sarah Vaughan, and a few others thrown in for a touch of variety. He enjoyed music, and when he wanted to get some musical point across, he would talk about some nuance of style that revealed the distinction between what he called "really singing" and a failure. He would say, "Now, listen to that there. Did you catch it? Hear what she did with that note?" With Grandma it was more likely to be:

"Did you hear that?"

"What?" I might ask.

"That. What she just sang."

"Yes."

"Well, what do you think of it?"

"It's okay, I guess."

"Well, that was garbage. She can't sing a note. That stinks. She's a fool."

Message across. We all choose our own pedagogical techniques.

Game shows are, well, game shows. I turned on my television the other day, and as I clicked through channels looking for something to watch I stopped long enough to hear an announcer say that the guest contestant was going to do something or other in 1981. Reruns of game shows? Well, why not? What difference does it make if the whole point is to watch people squirm, twist, sweat, blare, weep, convulse to get their hands on money and gifts, even if they end up being just "parting gifts?" (I won some of them myself once: a bottle of liquid Johnson's Wax, a box of Chunkies, a beach towel with the name of a diet soda on it, plus a coupon for a case of the stuff, and several boxes of Sugar Blobs — honey-coated peanut butter, marshmallow, and chocolate flavored crispies, dipped in strawberry flavoring for that special morning taste treat!)

Game shows in the fifties were different, more exciting. I thought the studio sets primitive even when I was watching them then. The clock on "Beat the Clock," the coat and crown on "Queen for a Day" — nothing like that mink on "The Big Payoff" that Bess Meyerson modeled — and that wire card flipper on "What's My Line" that John Charles Daly used — my, was it flimsy looking. The finest set of all, though, was on "The $64,000 Question." Hal March would stand outside the isolation booth, the door closing on the likes of Joyce Brothers, Catherine Kreitzer, and Gloria Lockerman, the music would play, and the clock would begin ticking down, like all game show clocks: *TOOT-toot-TOOT-toot-TOOT-toot-BUZZZZZZ*.

There were few opportunities to see black people on television in those days. I had watched "Amos 'n' Andy" when we lived in Chicago. But that show was a variation on a theme. Natives running around or jumping up and down or looking menacing in African adventure movies; shuffling, subservient, and clowning servants in local color movies (or any other sort); and "Amos 'n' Andy" were all the same thing: the perpetuation of a compelling, deadly, darkly humorous, and occasionally laughable idea. Nonfictional blacks on television were limited to Sammy Davis, Jr., as part of the Will Mastin Trio and afterward, or Peg Leg Bates on "The Ed Sullivan Show" on Sunday, or the entertainers who might show up on other variety shows, or Nat King Cole during his fifteen-minute program. Naturally, the appearance of Gloria Lockerman caused a mild sensation as we watched "The $64,000 Question," all assembled.

"Look at her," Grandma said.

I braced myself for the torrent of abuse that was about to be leveled at the poor girl.

"You ought to try to be like that," Grandma said.

"Huh?" I said.

"What did you say?"

"Yes, ma'am."

I was shocked, thrown into despair. I had done well in school, as well as could be hoped. I was modestly proud of my accomplishments, and given the price I was paying every day — and paying in silence, for I never brought my agonies at school home with me — I didn't need Gloria Lockerman thrown in my face. Gloria Lockerman, like me, on television, spelling. I was perennially an early-round knockout in spelling bees.

My sister understands all of this. Her own story is slightly different and she says she'll tell it all one day herself. She is a very good singer and has a superb ear; with our critical training, what more would she need? Given other circumstances, she might have become a performer herself. When she was about eleven Leslie Uggams was on Arthur Godfrey's "Talent Scouts" and was soon to be tearing down the "Name That Tune" runway, ringing the bell and becoming moderately famous. No one ever held Leslie Uggams up to my sister for image consciousness-raising. But my sister suffered nevertheless. She could out-sing Leslie Uggams and probably run as fast; she knew the songs and didn't have nearly so strange a last name. But, there she was, going nowhere in the Middle West, and there was Leslie Uggams on her way to "Sing Along With Mitch." To this day, my sister mumbles if she happens to see Leslie Uggams on television — before she can get up to change the channel — or hears someone mention her name. I told her I saw Leslie Uggams in the flesh at a club in New York. She was sitting at a table, just like the rest of us, listening with pleasure to Barbara Cook. My sister swore at me.

Grandma called her husband "Half-Wit." He was a thin, small-boned man who looked to me far more like an Indian chief than like a black man. He was from Iowa too, but that obviously did not account for enough in Grandma's eyes. He had a cracking tenor voice, a head full of dead straight black hair, reddish, dull brown skin, and large sad, dark brown eyes. His craggy face also reminded me of pictures I'd seen of Abraham Lincoln — but, like all political figures and American forefathers, Lincoln, to my family, was fair game for wisecracks, so that resemblance did Grandpa no good either. And for reasons that have gone to the grave with both of them, he was the most thoroughly henpecked man I have ever heard of, not to mention seen.

Hence, domestic scenes had a quality of pathos and high humor as far as I was concerned. My sister and I called Grandpa "Half-Wit" when we were alone together, but that seemed to have only a slight effect on our relations with him and our willingness to obey him — though I cannot recall any occasions calling for his authority. Grandma was Grandma, Half-Wit was Half-Wit — and we lived with the two of them. I have one particularly vivid memory of Grandma, an aficionada of the iron skillet, chasing him through the house waving it in the air, her narrow, arthritis-swollen wrist and twisted knuckles turning the heavy pan as if it were a lariat. He didn't get hurt; he was fleet of foot and made it out the back door before she caught him. My father's real father had been dead since the thirties and divorced from Grandma since the teens — so Half-Wit had been in place for quite some years and was still around to tell the story, if he had the nerve.

Grandma had a glass menagerie, the only one I've seen apart from performances of the Williams play. I don't think she had a unicorn, but she did have quite a few pieces. From a distance of no less than five feet I used to squint at the glass forms, wondering what they meant to Grandma, who was herself delicate of form but a powerhouse of strength, speed, and temper. I also wondered how long it would take me to die if the glass met with some unintended accident caused by me. Real or imagined unpleasantries, both in the home and outside of it, helped develop in me a somewhat melancholic nature. And even before we had moved to Ohio I found myself laughing and crying at the same time.

In the earlier fifties, in Chicago, I was allowed to watch such programs as "The Ernie Kovacs Show," "Your Show of Shows," "The Jackie Gleason Show," "The Red Skelton Show," and, naturally, "I Love Lucy." I was continually dazzled by the skits and broad humor, but I was particularly taken with the silent sketches, my favorite comedians as mime artists: Skelton as Freddy the Freeloader, Caesar and Coca in a number of roles, thoroughly outrageous Kovacs acts backed by Gershwin's "Rialto Ripples." My father was a very funny man and a skillful mime. I could tell when he watched Gleason's Poor Soul that he identified mightily with what was on the screen. It had nothing to do with self-pity. My father had far less of it than other men I've met with high intelligence, financial and professional stress, and black faces in a white world. No, my father would even say that we were all poor souls; it was the human condition. His mimicking of the Gleason character—head down, shoulders tucked, stomach sagging, feet splayed—served as some kind of release. I would laugh and cry watching either of them.

But my absolute favorite was Martha Raye, who had a way of milking the fine line between tragedy and comedy better than most. I thought her eyes showed a combination of riotous humor and terror. Her large mouth contorted in ways that seemed to express the same two emotions. Her face was a mask of profound sadness. She did for me what Sylvia Sidney did for James Baldwin. In *The Devil Finds Work*, Baldwin says, "Sylvia Sidney was the only American film actress who reminded me of a colored girl, or woman—which is to say that she was the only American film actress who reminded me of reality." The reality Raye conveyed to me was of how dreams could turn sour in split-seconds, and how underdogs, even when winning, often had to pay abominable prices. She also could sing a jazz song well, with her husky scat phrasing, in ways that were slightly different from those of my favorite singers, and almost as enjoyable.

There were no comedic or dramatic images of black women on the screen — that is, apart from Sapphire and her mother on "Amos 'n' Andy." And knowing Grandma and Grandpa taught me, if nothing else suggested it, that what I saw of black life on television was a gross burlesque — played to the hilt with skill by black actors, but still lacking reality.

Black female singers who appeared on television were, like their music, sacrosanct, and I learned from their styles, lyrics, and improvisations, lessons about life that mime routines did not reveal. Still, it was Martha Raye, and occasionally Lucille Ball and Imogene Coca at their most absurd, that aligned me with my father and his Poor Soul, and primed me to both love and despise Grandma and to see that in life most expressions, thoughts, acts, and intentions reveal their opposite polarities simultaneously.

Grandma died in 1965. I was away, out of the country, and I missed her funeral — which was probably a good idea since I might have been tempted to strangle some close family friend who probably would have launched into a "tsk, tsk, tsk" monologue about long-suffering grandmothers and impudent children. But, in another way, I'm sorry I didn't make it. Her funeral might have provided some proper closure for me, might have prompted me to organize her effect on my life sooner than I did, reconciling the grandmother who so hoped I would be a boy that she was willing to catch a Constellation or a DC-3 to witness my first few hours, but instead opted to take the bus when she heard the sad news, with the grand-mother who called me "Sally Slapcabbage" and wrote to me and my sister regularly, sending us the odd dollar or two, until her death.

I remember coming home from school, getting my jelly

sandwich and wolfing it down, and watching "The Mickey Mouse Club," my favorite afternoon show, since there was no afternoon movie. I had noticed and had been offended by the lack of black children in the "Club," but the cartoons, particularly those with Donald Duck, were worth watching. On this particular episode—one of the regular guest act days—a group of young black children, perhaps nine or ten of them, came on and sang, with a touch of dancing, "Old MacDonald Had a Farm," in an up-tempo, jazzy version. In spite of the fact that usually these guest days produced some interesting child acts, I became angry with what I saw. I felt patronized, for myself and for them. Clearly a couple of them could out-sing and out-dance any Mouseketeer—something that wasn't worth giving a thought to—but this performance was gratuitous, asymmetrical, a nonsequitur, like Harpo Marx marching through the Negro section in *A Day at the Races*, blowing an imaginary horn and exciting the locals to much singing, swinging, and dancing to a charming ditty called "Who Dat Man?"

I must have mumbled something as I watched the group singing "Old MacDonald." Grandma, passing through, took a look at what was on the screen, and at me, turned off the television, took my hand, led me to her kitchen, and sat me down at the table where she and Half-Wit ate, poured me some milk, and without so much as a blink of her eye, said, "Pay no attention to that shit."

Is it Maya? Or: Notes from Behind the Veil

DON'T GET AN allergy attack in Beverly Hills — for that matter, don't come down with any ailment that requires doctoring there — unless of course you are rich, have a solid health insurance policy that pays for everything, or are one of those people who believes that if it ain't expensive, it ain't worth having.

I had spent eleven years teaching American literature in several colleges around the country but I was rapidly becoming a classic burnt-out case. I had no grant, no paid sabbatical leave, and no job in sight when I decided to spend some time in Southern California. I went there partly because I had shown signs of terminal wanderlust — and the West Coast is the premier place in the U.S. for wanderlusting around — and partly because L.A. is such a mixture of fact, fantasy, and illusion that, as an Americanist, I felt I had to go. It's akin to going to Las Vegas, or Manhattan, or driving across Kansas or Nebraska: some things just have to be done if you consider yourself a bona fide Americanist. I came by the trip honestly: in keeping with the joke that claims that everyone in California really is from Iowa, I might have been born in Minnesota but the heavy Iowa presence in the family sufficed.

I was recuperating from an infection requiring the use of

an antibiotic, and after I stopped taking the medicine my lips swelled and I broke out in hives. Any dimwit could have guessed that I was having an allergic reaction, and considering the sort of medical history I have — long and involved — it should have been obvious to me. On many occasions I've had to be my own doctor because I've moved around too much to develop any long-standing relationship with a licensed practitioner. But, never having had a reaction to antibiotics before, I assumed that the incubation period had been too long. I thought I was probably allergic to my hand cream or bathing soap. It took me about ten days (after some serious scratching and after the pronunciation of some words became difficult) to go about finding a doctor. I found one — on the recommendation of one of those types who believes that if it ain't expensive . . .

I didn't have any health insurance at the time; I had no money and no job and my prospects for finding either were diminishing daily. With ten dollars in my wallet, and about a hundred in the bank, I drove to the recommended doctor's office in Beverly Hills.

Driving around L.A. was one of my few constant pleasures. I would charge the gasoline on a credit card (which was afterward rescinded) and go through Beverly Hills across Mulholland Drive, around and through Topanga Canyon down to the ocean, over to Malibu, back to Santa Monica, and back to my rented room near Culver City. Having been a habituée of eastern academic establishments — perhaps hanger-on might be more precise — I realized that I was supposed to dislike Southern California, love the Bay Area, and avoid national parks and kitschy places like Knott's Berry Farm and Disneyland. I do love the Bay area, never got to Yosemite, boycotted Knott's Berry Farm since it had enforced rather arrogantly an all-white policy when I was a child visiting California; I had seen Disneyland in 1956 and that was enough — but I also found L.A. to be a most interesting and beautiful place. On my drives I would think about how much money people seemed to have, how I didn't have any — still don't — and how I didn't know people with very much. Such wonderful houses, such flashy cars; I was a veritable Dorothy Gale in Oz. I had a nice car myself, but I couldn't help but notice that at any stoplight with more than three cars waiting for the green, one of them cost more than twenty thousand dollars (a lot of money at the time) and was no more than two years old. The percentages held true no matter how many cars reached the light, and actually went up on the side of luxury as more and more cars lined up. I never ceased to be amazed.

Anyway, I drove to Beverly Hills via my favorite street, Wilshire, and cut over to Santa Monica Boulevard and the area around Cedars Sinai to a medical complex housing my recommended doctor. All of the street meters were taken, so I drove to the complex garage, and on seeing the charges I prayed hard that I would be no longer than an hour and a half — ten dollars' worth. After that, the medical center could hold an automobile auction. I was carrying a clipboard with a tablet so that I could spend any waiting time writing yet another job letter. I was checked in by a friendly receptionist; I told her that I did have health insurance but this time I would pay on leaving, sat down, and began searching my brain for the right lines to snare a job.

The doctor's office was smaller and darker than I'd expected to see in Beverly Hills. There was a standard green tweed rug, one couch — early American (!) — several solid walnut-stained straight chairs with arms (I took the one right next to the door). I spent a few minutes surveying other people as they read magazines, stared blindly in front of them, or fidgeted. I wondered what was wrong with each, since I had not come to see an allergist, but rather an internist, to cut my potential losses in case I was not having an allergic reaction. The people waiting with me were not remarkable; no one I knew was there, no one who looked like a movie star, no one looking as if this would be one of the last stops before the grave. I took out my pen and started writing my job letter.

Is it Maya?

A half hour passed and I was ushered in to see the doctor, stopping first at a nurse's station to have my vital signs checked, and, of course, to be asked why I had come. Everything — apart from lips and rash — was normal. My blood pressure was lower than they expected for someone my age, weight, and race. I explained that I ran every day. The nurse said, "Oh." Then it was on to meet the doctor, who turned out to be about my age, cordial, wearing a mauvish plaid shirt under his white coat. He asked me the standard questions about allergies, what killed various members of my family, and inquired about my discomfort, which I thought was fairly obvious given the rash all over my body and my thickened lips. He then asked me about my work, where I had studied — the regular brand of questions I get because of a certain quality in my voice, a very deep resonance, that forces people to listen to me and get curious. This is a highly desirable teaching tool which, alas for those who don't have it, comes on the gene. I told him that I hoped to get work doing radio voice-overs, but that I didn't have the right contacts. (Not far from the surface of my thinking was the notion that everybody knows somebody in L.A. who's in the business. This guy's brother, for all I knew, could have been the radio voice-over broker of the West.) The doctor told me I spoke well.

My sister and I have the same voice. It's eerie. Had we the opportunities and desire, we could play audio twin-games. As it is, we are often mistaken for each other on the telephone. She used to be a French teacher, and a very good one too. When she visited France, the natives refused to believe she was from the States, insisting instead that she must be from Martinique because she had no trace of an American accent when she spoke, and she was fluent. They were just a tad shirty when she insisted she came from "She-cag-oh." It was probably Eartha Kitt who got her started on this French kick back in the fifties. We went to see "New Faces" with my parents in 1954, and my father had a number of Kitt's records. My sister even remembers all of the words to "*Sous Les Ponts de Paris*" and "Santa Baby" — no mean feat after over thirty years.

When my sister was just starting her teaching career, in order for her to become certified in the Chicago Public School System — as I have previously noted, a place to teach, perhaps, a place to matriculate, no — she had to go to an office in the Loop to fill out forms, talk to some Democratic Party politico in his position as sub-sub-superintendent, and then find out when certification exams were to be held, along with the other standard mumbo-jumbo. She waited in an office not unlike the Beverly Hills doctor's, except that I recall no pictures on the wall and surely there was one of Mayor Daley where she was. As my sister was ushered in to see the mucky-muck his secretary said, "Mr. Mucky-Muck, this is Miss Pemberton. My, she is articulate; she speaks so well."

There was nothing cutesy about the way my sister and I were raised. In the womb, we osmotically learned impeccable manners, and the occasions were rare, once on our own feet, when we had to be corrected about some breach of etiquette. None of those phrases I've heard mothers say to little children, like "magic words: please and thank you," ever crossed my mother's lips. I have since learned that there really are magic words, lots of them, and they are absolutely not "please and thank you." They are words that give rise to phrases like, "She speaks so well," or "My, she is articulate," or "Where did you say you are from?" These are, of course, northern, urban versions of their less delicate and more direct southern equivalents, like, "You mus be from the nawth," or "You ain't from 'round these parts," or "Ain't your mama the one who cleans for Pastor and Miz Hayes?" The proper retort to both northern and southern versions is "Your mama," but impeccable manners have a way of stifling spontaneity.

Several years ago a young black woman was being interviewed on one of the morning news/entertainment programs. It seems this young woman had not only recognized a former Chief Justice of the Supreme Court in a store but also had

27

walked up to him to engage in some conversation about, I believe, the disparity between blacks and whites in their cultural expectations — something like that. The woman had her four and a half minutes on screen, then the camera segued to our hostess, who noted to her partner, "My, she's so articulate, she speaks so well."

Same thing happened as I watched the 1986 World Figure Skating Championship finals. Every few seconds, it seemed, broadcasters noted with amazement that the black soon-to-be-champion, Debi Thomas, could skate so well and go to Stanford to study medicine too! And, as the camera superimposed a shot of the East German loser over the championship-winning performance so the audience could miss a few of Debi's jumps and twirls, the commentators allowed as how Debi was articulate to boot. Wow.

Actually, I prefer my fourth grade teacher's approach. There were two of us black girls in a class in Dayton, just three years after *Brown v. The Board of Education of Topeka.* On the last day of class, as we picked up our report cards and honors certificates, she boomed to us and to the rest of the amassed class, in her patented way of spitting through very large teeth, that we were pretty smart for colored girls. I do know what magic words are.

My doctor, after about five minutes of checking my yesses and nos, received a phone call, hand-signaled to me that he would be a few minutes, and talked for about twenty to a colleague. I perused the wall, checking his credentials, finding them to be acceptable but not overwhelming. I thought about how well I spoke, chalked it up to nature, nurture, and the rampant Episcopalianism that had me mouthing lines like, "We acknowledge and bewail our manifold sins and wickedness, which we from time to time, most grievously have committed, by thought, word, and deed, against thy Divine Majesty, provoking most justly thy wrath and indignation against us," from the age of six.

I looked at the doctor's shirt and thought about a madras suit I'd worn to death as a teenager that was about the same color. It had been a present for my seventeenth birthday; I got a watch too. Three weeks later, after a series of unlikely and surprising events, I was wearing the suit, standing in a massive ballroom in New York City with about 150 other American teenagers, about to embark upon a year of living and studying abroad. With the students were parents and siblings. My father was with me. Everyone was huddled along the periphery of the ballroom in small family groups. There was much buzzing and humming. Suddenly, a short, bouncy, heavyset woman dressed in a muu-muu — who looked to be the clone of Juanita Hall as Bloody Mary — came racing across the emptiness of the ballroom's center, capturing the attention of all, clapping her hands and waving them in the air, with a bead on me. She stopped inches short of my chin and screamed in my face, half-turning to the rest of the amassed group, "So very, very happy to see you. We're so glad to see you." I could hear the whispering around me: "Who is she?" More buzz and hum. Then it died down; people reverted to their family poses, I climbed out of my shoes and looked up at the quizzical expression on my father's face. Soon after, we were being welcomed one and all and congratulated for having been chosen to be American ambassadors abroad. Later, after the reception, several people asked me who I was; I pointed to my name tag with a quizzical look not unlike my father's.

The doctor kept talking on the phone.

I then thought about a poetry reading I'd attended a few years before at a college. A very famous American poet — alas, now dead — read for an hour or so. I was a new member of the sponsoring department, so I was invited to attend the requisite reception following the reading. A sultry September day had turned into a stormy evening and everyone was out of sorts, doubtless from want of drink. I entered the appointed living room, got myself some bourbon, and sidled over to the only other junior faculty member I could recognize. We began the regular "How'd you like the reading?" conversation when an elderly woman, dressed to the nines in a white, ornate dress and dripping with pearls — on what was clearly not her first martini — came up to me, stopping just inches short of my chin, and spoke. She had a fine, patrician face, thin nose, high cheekbones, arching eyebrows, and just the hint of a smirk that might or might not have been the natural turn of her mouth. In an unexpectedly melodic alto voice she slurred, "And I shuppose you're Toni Morrison."

Breeding won out. I said no.

She then said, "Then I shuppose you're the new member of the department."

I said yes.

She went away. I could have tripped her, but I didn't. Toni Morrison had been seen in those parts on a couple of occasions, and all things considered, I didn't mind; I probably would prefer to be Toni Morrison.

Just a few months ago I was sitting in a quiet New England inn, having some dinner with myself. I caught the eye of a couple across the room. They were prosperous looking; he had a flowing white beard, perhaps the most handsome one I've ever seen; she looked so much like Myrna Loy that I kept stealing looks their way. Obviously my surreptitious glances prompted something: the man came over to my table, introduced himself, gestured toward his wife and gave her name. He asked me if I were the piano-player and singer, So-and-So. I don't remember who it was that time.

My father, who from certain angles and at certain times vaguely looked iike Count Basie — and I mean vaguely — was often mistaken for him. I think it was the mustache. And I think my mother in her wedding picture looked like Loretta Young. But that's something entirely different.

The doctor finally stopped talking on the phone. He apologized again and asked me if I had taken any antibiotics recently. I told him I had. He reached into his desk drawer and brought out several sample packets of Benadryl and told me I'd be just fine. I left his office.

I stopped at the receptionist's desk and asked for the charges, taking my checkbook out of my purse. She said, "That will be a hundred and ninety." My left eye twitched just a little. I asked if I might pay half then and half later, an arrangement that was acceptable, and I wrote out a check. (It later bounced, not because the money wasn't there, but because of banking procedures in Los Angeles that had me regularly fantasizing terrorist attacks on a certain branch of First Interstate.) The receptionist had another form for me to complete and I sat down in my chair next to the door to do the work. We had a small bit of conversation as I wrote. A woman in a flowered dress came out of the doctor's area as I conversed with the receptionist. She looked at me, waved at the receptionist, and left. As I sat completing the form the woman came back to the office, cracked the door so that only I could see her, and asked me in whispered tones, "Is it Maya?"

I looked up, knowing that nothing could shake me after the news of the bill, and with a smile on my face I whispered back, "Does a dog have Buddha nature?"

Do He Have Your Number, Mr. Jeffrey?

DURING THE FALL of 1984 I worked for three weekends as a caterer's assistant in Southern California. Like lots of others seeking their fortunes in L.A., I was working by day as a temporary typist in a Hollywood film studio. I was moonlighting with the caterer because, like lots of others, I was going broke on my typist's wages.

Though the job was not particularly enjoyable, the caterer and her husband were congenial, interesting people who certainly would have become good friends of mine had I stayed in California. I spent my three weekends in basic scullery work — wiping and slicing mushrooms, mixing batters, peeling apples, tomatoes, and cucumbers, drying plates, glasses, and cutlery. Greater responsibilities would have come with more experience, but I had brushed off California's dust before I learned any real catering secrets or professional gourmet techniques.

One exhausting dinner party, given by a rich man for his family and friends, turned out to be among the reasons I brushed off that California dust. This dinner was such a production that our crew of five arrived the day before to start preparing. The kitchen in this house was larger than some I've seen in fine French restaurants. Our caterer was one of a new breed of gourmet cooks who do all preparation and cooking at the client's home — none of your cold-cut or warming-tray catering. As a result, her clients had a tendency to have loads of money and even more kitchen space.

Usually her staff was not expected to serve the meal, but on this occasion we did. I was directed to wear stockings and black shoes and I was given a blue-patterned apron dress, with frills here and there, to wear. Clearly, my academic lady-banker pumps were out of the question, so I invested in a pair of trendy black sneakers — which cost me five dollars less than what I earned the entire time I worked for the caterer. Buying the sneakers was plainly excessive but I told myself they were a necessary expense. I was not looking forward to wearing the little French serving-girl uniform, though. Everything about it and me were wrong, but I had signed on and it would have been unseemly and downright hostile to jump ship.

One thing I liked about the caterer was her insistence that her crew not be treated as servants — that is, we worked for her and took orders from her, not from the clients, who might find ordering us around an emboldening and socially one-upping experience. She also preferred to use crystal and china she rented, keeping her employees and herself safe from a client's rage in case a family heirloom should get broken. But on this occasion, her client insisted that we use his Baccarat crystal. We were all made particularly nervous by his tone. It was the same tone I heard from a mucky-muck at my studio typing job: cold, arrogant, a matter-of-fact "you are shit" attitude that is well known to nurses and secretaries.

I had never served a dinner before that one — that is, for strangers, formally. I had mimed serving festive meals for friends, but only in a lighthearted way. And, when I was a child, my family thought it a good exercise in etiquette — not to mention in labor savings — to have me serve at formal dinners. "It's really fun, you know," they would say. I never handled the good china, though.

I didn't mind cutting up mushrooms or stirring sauce in some foul rich man's kitchen for pennies, but I certainly didn't like the idea of serving at this one's table. I saw our host hold up one of his goblets to a guest, showing off the fine line and texture. There were too many conflicting images for me to be content with the scene. He was working hard on his image for his guests; I was bothered by the way I looked to myself and by what I might have looked like to the assembled crew, guests, and host. I couldn't get the idea of black servility to white power out of my mind.

The food was glorious. I recall serving quenelles at one point, followed by a consommé brunoise, a beef Wellington with a carrot and herb based sauce that I stirred for a short eternity, vegetables with lemon butter, and a variety of mouth-watering pastries for dessert. We worked throughout the meal, topping up wine and coffee, removing plates, bumping into each other. As long as I was doing this absurd thing I decided to make some kind of mental work attend it. I made the entire scene a movie, and as I served I created a silent voice-over. At one point, after the quenelles and the entrée and before the coffee, the table of eight sat discussing literature — a discussion of the "what'd you think of . . ." variety. My professorial ears pricked up. I discovered that one member of the party had actually read the book in question, while a few others had skimmed condensed versions in a magazine. My voice-over could have vied, I thought, with the shrillest Bolshevik propaganda ever written.

PEMBERTON (VOICE-OVER)

(haughtily)

You self-satisfied, rich, feeble-brained, idiotic, priggish, filthy maggots! You, you sit here talking literature — why, you don't even know what the word means. This is high intellectual discourse for you, isn't it? High, fine. You are proud to say, "I thought the theme honest." What, pray tell, is an honest theme? It might be better to consider the dishonesty of your disgusting lives. Why, here I am, a Ph.D in literature, listening to this garbage, making a pittance, while you illiterate pig-running-dogs consume food and non-ideas with the same relish.

Oh, I did go on. My script was melodramatic, with great soliloquies, flourishes, and, for verisimilitude, an eastern European accent. My comeuppance came as I dried the last of the Baccarat goblets. The crystal, no doubt responding to the dissonance and intensity of my sound track, shattered as I held it in my hand. The rest of the crew said they'd never seen anyone look as sick as I did at that moment. The goblet was worth more than the price of my trendy sneakers and my night's work combined. I decided to go home.

I drove slowly back to my room near Culver City; it was well past midnight. I had the distinct sense that I was the only sober driver on the Santa Monica Freeway that night, but given the weaving pattern of my driving — to avoid the other weavers — I fully expected to be picked up and jailed. Then, some alcohol residue from the broken goblet would have transported itself magically into my bloodstream to make me DWI, just as the goblet had reacted to my thoughts and sacrificed itself in the name of privilege, money, and mean-spiritedness. I made it home, feeling woozy as I left my car.

I didn't have to pay for the goblet; the caterer did. She was insured. I worked another party for her — another strange collection of people, but a more festive occasion — and I didn't have to wear the French maid's outfit. I got to stand happily behind a buffet, helping people serve themselves. I think back on my catering experience the way people do who, once something's over, say that they're glad they did it — like lassoing a bull, riding him, then busting ribs and causing permanent sacroiliac distress. The job was just one of many I've had to take to make me believe I could survive when it was obvious that I was going further and further into the hole. I never had more than ten dollars in my wallet the entire time I lived in

L.A., and not much more than that in the bank. Perhaps there's something about L.A. that makes working unlikely jobs—jobs your parents send you to college to keep you from having to do—all right and reasonable, since very little makes sense there anyway, and surviving means bellying up to the illusion bar and having a taste with everyone else.

L.A. has been like that for a long time. It did not occur to me that night, as I moved from one dinner guest to another dressed in that ludicrous outfit, that I might have created some other kind of scenario—linking what I was doing to what my mother had done nearly fifty years before, probably no farther than ten miles away.

It was in the middle thirties, Los Angeles. My mother's employers supplied her with a beige uniform with a frilled bib, short puff sleeves, and a narrow, fitted waist. The skirt of the dress was narrow, stopping just below the knee. She wore seamed stockings and low pumps, black. And her job, as far as she could ascertain, was to just be, nothing else. The couple who employed her—the husband wrote screenplays—had no children, and did not require her services to either cook or clean. I suppose they thought that having a maid was a requirement of their social position. So, Mother got the job. She is fair-skinned, and at that time she wore her dark, wavy hair long, in large curls that gathered just below her neck. I've seen pictures from those days and see her most enviable figure, an old-fashioned size ten, held up by long legs that, doubtless, were enhanced by the seamed stockings and pumps. Her employers were quite proud of her and thought she looked, they said, "just like a little French girl." When I was very young and filled with important questions, Mother explained to me that she thought it "damned irritating that whites who knew full well who they were hiring and talking to went to such lengths to try to make blacks into something else. If they wanted a little French girl, why didn't they go out and get one?" Ah, the days before *au pairs*. Well, I knew the answer to that one too.

Mother had moved to L.A. with her mother. Nana had decided to leave Papa, tired of his verbal abusiveness and profligacy. There were various cousins in California, and I am sure the appeal of the West and new beginnings at the start of the Depression made the choice an easy one. Both of my parents told me that they didn't feel the Depression all that much; things had never been financially good and little changed for them after Wall Street fell. The timing seemed right to Nana. Her other daughter, my aunt, had recently married. My mother had finished her third year at the university and, I bet, got an attack of wanderlust. She went with Nana to help her — and also to get some new air. The circumstances accommodated themselves.

I remember my shock when I learned that Mother had worked as a maid. I had always known that she had lived in California, but as a child, it never occurred to me that she would have had to "do something" there. It was not so much that my middle-class feathers were ruffled by the revelation as that I found it difficult to see her in a role that, on screen at least, was so demeaning and preposterous. Mother simply did not fit the stereotype I had been fed. And, to make matters worse, Grandma had taken pains to inform my sister and me when we were little girls that we should avoid — at all costs — rooming with whites in college or working in their homes. Her own stints as a dance-hall matron had convinced her, she said, that whites were the filthiest people on earth. The thought of my mother cleaning up after them made me want to protect her, to undo the necessity for that kind of work by some miraculous feat of time travel, to rescue her from the demeaning and the dirty.

Mother's attitude about her past employment was more pragmatic, of course. She explained to me — as if I didn't know — that there were really no avenues for black women apart from "service," as it was called, prostitution, and, perhaps, schoolteaching. Nana had no higher education and Mother's was incomplete, so service was the only route they could take. Mother also assured me that she had not cleaned unimaginable filth, but rather, with nothing else to do, had sat all day long reading novels, memorably *Anthony Adverse* by Hervey Allen, a big best-seller of 1934. My image of Mother became brighter, but in some ways more curious: there she was, imagined as a French maid by her employers, but really a black coed, lolling around a Los Angeles home reading *Anthony Adverse*. That's one far cry from Butterfly McQueen as Prissy in *Gone with the Wind*.

All good things must come to an end, as they say, and Mother's job did one day. She had been dating a man, she says, "who was very handsome, looked Latin, like Cesar Romero, but he was black too." Talk about images. He arrived to pick her up for a date as she got off work. He inquired after her at the front door — oops — and there went the job. Seems the little French maid's Spanish-looking boyfriend should have realized that no matter what black might appear to be, it better not act other than what it was. A slip in racial protocol, a lost novel-reading employ. "So it went," Mother said. After that incident she decided to look for a different kind of work and she began selling stockings for the Real Silk Hosiery Company, door-to-door.

Mother was lucky. I suspect that she and Nana might have had a tougher time if they had been brown-skinned, for contrary to many images from movies, white employers — if they were going to hire blacks at all — preferred the lighter-skinned variety. This was true of professions as diverse as chorus girls, maids, schoolteachers, waitresses, and shop clerks, an implied greater worth as blackness disappears drop by drop into ginger, to mocha, to "high yellow," to white. This scale was intraracially internalized too, making a shambles of black life from the earliest slave days to the present. These gradations also made color-line crossing a popular black sport, particularly since white America seemed to be at once so secure and satisfied in its whiteness and so ignorant of who's who and who's what. Blacks existed only as whites saw them, blackness affirming white racial self-consciousness and nothing else. This is what Ralph Ellison's invisibility is all about; it is what we have all lived.

In the evenings and on weekends, Mother and Nana used to go to the movies; they both were hooked and on location for Hollywood's Golden Age. I love movies too. It is on the gene, as I frequently remind myself as I sit watching a vintage B from the forties for the fifth time or so when I ought to be reading a book. A major chunk of my misspent youth involved watching them. When I should have been reading, or studying mathematics, or learning foreign languages — like my more successful academic friends — I was hooked on three-reelers.

During my youth Mother was my partner in all this. When I was in kindergarten and first grade on half-day shifts, I never missed a morning movie. When we watched together I would barrage her with important questions: "Who is that?" "Is he dead?" "Is she dead?" "Who was she married to?" "Is this gonna be sad?" Mother was never wrong, except once. We were watching an early Charles Bickford movie and I asked the standard heady question: "Is he dead?" Mother said, "Oh, Lord, yes. He died years ago." Several years later I came home triumphantly from a drive-in and announced that I had seen Bickford in *The Big Country* and that he looked just fine and alive to me.

Of course, hopeless romanticism is the disease that can be caught from the kind of movie-going and movie-watching my mother and I have done. There she was, with her mother, frequently a part of the crowd being held behind the barricades at Hollywood premieres, sighing and pointing with agitation as gowned and white-tied stars glided from limousines into rococo movie-houses. Both she and Nana read screen magazines — the forerunners to our evening news programs — that detailed the romantic, hedonistic public and private exploits of Hollywood's royalty. It was a time when my mother, as French maid reading *Anthony Adverse*, had to wait only a few months before the novel burst onto the screen, with glorious illusionary history and Frederic March swashbuckling his way into the hearts of screaming fans. The stars were part of the studio system and could be counted on to appear with frequency, even if the roles appeared to be the same and only the titles, and a few plot twists, changed. (I am convinced, for example, that the 1934 *Imitation of Life* was remade as *Mildred Pierce* in 1945, the major change being that the relatively good daughter of the former becomes the monster of the latter. Louise Beavers and Fredi Washington in the black theme of *Imitation of Life* only slightly alter the major plot.)

Mother's was the perfect generation to see Hollywood movies when they were fresh, new, and perhaps more palpable than they are now — when comedies of remarriage, as Stanley Cavell calls them, and historical adventures and melodramas dominated the screen, when westerns and political dramas were self-consciously mythologizing the American past and present, and when young French maids and their mothers, along with the impoverished, the disillusioned, the lost, and even the comfortable and secure, could sit before the silver screen and see a different world projected than the one they lived in. And they could dream. Mother loves to sketch faces and clothing, using an artistic talent inherited from Papa. She marveled at the stars and their sculpted (sometimes) faces, and would draw from memory the costume designs that made the likes of Edith Head, Cecil Beaton, and Irene famous.

Hopeless romanticism was the threat, but neither Nana nor Mother — nor I completely — succumbed to it. They never confused reality with anything they saw on either the big or the small screen. And they taught me what they believed. They both warned me, in different ways and at different times, to be wary of the type of people who wake up to a new world every day (and I've met some) — people with no memory, ingenuous, incapable of seeing either the implications or the connections between one event and another, people who willingly accept what the world makes of them on a Tuesday, forget as night falls, and wake up on Wednesday ready to make the same mistakes. It might have been some of that ingenuousness that produced my feelings of discomfort when I learned that Mother had been a maid, and she understood how I felt.

My mother always deplored the depiction of blacks on screen. She saw their roles as demeaning and designed to evoke either cheap sentimentality, cheap laughter, or cheap feelings of superiority in the white audiences they were aimed at. And, although she says she didn't see many of them, Mother loathed the all-black B movies Hollywood made for the "colored" audience, where the stereotypes were broader and more offensive to her, and where the musical interludes did no justice to real talent, she said, but trivialized it. She even hated musical interludes featuring black performers in the standard white A and B movies. She was — and still is — cold to arguments that say talented black performers needed to take any work they could get, and that black audiences were encouraged and happy to see black Hollywood stars no matter what they were doing. Mother countered that Hattie McDaniel's acceptance speech, when she won an Oscar for her role as Mammy in *Gone with the Wind*, was written for her, and that McDaniel was denied the status of eating dinner with her peers that night.

We have talked about all of this many, many times, particularly when I have felt it necessary to sort out my own complex and conflicting reactions to Hollywood movies. Like Mother, I have seen as nothing but illusion the world projected on the screen. But as Michael Wood notes in *America in the Movies*: "All movies mirror reality in some way or other. There are no escapes, even in the most escapist pictures. . . . The business of films is the business of dreams . . . but then dreams are scrambled messages from waking life, and there is truth in lies, too." Mother may have recoiled from black images on screen because they affirmed a reality she did not like. She could suspend her disbelief at white characters and their predicaments, she could enter the dream worlds of aristocrats and chorus girls living happily ever after, or dying romantic, drawn-out deaths, because there was some measure of inner life given these portrayals. The audience demanded some causal foundation to acts ranging from heroism and self-sacrifice to murder, duplicity, and pure cussedness. But black characters on screen, no matter how polished their roles, were ultimately as invisible as she was in her own role as French maid — a projection only of what the white world wanted to see, robbed of the implication of inner lives, nothing but glorified surfaces that really said everything about whiteness and nothing at all about blackness. It didn't matter to Mother if the characters were maids or butlers, lawyers or doctors, simpletons or singers. I knew there was an inner life, a real person in my mother — passionate and shy, lacking self-confidence but projecting intense intelligence and style — and that she had no business being anybody's French girl. The "truth in lies" was that Hollywood rent from us our human dignity while giving us work, as it sought to defuse and deflect our real meaning — a potentially dangerous meaning — in American life.

Mother found these invisible blacks painful to watch because they were so effective as images created in white minds. These complex feelings are on the gene too. I find Shirley Temple movies abominable, notwithstanding the dancing genius of Bill "Bojangles" Robinson. In *The Little Colonel* young Shirley has just been given a birthday party; there are hats and horns and all sorts of scrubbed white children celebrating with her. At some moment — I refuse to watch the film again to be precise — she gets up and takes part of her cake to a group of dusty and dusky children who are waiting outside in the backyard of the house. The only reason for their existence is to be grateful for the crumbs and to sing a song. There can be no other motivation, no reason to exist at all, except to show the dear Little Colonel's largesse and liberal-mindedness, befitting someone not quite to the manor born but clearly on her way to the manor life.

I was watching an Alfred Hitchcock festival not long ago. Hitchcock films are some of Mother's favorites. She likes the illusions and twists of plots, the scrambling of images light and dark. I realized that I hadn't seen *Rear Window* since I was a little girl, and that at the time I hadn't understood much of what had taken place in the movie. I was very interested in it this time around. There was James Stewart, as Jeffries, in the heaviest makeup ever, with his blue eyes almost enhanced out of his face, looking at evil Raymond Burr through binoculars in the apartment across the way. I was letting the film take me where it would; I created an *explication de texte*, noting how the film raises questions about voyeurism and images. Indeed, Stewart, in looking at the world from his temporary infirmity, is only content when he places a narrative line on the lives of the people on the other side of his binoculars. He is, in a sense, reacting to images and attempting to order them — as we all do.

At a crucial moment in the movie, Stewart realizes that he is in danger. The evil wife-murderer and dismemberer, Burr, knows that Stewart has figured out the crime. Stewart hobbles to the telephone, trying to reach his friend, Wendell Corey. Corey isn't in, but Stewart gets the babysitter on the line — who speaks in a vaudevillian black accent. He asks her to have Corey call him when he returns. The babysitter asks, "Do he have your number, Mr. Jeffrey?"

I called my mother to tell her that I had an interesting bit of trivia from *Rear Window*. She became angry when she heard it, said she was appalled. "He should have been ashamed of himself," she said of Hitchcock. Into the white world of *Rear Window* and questions of imagery, it was necessary to place a familiar black image — and this time it didn't even have a face.

Mother and Nana left L.A. in 1937. Working in service and selling silk stockings could not provide enough money for them to survive. They went back to the frozen North. Mother married in 1939; Nana returned to Papa and stayed with him until he died in 1967.

Nana and Papa both moved to L.A. in 1950, Papa then a semi-retired architect. They had a beautiful home on West Fourth Avenue. It was right in the middle of a two-block area that became part of the Santa Monica Freeway. One morning, on my way to a catering job, I drove my car as far as I could, to the fence above the freeway. I got out and thought long and hard about what had been lost — beyond a house, of course, but their lives gone, part of my youth as a little girl visiting in summers, and dreams about what life could be in the semi-tropical paradise of Southern California where they made dreams that seduced the whole world.

On Andrew Wyeth,
Checked Suits, Broken
Hair, Busted Dreams,
and Transcendence

I DON'T KNOW what to do when the temperature is eighty degrees and the calendar tells me it is November. Fall was a failure for me in Los Angeles. I didn't know how to dress for it. On one of these hot, Southern California fall days, when I wasn't working as a temporary typist at Universal Studios, I drove over to Ocean Avenue in Santa Monica, found myself some bench space, and gazed at the ocean, and at the people watching the ocean, for an entire morning. At lunchtime I began to feel guilty about having wasted so many hours doing nothing constructive. So, instead of searching for cheap food—which is not easy to find in Santa Monica anyway—I pulled a book out of my canvas Barnes and Noble catch-all bag and continued my struggle through *La Chambre Claire* by Roland Barthes. I do not usually read anything in French anymore; I can't. But something had gotten into me on another hot November day, when the proprietors of an upscale bookstore looked at me as if I were a Japanese beetle invading their rose garden, and I'd impulsively grabbed the book and taken it to the check-out counter with nothing short of pure murder in my eyes. I probably carried it around in my bag to ward off any stray lordly looks that might come my way, as a prospective victim holds up a cross to Dracula.

Without benefit of a dictionary, I found Barthes hard going, but I pressed on, feeling that I was getting a strong sense of his message, if not his substance. I am interested in photography, and Barthes' comments on how he viewed "the Photograph" as he put it, were provocative and depressing. At the very end, Barthes says:

> Telles sont les deux voies de la Photographie. A moit choisir, de soumettre son spectacle au code civilisé des illusions parfaites, ou d'affronter en elle le réveil de l'intraitable réalité.

(In the Richard Howard translation called *Camera Lucida* this reads: "Such are the two ways of the Photograph. The choice is mine: to subject its spectacle to the civilized code of perfect illusions, or to confront in it the wakening of intractable reality.")

That much I understood, and sitting on Ocean Avenue as the dusk of another hot, November day approached, my soul felt as damp and as drizzly as it had on many a late New England fall afternoon. I returned to my car and drove toward home, wanting to disagree with Barthes, but knowing that I had not understood him enough to frame an intelligent reply. I vowed to find a translation, but this time preferably from storekeepers other than those who had, with unconcealed bemusement, sold me this original. Barthes and the notion of the photograph and ideas of other images stayed on my mind.

I don't know why my sister and I were driving across Chicago Avenue at around one o'clock on a recent Palm Sunday afternoon. Chicago Avenue passes Cabrini Green, an all-black housing project made nationally famous for a few days in 1982 when Jane Byrne, the mayor of Chicago, decided to spend a week there. Business as usual in Cabrini Green is extreme poverty and its accoutrements: rape, murder, gang warfare, and a despair that has no words to express itself or be expressed, except, perhaps, perpetual. When Byrne was there, things were quiet.

We were waiting at a red light at Chicago and Orleans when we saw five young children — stairsteps, with the oldest only about eleven — crossing the street. It was a Chicago-brisk, gray Sunday afternoon, and the weather was changing from tenacious winter to blustery, cold spring. Threatening navy blue nimbus clouds reluctantly gave way in spots to an eerie yellow sun that edged through. The clouds blew eastward, moving so fast that the involuntary response of a skywatcher was to grab hold of something solid and plant her feet firmly on the ground. The wind wanted more than the children's haphazardly buttoned coats and hatless heads could provide. The eleven year old was attempting to impose order on the other children, each of whom carried a single palm. It was a hopeless task, as the four siblings — we assumed they were siblings — broke ranks and, without skipping, jumping, or running, maintained an ordered disorder that caught and seared our eyes. They seemed more like specters, off the ground, gliding to music — Debussy's *Danses sacrées et profanes*. There were old eyes in their baby faces.

Neither my sister nor I are mothers, but she gave a low, succinct grunt, and I, in the same tone, said quietly, "uh-huh." And we both wanted to grab and hold, not the smallest — who looked to be about three — but the eldest, who was trying so hard to corral the brood of cold and surrealistically lifeless children crossing a wide, ugly Chicago street on their way home to Cabrini Green from, most likely, the nearest Catholic parish. As we drove on we mutually concluded that kidnapping was not the answer. We also wondered if we would have felt differently had an — had the — absent parent been leading them or bringing up the rear.

When I was in about the third grade, I recall my teacher explaining to the class, during our social studies section on health, that being poor was nothing to be ashamed of, that having only one dress simply required the labor of frequent laundering. And that owning one pair of shoes meant that they should be kept shined and well-soled; she said that being poor was not synonymous with leading a blighted life. Places like Cabrini Green and its even more notorious sister (brother/cousin?), Robert Taylor Homes, give the lie to this, just as some other children I saw outside a train window one day, playing on a porch somewhere between Martinsburg and Harpers Ferry, West Virginia, half-naked with swollen bellies, looked anything but noble and proud in their rural poverty. On watching the children in Chicago, I assumed that they were statistically correct: siblings with different fathers, living with a single mother, maybe only barely old enough to be their mother.

We returned to my sister's apartment, where our mother had spent the afternoon reflecting on the depressing side of holidays. She had been weeping, thinking of our departed dead. The remainder of the afternoon was subdued; we acted as if we had all been struck with a powerful inertia. We didn't even want to hear the old hymns again.

It was not always that way. Palm Sunday was the beginning of Easter Week, when school was out, when on the Sunday eve the whole family went shopping. My sister and I would get patent leather shoes, new underwear and anklets, bonnets, purses, and a dress or suit for Easter. My sister, who was a devotee of church choirs — and who often had an alto solo in "The Palms" — would be excited about the forthcoming two weeks' worth of the best sacred music this side of Christmas. Palm Sunday was the only day when, as a child, I felt truly equal in church, for I too was given a palm to be saved for Ash Wednesday, when it would be burned with oil and anointed on my forehead. "All glory, laud and honor to thee, Redeemer King! To whom the lips of children made sweet hosannas ring."

Palm Sunday was also the beginning of spring eating week. My father, who so loved holidays, would have planned a table full enough to invite a whole floor of Cabrini Green residents to dine, with enough left over for Monday lunch.

My sister is a photographer of things, I of people. She loves French and the linguistic side of her foreign language education. I always loathed the grammar and vocabulary drills, but loved the fiction and poetry. She is an optimist, I a fatalist, although she sees these traits reversed in us. She drinks her coffee black; my first cup must have milk and sugar. I am five feet eight and have the build of Nana; she is five-two and structurally resembles Grandma and my aunt. Apart from these differences and in spite of the five years that separate us, we are very much the same. I don't think we look alike, but barbers claim we have the same shaped head, and once a friend of my sister's — a perfect stranger to me — accosted me on a train and asked me if I were her friend's sister.

Our lives have been different. As I went traipsing into the groves of academe, she taught French for sixteen years to, perhaps, the South Side cousins of the Cabrini Green children, because she insisted that black inner city youth have as much right to learn the language of their French-speaking black cousins in Martinique, Chad, Haiti, and elsewhere, as white children do of their Jean-Claudes and Maries of Paris. After sixteen years her despair became too great, not at the children and their French — for barely a week goes by without some terribly aged person greeting her on the street to reminisce about her classes — but at the school system itself and its bureaucracy. She left her love of teaching and of French to work for a community-supporting bank. But she misses the French and the students. She frequently writes me letters in French, and I write back a patois translatable only by her. She is not much of a reminiscer herself, but she will occasionally wonder how she managed to survive as a young teacher who was out on the town when not in classes, and who, on at least one occasion, had to hit the pavement, dodging the bullets of rival gangs who had mistaken the school parking lot for the OK Corral. Sometimes, if I happened to be in town over a holiday break — say, Easter Week — I would go with her on the last day of classes, helping her carry her briefcase, camera, and the baritone ukelele and tape recorder with which she taught the students their black French-speaking cousins' songs. (My sister was some cross between Eartha Kitt and the Singing Nun.) I have always admired her willingness to stay put and work in the trenches. She has always envied my agility in getting out of them. We are the greatest of sisters now, loving, loyal, and playful. It was not always that way, though.

According to the story — clearly not my own — my sister, having seen the baby sister of her friend Linda, pleaded: "Oh, Mommy, pleeze, can I have a little sister? Oh, I would just love to have a little sister!"

According to the story — not mine, I was too young to remember — my mother told my sister the following: "Now, watch your baby sister on the table. She can't control her movements, so don't turn your back because she might fall off." I have attributed my lifelong struggle with physical awkwardness, and my lifelong sense that something dreadful is imminent, to the fall.

According to the story — again, not my own, I was still too young to remember — my mother told my sister: "Now, watch your little sister. Don't let her go so fast in that rocker. The stool is too close to the rocker anyway, and she might hit her head rocking so fast. You'd better move the stool." As I was rushed to the emergency room my mother was sure I'd lost my left eye, the blood gushed so violently from my forehead just above it.

According to the story — mine — my sister, willfully, and with malice aforethought, pushed me down the stairs on a Saturday morning in the spring of 1952 at 223 West Ninety-fourth Street, Princeton Park, Chicago. My head hit every step, but my father — who was not usually fleet of foot — caught me before I rammed into the door at the foot of the stairs. This may explain why some people call me Pooh. Regardless, the damage from this incident was a permanent fear and loathing of this world, and, for quite a while, of my sister in particular.

According to the story — mine again — I asked my mother when I was eleven, "Did you have me because I was asked for?"

Mother said, "Well, dear, to be frank, we hadn't exactly planned on you."

"Does that mean I'm an accident?" I asked.

"Well, yes, dear."

The same year I learned of the circumstances of my nascence my mother sat me down to tell me the facts of life. My sister stood by as a kibitzer, making faces and adding adolescent misinformation until Mother stopped her. I remember how Mother placed me at the dining room table, pulled out a pamphlet prepared by the Modess Company for such cosmic moments, and read it to me, showing me the diagrams of a uterus, vagina, fallopian tubes, eggs, and an elastic sanitary pad belt. I believed that I understood everything, but later my sister had to tell me the connection between the sexual act and babies. I understood about sperm and eggs; I wasn't even curious about how the former got to the latter.

My mother often exhibited extreme serenity, extraordinary calm, in her pedagogical techniques. I remember her telling my sister at thirteen — when disturbing numbers of her schoolmates were becoming pregnant, exhibiting the fifties version of the eighties epidemic — that she would rather see us both dead than pregnant. Mother said it so calmly and matter-of-factly. Some things from childhood stick: I cannot speak for my childless sister, but I took Mother at her word and, on considering the alternatives, I have clung to life as well.

Several hours after that talk my sister took it upon herself to give me a disquisition on the meaning of blood, the upshot of which was that in reality I was more closely related to her —

who, like me, shared the blood of both our parents — than I was to either of them. She said I was her closest relative. I wept.

Anyone who was there can tell you, and would be pleased to do so — those who are still alive — that my sister came out of the womb a diplomat, ready to entertain and please. She caused my mother scant grief during the pregnancy. From the slap on her back she began to gurgle, coo, and mug her way into the hearts of all. She smiled and soon talked, sang and danced, to the amazement and pleasure of various great aunts and uncles and family friends in the Twin Cities where our family lived at the time. At the age of three, tired of the provincial routine at home, she marched out of the house — headed west, of course — crossed one major intersection and was headed for another when a neighbor rescued her from herself and brought her back, crushing any incipient wanderlust before it got started.

On my bureau I have a hinged five-by-seven double picture frame with early pictures of my sister and me in it. I am about eighteen months old in mine, my sister is about two and a half years old in hers. She is sitting on an upholstered bench, in a white dress with a golden locket hanging in the front. A large bow is in her curled hair. Her right leg crosses under the left one, which dangles over the edge of the bench; her hands are resting on the bench, as if about to propel her just slightly forward. She is looking dead straight into the camera and has a broad smile on her face.

In my picture I am sitting in front of a photographer's screen, reluctantly. I, too, have on a white dress and a golden locket. There is a small bow in my short hair, my right hand is knotted into a fist, and I am about to try to punch out the photographer and cry. There is a look of profound skepticism on my face.

These early pictures are telling. My sister grew up to be known in some circles as the great diplomat, Miss Urban

League, Miss Personality, a clown, a performer. I learned to hide while watching the strange goings-on of people who my mother had to remind me were my Aunt and Uncle So-and-So, talking and laughing in the living room.

Barthes did not see "the Photograph" this way. He wrote, "I must therefore submit to this law: I cannot penetrate, cannot reach into the Photograph. I can only sweep it with my glance, like a smooth surface. The Photograph is flat, platitudinous in the true sense of the word; that is what I must acknowledge." But I have discovered that I cannot see it so.

There was nothing smarmy about my sister's appeal. She was, by all accounts, a delightful, happy child. And she was no fool — it shows in the picture. Her natural temperament she parlayed into a number of treats. Papa, who was an architect, would take a break from his boardwork and amble hand-in-hand with her to the corner candy store. Once there, he would point to a Fudgsicle or candy bar and ask her, "Do you want one of those?" Her standard reply was, "I want two, Papa!" And two she would get. She could have opened her own store with the chocolates from Papa and the cellophane-wrapped mints and rock candy that came out of black purses, opened by fingers in white gloves or holding fragrant hand-kerchieves, the wrapper slightly dusty from the leaking compacts of older aunts and other ladies who rewarded her good manners and her high spirits.

She developed a keen sense of propriety, an ability to mimic, and a mastery of language that have served her well. She has been known to walk through political, ideological, and racial mine fields, without so much as worrying about where her feet will tread. She learned it all very early. Her photograph defines self-confidence.

Shortly after her second birthday, my mother noticed a rash developing on my sister's arms, scalp, and neck. The doctor diagnosed her as having eczema. "Fairly common," he said. "She'll probably outgrow it in a couple of years." But the rash persisted, and soon the curled hair of her baby picture broke off and would not grow. Instead, patches of rough, angry skin smothered new growth. Across her forehead, neck, and upper lip, scaly and itching patches formed, as they did on the backs of her knees and elbows. For nearly twenty years she itched and scratched; the skin sometimes wept, and Mother had to tie her hands with gauze when she was little to keep her from tearing her skin to bits.

By the time she was ready for school, we had moved to Kansas City for the first time — nine years later we returned — and every morning my mother would walk her nearly a mile to Booker T. Washington Elementary School. The Benton School (Walt Disney's alma mater), as it was called in those days, was four blocks from our apartment and for whites only. Mother says she silently cursed every step of her four-mile day, and sometimes she came home and cried at the bravery of her child, who, often bandaged and generally uncomfortable, persisted in her high spirits and optimism, though she was ever a target for schoolyard taunts and ineffective salves.

Two years later we moved to Chicago, and my sister entered the third grade. A black dermatologist there started her on the long road to healing by identifying chocolate as the primary food culprit, aided by a highly-strung temperament and a genetic proclivity to allergies. It took time for various treatments to stop the weeping, for the chocolate habit to be broken in a home where the father was a bona fide chocaholic, and outside a home where being brave and trying to be impervious to the craven rantings and silent stares of little children took a toll on her nerves. I was there, though I don't remember, the day she was sent home early from school by her fourth grade teacher — a bully who spat through large teeth — with a note to my mother to wash the soot off my sister's upper lip. That was the same year I outgrew my asthma. Also in that year, three Spanish peanuts given to me by my piano teacher caused my first anaphylactic response to legumes and nuts.

Mother is a great weeper herself. On days when the vapors are out of sync and she needs a cry, she often thinks about my sister's childhood—of the gauze, of the fun she missed at parties, of the few chances to dance at the parties she was invited to—and how brave her daughter was, how optimistic and cheerful she remained about almost everything. Mother has long brooded on the nature of life, on womanhood, on the inequities of blackness, on being a mother with two brown, allergy-ridden daughters. She likes to think we are brave; we think she is.

But my sister's eczema, as physically marring as it was, remained an allergy, not a handicap, in spite of the boorishness of children and adults alike. My sister realized early that she was as victimized by those who reacted to the color of her skin as those who laughed at its discolorations. She remained "Miss Personality" in public and my personal tormenter in private. For underneath her cheery aspect lay a mean temper, inherited from every possible side. She always had to have the last word, regardless of the peril involved in doing so. I would watch her in pitched battles with my father and mother. A typical routine of my sister's went like this:

"But you said I could," she would whine. I hid within earshot, amazed at her insistence on carrying points further. I thought she was insane and I was determined to learn from her mistakes. I would develop alternative strategies when I grew older.

"I said nothing of the sort," Mother would say.

"Yes, you did," my sister would retort.

"Don't contradict me!" Mother was getting hotter.

"You forgot, that's all," my sister would sass.

"I told you not to contradict me. The issue is closed!"

"The issue is closed," my sister would mimic (*sotto voce* and whining).

Mother would then rush for her and give her a few hand pats on the rear—painless and for the most part catalysts for paroxysms of boo-hoos from my sister. This insane child

55

would then continue to repeat the last lines, sassing, and I am sure that had my parents been given to real violence, she would have limped, as she scratched, her way from childhood to adulthood.

I was afraid of her, and witnessing her battles with my parents made me wary of her. (So we had been instructed to treat the certifiably insane.) As I grew older, I learned to yell at my parents and sass — what else can an adolescent do — taking on her brand of contentiousness with the same results. Grandma may have threatened to put my sister in a convent, but my father prophesied that my mouth would be the death of me.

When I was eleven I declared war on my sister. From the first time she had been allowed to babysit for me (I awaited the inevitable right hooks and punches on my arms, the tripping, and the pulling of my hair), through to her predictions of the apocalypse at the sound of a siren, she had had the upper hand. I was always terrified, invariably throwing up as soon as the door shut on my departing parents, vainly threatening to "tell" when they came home, crawling under the davenport to escape the apocalypse. But when I was eleven I had already grown taller than she was. One day I came home from school after a heavy wet snow, changed into my play clothes and formed one hundred snowballs, which I lined up on the walk to our house. I waited for her to round the corner, but somehow the work and the anticipation of her arrival spent me, and the only thing that happened to the snowballs was that she photographed them. My sister, with a love of French, has an understanding of symbolism; she resorted solely to psychological abuse from then on. And I retained an overwhelming sympathy for younger sisters, believing that older ones are dangerous and should be watched carefully at all times.

I refuse to believe that I had anything to do with my sister's eczema, even though the notion sometimes would cross my mind. She was quite simply determined to make me pay for being born and ruining her family hustle. There was compensation, however. She perfected her extraordinary sense of humor, and, when she was game, we played together. Watching our favorite comedians, she practiced their moves. We developed our own versions of French, Japanese, Slavic, German, and Spanish languages after seeing Imogene Coca and Sid Caesar. We carried on long conversations in our gibberish, concentrating on tone and inflection for coherence. She became a clown, masterfully straddling the line between the sublime and the absurd, and became a far cry from the little girl being walked to school by a deadly serious and pissed-off mother.

Barthes writes, "Consider the United States, where everything is transformed into images: only images exist and are produced and are consumed." There's plenty of truth to that. He goes on to say, "What characterizes the so-called advanced societies is that they today consume images and no longer, like those of the past, beliefs." For example, I have no trouble making people understand me if I refer to the television image of John Dean testifying before the Watergate Committee. But very few people can locate my irony when I use the phrase made famous by the Watergate hearings: "to the best of my knowledge."

But Roland Barthes was a Frenchman who had the kind of Gallic self-confidence and arrogance that I find nothing short of outrageous. I am a black female American, born at midcentury into the midst of a barrage of images. There are the white images that reinforce what I am not and the black ones that are supposed to define blackness, and that are in some ways naturalistic, always symbolic of the whole, designed to elicit pity, fear, or cheap sentiment. They are always there to defuse and displace the potential meanings of black life. In Hollywood films and television dramas the black male image is the sum of Uncle Tom, Jim, Lucas Beauchamp, Babo, the "nigger" in the background — in the kitchen, the barn, the repair shop, the railyard, the jail, the streetcorner, the woodpile — or in the foreground spiking the ball, dancing the step, uttering the oath. For the black woman the range moves from Aunt Jemima on the pancake box to Dorothy Dandridge in *Carmen Jones* — dressed only in panties and bra in one scene, in an age when white leading ladies hardly suggested the existence of underwear.

I once heard a black student complain to a white colleague: "I'm a minority; I can't write a good paper. I need extra help." *Minority* is a word for statisticians, not a self-identifier for their victims. The word robs those in minority groups of their special racial and ethnic histories, and teaches them to view themselves, their families, and even their existences as fundamentally problematic. In 1925 Alain Locke in *The New Negro* expressed his great hopes for the New Negro Movement when he said:

> Negro life is seizing upon its first chances for group expression and self-determination. . . . it must be admitted that American Negroes have been a race more in sentiment than in experience. The chief bond between them has been that of a common condition rather than a common consciousness; a problem in common rather than a life in common.

By the early 1980s that black student had removed herself more than verbally from any potential common consciousness and the liberation it might bring. I chalk it up to the images she had seen and internalized of what she supposed herself to be.

I remember reading *Jet* about the lynching of Emmett Till. It might have been the first *Jet* I read cover to cover; the news of Gloria Lockerman's spelling triumph was in the same issue. His death created a pall over my family — not in easily discernible ways, but it seemed we carried ourselves differently. Nobody said very much; our eating and sleeping were desultory and fitful. The photograph of Till's mutilated body bore little relationship to anything human I'd ever seen. I looked at it, trying to find a face, but it was just a mass of protoplasm. The next time I thought about it I was in a college biology lab final looking at unknowns through a microscope. The lab instructor, a sadist, had put various items like rubber bands and parts of sandwiches on slides to fool us. The peanut butter and jelly sandwich made me think of Emmett Till. I felt disgust and nausea.

And as I grew older, I retained the images of other lynching victims, of spitting grandmothers in Little Rock, Arkansas, of Dobermans and German shepherds hungry for black bodies throughout the South, of fire hoses, of black choirs singing "Lift Every Voice and Sing"—images of cursed battles that had all the earmarks of Pyrrhic victory written upon them long before time and administrations and supreme courts could attempt to blot them out.

I even knew a guy who had a huge, ghastly photograph of a lynched and mutilated black man on the wall above his living room couch. He admitted to its having been a political statement, that it kept him angry; but angry was clearly all that he was. I wondered if he ever *did* anything.

Behind me, as I sit writing, I have an eighteen-by-eighteen framed photograph from the March on Washington, 1963, a copy of a print given to my father by his friend Whitney Young. Camilla Williams, dressed in a black dress with a string of pearls and a large black hat, is singing "The Star-Spangled Banner," her mouth open on what might have been the "through the perilous fight" line. Directly behind her, A. Philip Randolph wipes his left eye with a handkerchief, and in the foreground, with their hands over their hearts, are Young, Martin Luther King, Jr., and Walter Reuther. King's hand, however, is in a relaxed fist, grabbing his left lapel. Stokely Carmichael is in the background behind Camilla Williams' hat, and so is a white man in dark glasses who looks menacingly and nerve-wrackingly like both James Earl Ray and the FBI agent provocateur in the Birmingham bombings. I often stare at the photograph, realizing that within minutes of its taking King will deliver one of the greatest speeches of all time; that within a few years of its taking Randolph,

Young, King, and Reuther will be dead; that Whitney Young, a few years before it was taken, sat in my parents' living room and for once I didn't hide; that his successor as Urban League head, Vernon Jordan, kissed me on the cheek once (several years later and a few years after the picture was taken someone shot and nearly killed him); that as it was being taken I sat in front of the television in a hip-to-ankle cast on my left leg, watching the March on Washington, wishing I'd been there; that I am who I am because when I look at the picture I redeem myself, my history, from the flatness of a piece of chemically-treated paper exposed to light, and I redeem the photograph from the category of mere "image" — since that word, too, has become hopelessly entangled with advertising propaganda in which an image is something really designed to veil the truth. I am not without anger when I look at the photograph; I'm also not without joy. Most important, I am conscious that some spirit, some idea, some reality has both defined and transcended a particular moment in August 1963, and that every time I look at the photograph I am somehow made more able to withstand the lesser images that bind the culture's mentality.

I must disagree with Barthes, turn his words around and say, "I can penetrate, I can reach into the Photograph." I must. I am sure others who see photographs feel differently, and agree with Barthes that "society is concerned to tame the photograph, to temper the madness which keeps threatening to explode in the face of whoever looks at it." I enjoy the taste of the powder.

A painting is, naturally, not a photograph. Barthes says that "painting can feign reality without having seen it." He certainly is right there, for I have a print of the painting *Day of the Fair* by Andrew Wyeth that proves it. I bought it along with two other Wyeth prints, two views of the same black man, in 1970. In *Day of the Fair* a young black girl is sitting in a straight chair, in a bare room, with the bottom portion of a window reflecting the brightness of the day outdoors. The framed print hangs on the wall opposite my March on Washington photograph.

A few years ago the American art world reacted with surprise to the news that for fifteen years Andrew Wyeth made many drawings and paintings, called the Helga paintings, named for their model, that were unknown to just about everyone. Even Wyeth's wife did not know he had painted them. According to an article in the *New York Times*, Mrs. Wyeth says Helga "informed and inspired his other work." And she is quoted as saying of one particular painting:

> It's a remarkable painting. . . . There's Helga, but she's a negress. He told me, "It just didn't work with Helga," but he was very tight-lipped. I don't know and I don't pry. Not if the work is "Barracoon."

Day of the Fair precedes the Helga years, and *negress* is a term so archaic and suggestive of the jungle that I was taken aback by the entire quote. But it is conceivable to me that some emotion with its source in some place outside of black life, and specifically apart from that of an anonymous black girl, found its only expression through her.

The painting could be a portrait of my sister when she was fourteen, when eczema ravaged her body. The figure in my print is an adolescent, dressed in a three-piece dark green or black checked suit. The suit looks worn, a hand-me-down from another age, perhaps, another sensibility. The girl's head is bending slightly down, her mouth taut. A single white hair-band crowns the top of her head, bridging brittle, stumpy black hair that won't grow; she has short bangs. Her hands are in her lap as she faces away from the window, and they are expressive. The left hand is open, the four fingers bending slightly together, the thumb flexed in the opposite direction, while the right hand is in nearly a fist; but it is relaxed, as it seems to be in motion — patting, thumping the open palm of the left hand. The hands retrace all the steps that led to this bare room and this chair and a fair that meant so much — earlier, while dressing — that is now a dashed dream to add to all the others in a young black life. The bare walls surrounding the girl are variations on shades of gray; the light from the window that hits them nearly silhouettes her figure in the foreground. The light on the window gives the room an aspect of a prison, the shadow of the mullion suggesting prison bars.

I cried when I first saw the print. My sister cried when she first saw it too. She said, "That's me, you know." I told her that was why I bought it. It said everything about Mother's brave little girl.

My mind does not require the framed print, but my heart does. I rarely cry when I look at it now, though. And I realize that if the girl in the painting were white, the emotion expressed would be sentimental and transient, without the power that the blackness and its historical meanings and racial longing bring to it. I look at it in a terribly private way because I see it as my sister, and remember a time in her life when it seemed that her eczema would be permanent, would destroy a vibrant life. But then, too, after a few seconds, after I have located my sister and her adolescent misery, the print ceases to be her, and becomes *Day of the Fair* again. My sister has spent her life denying the helpless sorrow of the girl, and has transcended the bad times — so much so that I half expect the print to move. For if it really were my sister on that paper, she would look up in her plaid suit at the viewer and giggle. The print's emotion overwhelms, but its profound sadness and imprisonment are only transient. My sister, the clown, animates it and redeems it.

My favorite Palm Sunday hymn is "O Sacred Head Sore Wounded," adapted and supplied with harmony by J. S. Bach himself. My favorite lines: "What sorrow mars thy grandeur? Can death thy bloom deflower? O countenance whose splendor, the hosts of heav'n adore!" There is something in Passiontide that lends itself to my personality, a ritualized laughing and crying all at the same moment — Christ entering the city to the hosannas of the crowd only to be crucified in a few days. And I think about those five children with their palms on Chicago Avenue and recognize that the image their procession burned into my mind is useless to me unless I can redeem it. For seeing them as pathetic specters, gliding toward the obscenity of their housing-project home, makes them dead to me — and they are not. It is not romanticism, or madness, or transcendentalism that allows me to consider them alive, not statistical minority children fending for themselves while their mother, somewhere else, could give a hoot. They are not flat on some page of my memory, but attest to the truth and the lies about people living blighted lives. And for all I know (and this is not madness either) someone is — some ones are — eagerly waiting for them to come home.

On the Lower
Frequencies

Who knows but that, on the lower frequen-
cies, I speak for you?
                        RALPH ELLISON

SOME OF THE most loved anecdotes in my family are those that
feature my parents and sister as thespians. My family is filled
with fine actors all of whom have a great sense of comic timing. My mother is a woman of high drama as well as comedy,
who uses her hands graphically to depict scenes, whose eyes
widen at the climactic moments, whose voice reveals nuances
of language with ease. She is also very shy, and was nearly a
terminal case in her youth. Much of this reserve she outgrew
over the years, but there is plenty left, and she has suffered because her shyness has been taken for aloofness by people dis-
posed to think that way. Nothing is further from the truth; she
is just shy and concentrating on other things. One summer
day, my sister and I went to pick her up from work. We sta-
tioned ourselves at opposite ends of the block and walked toward her, each of us addressing her as we walked past her. She
made no response to our greetings and kept looking for our
car in the street. Had she had a bit more feistiness and arrogance, I fully suspect — the sorry state of employment for
black actresses notwithstanding — that she might have become moderately famous. Then, too, she might have become
a great painter if she'd stuck with that.

Mother's dramatic career peaked in a play called *The Other Woman*, presented in St. Paul sometime in the early 1930s. Mother was a student at the university, but theater with blacks was something that black fraternities, sororities, and independents put on in the black community in town, not on campus. As the story goes, Mother brought down the house and surprised everyone who knew her by sashaying, eyebrow-lifting, and cigarette-smoking her way through the lead of the play. Dressed in red, she played her final scene for all that it was worth, so much so that Tallulah Bankhead and Bette Davis would have looked on as tyros at a tryout as she puffed her cigarette, threw back her hair, and, with a suitor-shriveling line, vamped off the stage. She got raves, but abruptly ended her career. It was briefly revived in Hollywood, but that's another story.

Members of my family were, and are, a flexible lot on most issues. But on the subject of fraternities and sororities we have our passions. My mother and sister deplore them. I hate them; I find them useful only in asserting unpleasant realities, like banal group-think, one-upmanship based upon the acquisition of material goods, backbiting, and other forms of social regression.

My father felt differently. I suppose I must admit that "Greek" life in earlier decades had its place for black youths otherwise shut out of the social lives of their colleges and universities — particularly those who attended predominantly white schools. A man I knew who had gone to Harvard during the sixties told me how important it was to have a fraternity life with other black men at Boston-area colleges. There was no other guaranteed social milieu. He gave up the activity after graduation, but he still remembered it fondly. And I am sure fraternities and sororities gave countless young black people a lift in the face of the racial status quo at their colleges and universities. I refuse to go much further with it. Several years ago, I saw a group of black fraternity pledges marching down the main road of the campus where I taught. Their heads were shaved in a peculiar design, they wore military fatigues, and they were being called obscene and racially degrading names by their older frat "brothers." Their march made the front page of the university's daily, much to the chagrin of some black students. They were angry that the picture had been taken. My response was that both the pledging and the anger at a public event having been caught publicly were both profoundly off the point. But my father enjoyed his fraternity life when he was young, and as he grew older, the yearly holiday dances and picnics were fun. He was a Q, an Omega Psi Phi.

My family are great singers, too, and my father's tenor-baritone was smooth and rich, even though he smoked too much. His triumphant stage moment was really a combination of two: the first in a fraternal drag review, where he is reported to have had them screaming from their seats, dressed as a young thing, mouthing, "tee hee"—the sort of story I found sidesplitting when I was a child, but which began to bother me in vague ways with subsequent airings—and the second in a talent show evening when he sang "Brother, Can You Spare a Dime?" This Gorney and Harburg tune might well be called an anthem of the Great Depression, and like most American phrases, songs, and evocations of dreams or despair, when sung or spoken by someone black, it becomes an entirely different, extra-ironic experience, the most dramatic of which I've ever heard being Ray Charles singing "America the Beautiful." But here was my father, in a blue suit, standing in the center of a bare stage singing "Brother, Can You Spare a Dime?" gesturing with his arms and hands, dramatically—perhaps melodramatically—evoking the once-proud builder of railroads, Al, now looking for spare change, and capturing the sorrows of the Depression audience, singing their woes for them—with his fly unbuttoned. How I've longed to time travel to that moment so that I might laugh and cry at the same moment with him. I think my mother liked telling the story because every time she did he made a bit more peace with it, and came to laugh at the story's comic dimensions as heartily as the rest of us. I'm sure his arms were stretched completely out at the climactic, crescendoing lines of "Hey, don't you remember, it was Al—it was Al all the time. Hey, don't you remember, you're my pal? Brother, can you spare a dime?" Smarmy children like me, fresh from Psych 101, had a field day with that one.

My sister shares my feelings about "Greeks," but when she was a young teenager, the greasepaint's smell was too strong for her to resist in the face of mere principle. We lived in Dayton during her first two years of high school, and one of the black sororities put on what it called a "jabberwock," a revue of music, plays, and sketches. Prizes were awarded the best in each category. My sister had a small role as a maid to a rich family. I was there; I remember that she did bring down the house with one word. In her resonant voice—and as she later told me, "thinking Butterfly McQueen with dulcet tones"— she stretched the question "Ma-am?" to five syllables and the audience roared. Major roles, bit parts, one-liners, one-worders—they all did very well.

My own short theatrical career was not in independent productions that served an entire black community. I was Mama in *A Raisin in the Sun* in college. I was eighteen, and I believe my only claim to fame was that I forgot three pages of dialogue halfway through the first night, realized what I had done, and quickly ad-libbed all that had been lost. And I did appear in a faculty show of Gilbert and Sullivan's *Patience* once, but that's really off the point. I wasn't involved in buttressing the pride and self-worth of a black community in my role; neither was the college community an exilic one, separated from a white mainstream and its amusements.

During the Christmas season my sister and I occasionally accompany Mother to brunches or eggnog sips held by former Minnesotans who live in the Chicago area. I recall one late afternoon, sitting in the small quarters of a retirement apartment, having more fun than I've had in years, listening to ten or so septuagenarians happily, with much laughter and some contradiction, reminisce about their youths. One of Mother's friends — a dynamo with sparkling eyes and a razor wit — said laughingly, "We had such fun in those days. Nobody had any money; we ran in big groups. Everything was relaxed. If you didn't have a boyfriend you would just latch onto one of the stray fellows who was always around, and if you did, it didn't mean much. We would go caroling, tobogganing in the winters, and all year long there were dances. It was a hell of a lot of fun."

Later, I asked my mother, because she was a famous brooder and shy person, whether she had experienced such out-and-out fun, and she had to admit, "Well, yes." I think now of the quality of foreignness in those stories because I never had that kind of fun as a teenager or young adult. And what I noticed about the reminiscences of Mother's friends was that though certainly there was nostalgia for this Americana it was also obvious that they still knew how to have fun. And I was witnessing it; I was part of it. My experiences, thirty and forty years after their fun — in an ostensibly more racially relaxed world — were not so joyous. The only event in my youth even approaching one of those Minnesota outings was a trip I took to the Missouri State Fair in Sedalia with three of my friends. We saw the livestock, the food, the 4-H displays, and the cheap carnival contests and acts. There was no love, not the puppy kind at least, in our foursome of two girls and two boys, but I knew that things were just a bit off when the boys won huge stuffed rabbits and refused to give them to us. It seemed to me then that they insufficiently understood the game and us: we wanted the rabbits for no reason beyond the fact that a girl is supposed to come home with a stuffed animal from a fair. Not getting them gave them a kind of reversed and ironic significance.

Our adventure became absurd when we realized that we had missed our appointed bus back to the city. Sedalia's county in those days refused to go on daylight savings time, rendering the bus schedule useful for only the farm-minded cognoscenti. Afraid of parents' ire and embarrassed that seventeen year olds with our collective self-images could be so stupid, we went around the fair looking for black people who might be willing to sign for a rental car. We must have been quite a show to watch as we tried to convince one particular elderly lady that we were upright, trustworthy, and God-fearing. Needless to say, we took the midnight bus home, where the boys expected to meet stern fathers with pursed lips. I calculated that to be the flip side of insufficiently under-standing the game. Their concerns added significance where there was none. My father had long since gone to bed and Mother, the night owl, was merely watching her regular late show. My father laughed the next day when I told him there had been trepidation on the part of the boys. He said that he trusted me more with them than with my girlfriend — which was not an insult to my girlfriend, but meant that he under-stood that there was no significance at all in the four of us go-ing to the fair. He thought two bold girls were liable to get into all sorts of trouble. The only fun of the story is in retrospect, visualizing four black city kids wandering through a redneck carnival, looking for more than solidarity and kinship from rural, old black folks. Four black city kids were looking for a signature on a rental car form that would suddenly have made everything all right.

My friends and I did enjoy ourselves frequently, but it was so much with an eye to how we saw ourselves — forming a club called "Les Élus," and itching to conquer an indifferent and occasionally rabidly racist world. And our community, still exiled, seemed more self-conscious of what it was not than what it was. The reveling was spare.

My mother's friends even sang "Hail, Hail, the Gang's All Here," when they met in the old days and at Christmas. I remember the first time I heard the song. Nana and Papa had moved to Los Angeles after he had retired from the architect's office in St. Paul in 1949. They chose not to spend their later years in Minnesota (although they did move back briefly again, after the Santa Monica Freeway took their home in the early 1960s). My mother, sister, and I began our summer vacations there in 1951, when I was a strapping two, nearly three year old. I have seen pictures of my first days in Southern California, being held by strange women I can't remember, all of us smiling at Papa's rangefinder. There must have been a sharp, bright, unsmoggy California sun behind him, for we squint in the picture, looking straight out from the porch of the Spanish-flavored white stucco duplex Nana and Papa owned. I am a brown child, as is my sister, in what seems to this day to be a sea of whiteness. I remember mentally bonding with the only dark woman in the photo. I don't know who she was, but she walked with a limp, and my memory has placed leg braces on her, whether she had them or not. I think that reveals something about my feelings about race as a child. I suppose I felt that being black was a handicap and that I pitied the condition and had to sentimentalize it, so a gimpy lady becomes a tragic figure in leg braces. Doubtless she too was a member of the Minnesota Club, black and not-so-black exiles from the frozen North living out their days amid the palms.

Every summer the Club held a wonderful picnic in Griffith Park, a place that time and a less relaxed world have now made an unlikely spot for picnics of elderly Midwestern exiles. My grandparents, particularly Nana, were crack bridge players, and I remember that card tables proliferated among the wooden picnic tables that graced the shallow canyon where the festivities were held. I only vaguely remember other children, apart from my sister and me. And since I was rather shy and brooding myself, I stayed close to my mother and the glorious fried chicken, deviled eggs, baked beans, and potato salad that were always on hand at picnics, along with the California exotica of avocados, ice milk, and swollen, ripe peaches and plums. I recall once hovering around her, being shooed away, clutching a celery stick with one hand and pawing the sandy dirt with the other, when I turned around at the sound of the entire Minnesota Club singing, "Hail, Hail, the Gang's All Here," as the final members walked up, baskets, card tables, blankets, and chairs in hand. I thought the music strange, but the ditty stuck, and I sang it intermittently all afternoon.

I felt foreign there, I'm sure, mostly because I was a very young child among retirees. I was also distinctly brown among the fair. I was not yet an exile from the Middle West. I think of poor Sally Carrol Happer in Fitzgerald's "The Ice Palace," undone by her hapless holiday with Harry in the frozen North, lost in an ice palace, dying to go back home to sultry Georgia, where fun meant game-playing of an entirely different sort than that practiced by the "Hail, Hail" gang. Sally Carrol took the train from Georgia to the unnamed Minnesota, moving from what she saw as secure, warm, nurturing, to the cold and isolated.

> As she left the diner and swayed back into the Pullman she experienced a surging rush of energy and wondered if she was feeling the bracing air of which Harry had spoken. This was the North — her land now!
>
> "Then blow, ye winds, heigho! A-roving I will go," she chanted exultantly to herself.
>
> "What's 'at?" inquired the porter politely.
>
> "I said: 'Brush me off.' "

I love trains, although it is increasingly difficult to get to many places on them, and I've never told a porter to brush me off. Trains have always provided me with a sense of just how far places are from one another, in ways that driving a car or flying simply cannot. I look forward to trips from New York to Chicago because I have time to readjust to the fact that I am going to another region to be with my family. Whether or not we take the time to reminisce about the past in any way, our existences attest to it — to a history, a family, a race, a nation. When I feel the Broadway Limited rocking back and forth on tracks passing through the small towns of Pennsylvania, Ohio, and Indiana, across farmland, passing factories, I am reminded a bit more of who I am and where I came from.

I have memories of being a child, living near railroad tracks in Dayton, watching with awe the New York Central and the Pennsylvania New York to Chicago and St. Louis trains roaring past the single, unlighted railroad crossing, of it always being dusk, with the train black, ominous, naturally snake-like, with a white blur of faces in the speeding diner synchronized with the blaring Doppler effect on my ears.

By the time my train lurches past Gary and into Chicago's Loop, I am ready to be there. I've seen the backyards facing the tracks, the pick-ups piled to the sides, with clothes on the lines regardless of the weather, and main streets with hardware stores, a five-and-dime, a bar, and empty steel mills, and farms for sale—all the things my college classmate, Steve Goodman, evoked in his song "The City of New Orleans," his requiem for the passenger train. And there's more, because these images are of things most people I know have never seen; they think of these sights as belonging in a twilight zone of American history, circa 1890 to World War II. That's not how I see these images, though. As the train moves through the backyard neighborhoods, I remember running across the tracks, hoping I wouldn't trip, when I was chased home, sticks and rocks flying, one day after school; I remember pulling into the station in St. Louis, where the decaying black steel and glass canopy that hovered over the tracks was filled with holes and what looked like dangling moss, making me think of documentaries on war-torn Europe; I remember eating pancakes in the diner, a treat because our budget was small, scrunching through the desert dust that gathered on the syrup as Mother, my sister, and I rode the Santa Fe through Seligman and Kingman, Arizona to Needles, Barstow, and across the San Bernardino Valley to Los Angeles.

Things happen on trains that simply do not occur in other

situations. The people who ride them have chosen the train for many reasons—fear of flying, budget, a way of seeing scenery instead of whisking past on a four-laner, a chance to keep the kids from screaming, "Let's go there!" as the loaded car passes yet another "magic prehistoric garden" sign or killing each other in the back seat. Occasionally the captive population of a train turns into a temporary town filled with all the stereotypical characters one finds there. On a trip from California to Chicago I was in the club car, having a few beers and looking out the window, when I noticed a tiny woman stopping at every table, telling jokes, singing songs. She was deep into a drunk. She may have annoyed some of the travelers, but most, after a while, got into the spirit of her day and sang along, bought her drinks, dealt her in card games. She was still going strong as I walked through the club car on my way to breakfast in the diner the next morning. That afternoon, somewhere in Kansas, she detrained. As far as I could ascertain, the entire population of the train waved good-bye to her, my coach car tipping to the right as everyone moved to the windows to wave.

Train trips help me organize my thoughts, help me solve what sometimes seems the great riddle of self. I make use of the miles, not wishing to go back in time, but endeavoring to understand the structure of the present. Air travel disturbs me, physically and psychologically—it destroys my rhythm and undermines my questions. And driving a car across the country becomes a game of physical endurance—the car's and my own—involving little concern for miles and their meaning other than how many I've managed to pass since I last looked at the odometer.

I think of my grandparents when I ride, of how I miss them, of whether or not I knew them at all. My world and the communities I've lived in have been so different from that of the Twin Cities in the first half of the century or from the exilic Minnesota Club. Sometimes I think I am more of an exile by never having had a similar world and life. But train rides help

73

me destroy the gulf of foreign feeling at the sight and sound of the Minnesota Club, at the fun my parents and their friends had doing all those corny things, at missing theatricals in Midwestern cities where an open fly served to momentarily relieve the urgency of economic and racial despair. The last time I rode what used to be the route of the Atchison, Topeka, and the Santa Fe line, the Chief, the El Capitan, and the Super Chief (the all-Pullman train I never rode), now called the Southwest Limited by Amtrak, I thought hard about my grandparents and their lives and how the distances of space and time, of expectation and experience, between us must not have been so wide after all.

I own a battered seventh edition, 1907, of W. E. B. Du Bois's *The Souls of Black Folk*. I found it one day, along with a packet of letters, under linen napkins and sculpted green dessert plates at the bottom of a moving company dish barrel. I was helping to clear out the attic in my mother's home as we prepared to move her to Chicago. The book is autographed, "Very sincerely yours, W. E. B. Du Bois, Atlanta, Ga., November 9, 1909." Above the autograph is my grandfather's name, in his artistic Palmer-method penmanship. On the flyleaf I can see where pencil markings, made by a very young child, have been erased. And, amid the blank bits of paper spread throughout it — bookmarks, I assume — are a card for a roofing and paint company, "Modernize Your Home, Phone Nestor 1315," and two Christmas favor cut-outs, done by my mother and her sister. There are marginal comments throughout. Over Chapter Eleven, "Of the Passing of the First-Born," is written, "A Beautiful Chapter," naturally making me think that my grandfather was remembering the miscarriage of his first child and only son. *The Souls of Black Folk* is the great lyrical text of black America, blending philosophy, literary criticism, autobiography, history, politics, and commentaries on poetry, music, folklore, and religion. I recall that the first time I read it, in the 1960s, I was riveted by the foreword's opening lines:

> Herein lie buried many things which if read with patience may show the strange meanings of being black here at the dawning of the Twentieth Century. The meaning is not without interest to you, Gentle Reader; for the problem of the Twentieth Century is the problem of the color-line.

There it was, a nineteenth-century literary sensibility expressing one of the only twentieth-century truths I was certain I knew. And, although I could only imagine "the strange meanings of being black at the dawning of the Twentieth Century," I did have some experience with strange meanings in the late 1960s.

At the back of Papa's book, past the copious quotes and testimonials from publishers and newspapers, on the back flyleaves, is a long handwritten poem called "Beyond the Veil." I can find no source of it elsewhere and have concluded it must be Papa's composition. There are erasures, primarily at the ends of lines, where he decided to change the words for better rhyme and meter. He wouldn't have copied a poem that way. It is emotional, strident, derivative, sonorous, a nineteenth-century poem written by an architect, a self-taught ragtime piano player, a cigar-smoker, and inveterate letter-writer — not, perhaps, a poet. The fourth and last stanza reads:

> Afar the distant rumbling of mighty hosts with quickening tread
> Falls on my ears and serves to stir the souls of countless dead:
> To call the living to their feet, to rub their sleeping eyes and peer
> To see the lifting of the veil disclosing serried ranks of young and old
> Like valiant templars triumphant bearers of the cross of gold.

It's not a very good poem, but I do like the ambiguity of the image of eyes that have been sleeping in the third line, and prefer to think it is the newly awakened living, who are being made aware for the first time of possibility, and perhaps transcendence. Most likely Papa meant the dead.

The most famous, the most quoted part of *The Souls of Black Folk* is Du Bois's definition of double consciousness, and a place where Papa was moved to make brief marginal comments:

Du Bois	Papa
After the Egyptian and Indian, the Greek and Roman, the Teuton and Mongolian, the Negro is a sort of seventh son, born with a veil, and gifted with second-sight in this American world, — a world which yields him no true self-consciousness, but only lets him see himself through the revelation of the other world. It is a peculiar sensation, this double consciousness, this sense of always looking at one's self by the tape of a world that looks on in amused contempt and pity. One ever feels his two-ness, an American, a Negro; two souls, two thoughts, two unreconciled strivings; two warring ideals in one dark body, whose dogged strength alone keeps it from being torn asunder.	How True.

    The history of the American Negro is the history of this strife, — this longing to attain self-conscious manhood, to

merge his double self into a better and truer self. In this merging he wishes neither of the
older selves to be lost. He
would not Africanize America,
for America has too much to
teach the world and Africa. He
would not bleach his Negro soul
in a flood of white Americanism, for he knows that Negro
blood has a message for the
world. He simply wishes to
make it possible for a man to be
both a Negro and an American,
without being cursed and spit
upon by his fellows, without
having the doors of Opportunity closed roughly in his face.

This simple ambition
is slowly but surely
lifting the colored
American into the
ranks of achievement
all along the line.

I have no way of knowing when Papa read the book, how
many times, or when he made his marginal notes and
poems about color lines and veils. Either it was before World
War I when he and Nana, as young marrieds, moved from
Nebraska to Wyoming and back again, or after the war, when
they lived in Minnesota, when my mother and aunt would
have been coordinated enough to control scissors and make
Christmas bookmarks, each with a red construction paper
star, guiding their father to his place. On some days I would
like to think his comments were fueled by New Negro hopes
that accompanied the end of the war, when dreams of shatter-
ing the line, for good, found words that rose from pulpits, off
editorial pages of the black press nationwide, and from poets,
composers, painters, and musicians, either on their way to or
arrived at Harlem, New York, U.S.A. On other days, I realize it doesn't matter when Papa made his notes. Neither he nor
Du Bois needed the New Negro Movement to articulate their
thoughts on racial inequities and strange meanings.

As I rode the Southwest Limited toward Los Angeles, I realized that when or where or how Papa read *The Souls of Black Folk* would always remain an unsolvable mystery for me, even though I might enjoy creating a narrative line for my own pleasure from time to time. I thought about Jim Crow cars, the bane of black travelers for so many decades, of Du Bois having been refused a Pullman accommodation on the Cincinnati-Atlanta route of the Southern Railway in 1900, and of Papa getting a Pullman on the same train in 1913 because the conductor, on seeing Papa's Shriners pin, assumed he was white and asked him to dine. I recalled Du Bois's line from his 1940 *Dusk of Dawn, An Essay Toward an Autobiography of a Race Concept*, my favorite work of his after *The Souls of Black Folk*:

> It still remains possible in the United States for a white American to be a gentleman and a scholar, a Christian and a man of integrity, and yet flatly and openly refuse to treat as a fellow human being any person who has Negro ancestry.

And I thought about all the so-called gentlemen and gentlewomen I'd run across who fit the description to a T, whom I considered, and still do, ill-bred, because the mouthing of racist sentiments is most certainly a sign of that. I remembered Papa as a wonderful grandfather, full of stories, change in his pockets, cigar-band rings for my fingers, and cigar boxes, rich-smelling even when empty, for my pencils and crayons.

He is remembered by others as a man with extraordinary talent and temper, with little business sense and a tendency to verbally abuse my grandmother — a man who sometimes narrowly walked along the color line.

The more I think of Papa and Du Bois, of "strange meanings" then and now, of double-consciousness and blackness, I find myself tempted to put Papa's life — what little I know of it — as he did, into a perspective that goes beyond family to the large, dense, and complex history of black people in America. Papa had far more in common with Du Bois than he had with me. He was fifteen years Du Bois's junior and sixty-five years my senior. He was a man of obvious mixed blood, with a love of formal dress, order, professional discipline, and self-aggrandizement — a quality he despaired of in others. On hearing someone tout his or her accomplishments, he would unceremoniously break into the vain disquisition with the word "Song!" drawn out like a foghorn at sea. He was an architect who spent hours a day at his board, making plans that were more like paintings and blueprints that had the perfection and three-dimensionality of a computer-drawn, Lucasfilm star-warrior's trajectory.

Du Bois grew up in Great Barrington, Massachusetts, the scion of several generations of free, mixed-blooded blacks. He spent years studying at Fisk, at Harvard, and in Germany before he began a teaching career. Just after the turn of the century he formed the Niagara Movement, a precursor of the NAACP. Du Bois wrote essays, scholarly books, and a novel, and made the *Crisis* — the organ of the NAACP — his fief for decades. He wrote literary criticism, compiled information on lynchings, on the treatment of black soldiers in the army, and developed economic, social, and political theories designed to improve the conditions surrounding black American life. In *Dusk of Dawn* Du Bois wrote:

> Not only do white men but colored men forget the facts of the Negro's double environment. The Negro American has for his environment not only the white surrounding world, but also, and touching him usually much more nearly and compellingly, is the environment furnished by his own colored group. There are exceptions, of course, but this is the rule. The American Negro, therefore, is surrounded and conditioned by the concept which he has of white people and he is treated in accordance with the concept they have of him.

Papa lived at least partially as an exception to this rule. He lived in the netherworld of black professionals in white Minnesota and he claimed that he faced little discrimination in his life. He had pride in his work and was happy to be able to ply his trade. He might have passed, with Nana, as some more exotic admixture of white and something else. But he loved the black social world, with its conversation that could run easily from Cool Papa Bell and the Negro Leagues to Dr. Du Bois's latest column, all within minutes. He made razor-sharp comments about racism and America. And he loved taking his brown granddaughter, my sister, to the candy store to fill her with chocolates and sing silly songs to her. And he indulged his other granddaughter, me, who loved the smell of his automobile and would sit playing with the "clinker"—the lock—as he whisk-broomed the interior daily. Like Du Bois, he never thought of himself as anything other than black and talented.

Papa was born in Lawrence, Kansas in 1883, but when he was an infant his family moved to Omaha. Langston Hughes remembered Lawrence—he spent much of his boyhood there—as a highly segregated, unpleasant place in the early years of the century. I was in Lawrence only once, and I have an indistinct memory of a carillon and people chanting, "Rock Chalk, Jayhawk, KU." Papa's parents had six sons and six daughters, some of whom, in the large family scenario of the nineteenth century, died in infancy, others before adulthood—Mother says the handsomest and the prettiest, of course. When I asked her what Papa's father did, she told me she never knew, but that he had not been a farmer and that there had been no slaves on the line. She said Papa's father, by all accounts, was a mean and vain man, the son of an Englishman and a racially mixed woman, who was fond of proclaiming to his brood that he would look better laid out in a coffin, stone-cold-dead, than any of them could hope to appear in life regardless of how hard they tried.

Papa's father, I learned from one of the letters in the packet I found—he kept copies of what he wrote—drove an ammunition wagon for the Union Army at the age of fifteen. Papa's mother taught school in "either Kirkwood, Mo. or Webster

Groves, or both," until she married. (I once saw a documentary called *Sixteen in Webster Groves* and I shuddered for days afterward at the banality and narrowness of the teenagers interviewed and their dreams.) Papa's great-grandmother, Agnes Bledsoe, died with a measure of Americana fame. Many years after her death Papa wrote a friend, partially drawing from her obituary:

> Mrs. Agnes Bledsoe, the oldest citizen in Nebraska, died yesterday at the authentic age of 108 years old. She was born in Virginia in 1787. She and her mother were free persons. The mother worked as a maid for the Pendelton family of Virginia. When this Agnes Bledsoe was a child of five years old, she and her mother were taken to an open-air gathering where President George Washington was the guest speaker. Just prior to the end of this meeting, the chairman of the proceedings announced that the President would be glad to answer any questions. Since the Pendeltons were very close friends of the President's family, Mrs. Pendelton said, "Mr. President, I have with me a little five year old girl who wishes to shake hands with you. May I bring her up?" According to this . . . article printed by the Omaha *World Herald* in 1895, President George Washington stooped down, shook hands with this child, then picked her up and kissed her.
>
> I doubt very much if there is even a handful of people, still living who ever saw or read this remarkable commentary on the life and death of my great grandmother, Mrs. Agnes Bledsoe. One of my older brothers . . . who passed in 1959 at the age of eighty-six, had for years a yellowed clipping of this 1895 newspaper article, but we have, so far, been unable to find it.

My friend Kathy, who knows something about genealogy and the techniques of mapping one's ancestry, says that the names Pendelton and Pemberton, for all intents and purposes, should be considered the same name. This makes for an interesting, if unlikely, potential arena for both sides of my family to have met—the Pembertons, about whom I know practically nothing, might have been around Mrs. Agnes Bledsoe, great-grandmother to grandfather Wigington.

In 1895, Papa was twelve and loved to draw. He was developing a talent that would win him three first prizes, in charcoal, pencil, and pen and ink, at the Trans-Mississippi World's Fair in Omaha in 1899. In 1895, Booker T. Washington addressed the Cotton States and International Exposition in Atlanta and was hurled into the national limelight with, among other things, the remark that "In all things that are purely social we [blacks and whites] can be as separate as the fingers, yet one as the hand in all things essential to mutual progress." In 1895 Du Bois, fresh from three years in Europe, telegraphed Washington with words and sentiment he was rarely, if ever, to repeat to the man's face: "Let me heartily congratulate you upon your phenomenal success at Atlanta—it was a word fitly spoken." And in 1895, somewhere in Omaha, the oldest Nebraskan then on the books, my great-grandmother to the fourth power, kissed by Washington—George, that is—died.

By 1900, the year Du Bois, among other things, wrote the Southern Railway to ask that it clarify its position on race and Pullman cars, Papa was studying art, architecture, and engineering, privately, because two of his grade school teachers had given him a scholarship after his success at the 1899 Fair. And during the next few years he found time to travel back to Kansas, to court my grandmother, a pretty mixture of Cherokee, black, and white who had been born and raised outside of Atchison, a railroad town to the northeast of Lawrence.

My grandparents married in 1908, five years after the publication of *The Souls of Black Folk*, and they went off to Sheridan, Wyoming. I used to wonder how in hell they got to Wyoming, but judging from some of the places I've ended up myself, I know better than to ask. They were simply going to find a fresh place to start, where one of Papa's brothers-in-law ran a dry-cleaning business, and where newlyweds might begin in a territory potentially light years away from the Middle West. They left after a year, headed back east instead of opting to continue westward in the middle of that long era between the Gold Rush and the Great Depression.

While in Wyoming, Papa won his first architectural competition. He wrote,

> One morning at breakfast we read in a small weekly paper that Dr. James E. Shepard was planning to build an Administration Building, a Men's Dormitory, a Women's Dormitory and a new home for himself in Durham, North Carolina. At that time he was President of a School called The National Religious Training School. I did not know him personally and he did not know me at all. However, I sent him a long night-letter telegram, asking him if an Architect had been selected? He sent me a reply immediately with complete information, saying that an Architect would be selected through a competition. A few months later he advised me that I had won the competition. Eventually, many years later, this School became what is now North Carolina State College for Negroes. This result reminds me of a sage statement once made by Dr. Booker T. Washington. It was, "Take Fast Hold of Education, For She is Thy Life."

Back in Omaha, Papa worked for a large firm, still as an apprentice, and later opened his own office. He and Nana had two healthy daughters and in 1914 the family moved to St. Paul, where Papa, through competition again, became the Senior Architectural Draftsman of the city, and later the Chief Architectural Designer. He went on to design high schools, grade schools, park buildings, a famous water tower, and ice palaces, which he called "my babies," for the St. Paul Winter Carnival.

I think about Du Bois. By 1900 he had finished his landmark study called *The Philadelphia Negro*, and he was about to write *The Souls of Black Folk*. He was laying the groundwork for the Niagara Movement. He no longer congratulated Booker T. Washington, but castigated him for what he saw as Washington's accommodationist stance in the face of ever-closing doors of opportunity, and thought Washington passively accepted a dangerous revisionist history of the black American experience that justified slavery and revealed "scientific" proofs of black inferiority. (This kind of history comes from a mentality not unlike that of a letter-writer to the Chicago — where else? — *Tribune* I read not long ago. The author was congratulating South Africa because it is, he said, a society that works well, while black-governed Africa is corrupt. Slave societies often run well, and, after all, Mussolini did keep the trains running on time.)

In the early part of this century, Du Bois was helping to create a language and forge a sensibility that would, if internalized by blacks, allow them to liberate themselves from the debasing definitions of blackness created by white America. And Papa was writing letters about his own experience in St. Paul:

> Each night, year after year, I thanked Almighty God for granting me some degree of ability, a stout heart of courage, a mind of sincere understanding, a sound and liberal appreciation of my good neighbors, a hope and trust that man's inhumanity to man in some areas of my country would stop NOW, not next year, not a generation from now, but NOW.

Papa was one of Du Bois's Talented Tenth, working, hoping, striving for a kind of success that would break down the barriers of racism. He lived with Du Boisian double-consciousness. He believed, like Du Bois, that the principles forming the underpinnings of American society were wonderful, but that the hypocrisy of reality was nearly unbearable. He wrote Franklin D. Roosevelt, petitioning for the decent treatment of black soldiers in 1941, as part of the March on Washington Movement:

> We thank God that we have America and we feel as much a part of it, and we are a part, even as though we're its rich soil. We ask, even if the act outranks the Magna Carta and

parallels Lincoln's Emancipation Proclamation, that you will find full cause today, in the most critically dangerous period of our national history, to act, that it cannot and shall not be said that this urgent and fundamental petition failed and that America failed so many millions of its loyal citizens. Finally we ask that wherever it can be found by investigation and proof that Negro soldiers or sailors of this nation have been or are being subjected to undemocratic, illegal or vicious attacks due to color or racial discrimination that such practice and procedure shall stop even if it or they require an executive order from the president.

And commenting on the election of John F. Kennedy in 1960, Papa wrote to a friend:

> If President-Elect Kennedy, after inauguration, has the determination, the courage, the honesty, the desire and the ability to produce among other important matters, an equitable Civil Rights Bill, I shall wire him my sincerest congratulations, and I shall thank God for a strong, forthright, able and God-fearing President. If he cannot manage this, then I shall have to fall back on President Eisenhower's most outstanding domestic achievement, the desegregation of our Capital City, Washington, D.C. — No other president in our whole history ever had the courage and foresight to bring about desegregation in Washington. We were the laughing stock of the world as to segregated Washington.

In 1912, when Papa was making blueprints, Du Bois was no longer considering the Republican Party, in Frederick Douglass's terms, "the ship, all else is the sea," and was justifying a vote for Woodrow Wilson, the man who was to oversee the segregation of Washington. And in 1963, when Du Bois was dying on the eve of the March on Washington, Papa had written a friend not a week before: "Nobody ever gives the underdog full equality in anything. He has to fight for it, even if somebody gets hurt."

On my paperback edition of *Dusk of Dawn* is a photograph of Du Bois, looking very distinguished, holding a pair of glasses. In 1917 he received a letter from the Garrett Distributing Company of Mt. Sterling, Kentucky, asking him if he would give permission for his name to be used on one of the company's "private brands of cigars," and his "photograph on box labels and cigar bands." Du Bois wrote the company, "Gentlemen: I have no objections to your using my name on one of your brands of cigars providing the cigar is not too bad."

Papa not only smoked cigars, he chewed them. He would light them only occasionally. I remember the backyard of their Los Angeles home as a place where figs, avocados, and peaches would drop to the ground, to join the snails and cigar ends Papa would clip off with his pocket scissors whenever an end got too soggy, to become, after he raked, a rich California compost. It would be nice to think that Papa smoked a Du Bois–brand cigar around 1918, but I doubt if he did, if they ever existed or were distributed. Still, the cigars, the sentiments, the cultural interpretations, the voice, the childhoods, the high-seriousness, the dreams of their lives link Du Bois and Papa in my mind, and I believe I understand each of them better by having read one extensively and touched the life and letters of the other.

Several years ago my mother and aunt went to St. Paul for ceremonies designating the Highland Park Water Tower a historical landmark. It was one of the designs of which Papa was most proud. Clearing out Mother's attic and finding hidden treasures, I found another — a painting of one of Papa's "babies." The castle is huge, with bright lights showing the intricate brickwork design, beckoning north country revellers to enter its mammoth, fairy-tale rooms. It is a wonderful painting to me, a testimony to Papa's artfulness and to lost causes: an ice palace, a temporary place designed to evoke romantic dreams of princes and princesses proclaiming their sovereignty over a frozen North — painted, designed, and construction overseen by my black, cigar-chewing grandfather.

I have never been to a St. Paul Winter Carnival and there was a time when I could not have imagined what one might have been like. I am sure it never would have occurred to Sally Carrol Happer that a black man could have designed a building like the one that brought her so much woe. But remembering the long lost moments of my mother as vamp, and my father as Al, I find that I need not have been there to understand what it felt like to see the ice palace, to feel it, to know well its designer. I get closer to a particular black life and a particular personal history, carved out of the ice and snow of the plains, foreign from the South and its particular kinds of heat. And I begin to feel warmer and more secure.

The Koan of Nana

THE LETTER READS, in part:

This communication is in regard to the recent decision of the Indian Claims Commission, which concluded that the Cherokee Nation is entitled to an award of $14,789,476.15 as payment for inadequate compensation for its lands in Oklahoma, known as "The Cherokee Outlet Act of March 3, 1893." . . .

I am respectfully requesting full information from you, relative to this important matter, particularly in view of the fact that I am a direct descendant of two of the names that appear on the "Kerns-Clifton Roll." These names appear as follows, Lizzie Johnson, Kerns-Clifton Roll No. 3991, Page 161. Lizzie Johnson was my mother. The other name appearing on this roll, is Mary King, Kerns-Clifton Roll No. 1631, Page 65. Mary King was my maternal Grandmother.

Knowing that the final act relative to the distribution of the long-delayed $14,789,476.15 award to the Cherokee Nation, and appropriated by the Supplemental Appropriation Act of the 87th Congress, First Session, Document No. 56, I am herewith requesting and applying for the proper and required Heirship Blank or Blanks.

My Heirship Claim, herein and hereby made, is based on

Lizzie Johnson, my deceased Mother, and on Mary King, my maternal Grandmother, deceased.

It was a valiant attempt, but Nana failed to get any of that $14,789,476.15 — not even that final tantalizingly and perfectly absurd fifteen cents. Nana was not surprised. She had a greater understanding of how the world really works than almost anyone I've ever met. She was kind, loving, and sarcastic. She loved her grandchildren — perhaps her grandson, my cousin, a bit more than she did my sister and me, but it wasn't personal. For some people of her generation these emotions seemed to go with the territory, and my minding would not have changed them. Suffice it to say that I never consciously felt that we girls were less prized.

When I was young I always thought Nana looked the way grandmothers were supposed to look. Her hair was white, thick, with undulating waves in it. She wore grandmother shoes — sensible, sturdy, heavy-soled oxfords with two-inch heels. She wore housedresses and aprons with pockets for her handkerchieves and thimble. She had a farm girl's frame, although Mother says she never lived on a farm, and the softest palms I have ever felt in my life. Her skin was very fair, with high cheekbones and a jawline that curved to a point at her chin. Her nose was a serious one — a large, American Indian nose that matched her cheekbones. And her eyes were so large, so beautiful in their light grayish brown, that I found myself staring at them when I was a little girl. I remember the constant set of her mouth holding a smile — sometimes an innocent one, usually a worldly one filled with humor. I loved to watch her eat, her lips closing as she chewed, with the faint sound of dentures slipping. This plucked some almost inaccessible and peculiar aesthetic chord in me. The only thing she did that I actively disliked was to have us save our cloth napkins after a meal. I am, as my father was, a serious napkin-user, and I never wanted to touch the thing after a meal. The idea of using it two days down the line turned my stomach.

Nana reminded me of Jack Benny. She would place the palm of her hand on the side of her face, her little finger just touching the corner of her mouth, her head turned just slightly to the side, as she made one understatement after another. Maybe she got it from Jack Benny; maybe he got it from her. All I know is that Nana was devastatingly accurate in her sarcasm and would, on occasion, look you straight in the face and laugh at you with a "Hee, hee, hee," and her head would bob just a little with each "Hee."

She had suffered her share of unhappiness. When Nana was thirteen Lizzie Johnson died from a ruptured appendix. They couldn't get her to the hospital in time to save her. Nana's favorite brother, Walter, was killed in a hunting accident when he was a little boy. Later she married Papa and lived in St. Paul. Papa got his pay regularly, but didn't bring home enough of it, and was occasionally waylaid by card games and flashy women. This spawned arguments and enough dissatisfaction for her to leave him in 1933 and go to California. She lived a long time, to the age of ninety-two, but during her last few years she was an invalid, and my father and mother cared for her. When my father died, Mother did as much as she could on her own until it was obvious that Nana needed to be under professional care. One day she had managed to get out of bed and out of the house. She was found wandering in the front yard; Mother came home from work to rescue her.

Nana died of a stroke in 1980. I had not seen her since the Christmas of 1978; my aunt gave her a bell that Christmas, like the ones grade school teachers used to ring to call the cherubs in from recess. She loved the bell, and broke out into a long and sustained laughter when she first saw it — I have a photograph of her ringing it. It was a joyous moment for the four of us: my sister, my mother, Nana, and me, standing in her bedroom on Christmas morning, laughing and trying hard not to think about the empty beds that were all around us.

I was at an Ivy League football game becoming rapidly blotto. My old friend Maurice and I would sometimes go to games during the early 1970s, a period when Vietnam and Cambodia and Kent State and Jackson State and Nixon and Agnew and SDS and strikes and marches and curriculum reform were the most visible undergraduate concerns. Football was hardly in fashion, but we went to several games because I wanted to see what it was all about: the tailgate parties, the patrician style, both real and assumed, on the playing fields and in the stadia.

This game was cold and rainy. It was the Harvard-Yale game—I think. We were sitting near the very top of the stadium in Cambridge, sipping two thermoses' worth of fine Kentucky bourbon, neat. We might have been guzzling it. Just before halftime I went in search of a toilet; as I staggered back, my eyes caught a couple who were sitting a row or two behind us, on the other side of the aisle. The woman looked to be in her middle thirties, perhaps younger; I couldn't decide. She wore makeup tastefully, if in abundance. Her gloves were off, her left hand displaying a very, very large diamond ring, surrounded by reasonably sized smaller ones. I flexed my finger, wondering what kind of muscles a ring like that would develop. (The only muscled fingers I've ever seen belonged to Segovia. I could see them from the tenth row of Avery Fisher Hall.) The potential weight of the ring—not its stones, its cost, or its ostensible meaning—fascinated me, and I looked at it as only someone well on the way to being completely drunk can concentrate on minutiae. I smiled at her. She had frosted blond hair and she wore what looked to be a long silver fox fur. Sleek black suede boots were just visible below the hemline. She winked back at me and took another swig from the large silver flask she shared with, I assumed, her husband: an older man, perhaps in his late fifties, with thinning, silver-gray hair. He wore a double-breasted silver cashmere coat, a black scarf, and heavy black leather gloves that gave a muffled clap as he rooted for the Crimson. As I sought my balance in moving down the two or three steps to my seat, he put his arm around her, nuzzled her, and took the flask from her hands.

The game ended and one of the teams won. Maurice and I staggered up the steps and the woman smiled at me as we passed, and called after me, "Honey?" I don't usually answer to names like Honey, but I paused and looked back. She beckoned me to wait a minute for her. Maurice went on, saying he would meet me outside the stadium because he was in a hurry to find a john. I waited for the woman to stagger up to me. She pulled me gently by the arm and led me out of earshot of her companion, who was now in conversation with another man. Then, letting my arm go, she gestured toward Maurice, and asked, "Harvard man?"

I said, "Yes."

Then, with her still ungloved left hand, sweeping it from her head to her toes in an Elizabethan flourish — the way Bess Meyerson used to model the mink coat on "The Big Payoff" — she half-stuttered with a whisky breath and a whisky voice, "Honey, marry 'im. Marry 'im. See?" Her hand kept moving. "Marry 'im."

I smiled wryly, warily, and humbly, and said, "Sure."

Naturally I didn't. Marrying Maurice for his money would have become one of the greatest jokes in the history of the world; he has less of it than I do. And beyond a disinclination on each of our parts to view the other romantically, marriage would have spoiled a long-standing friendship that's still good. But I often think of the woman, the admitted gold digger, and the mind-set of women who feel that they've failed in life if they don't marry. This fear has reached crisis proportions among some women of my generation, so much so that only the other day I read a newspaper article that told the story of one who married a man she didn't love — in fact, didn't even particularly like — because she'd read statistics that proved her prospects of marriage diminished by quantum leaps with every age-producing day. She was thirty-two. I think about the silver-foxed lady and the desperate newlywed and realize how differently I was raised. Both my sister and I were urged to be fiercely independent of mind, of action, and of heart. For better or worse, we never developed the attitude or style that attracts gentleman callers. The last real date I had — movies, dinner, that sort of thing, my third in life — was in my last year of college. And the only times men have given me flowers have been for good luck at impending lectures, and once two gay men gave me a dozen roses on Valentine's Day because I had complained of never having received any.

My sister was married once, for ten years. That's her story, not mine. But marriage never became even remotely an issue for me. My wanderlust has rarely kept me in a place long enough to learn the names of my colleagues' children, let alone have a relationship, not to mention the fact that eligible men, marriageable men, black or white, are not a visible resource on America's college faculties, or, it would seem, even in their vicinity. I simply know that sometimes I wish I were married and most of the time I'm happy I'm not.

Not long ago I read Phyllis Rose's interesting book *Writing of Women*, and was much taken with the short essay on Simone de Beauvoir. According to Rose, de Beauvoir and Jean-Paul Sartre had, in some ways, a most enviable relationship — passionate, cerebral, intimate — with separate residences and no marriage certificate. She notes, "De Beauvoir was intensely skeptical about marriage, believing that it was virtually impossible for a woman who married or even lived with a man to escape the traditional female role of housekeeper and caretaker." I feel the same, if only because it is enough of a chore to take care of myself without considering the married alternative, and because I have met few men who can even begin to take care of themselves. But perhaps the caretaking is part of the deal, along with a number of other things I don't know anything about.

Nana provided me with some guidance in all of this. She was a voracious newspaper reader, from the front page to the last. Occasionally I would hear her chuckling over a soft news feature about some marital woe or other, or a letter to Ann Landers/Dear Abby. She would look up, hee-heeing, and tell the story. At the end, with all seriousness in her voice and the glint gone out of her eye, she would say, "There's a lot worse things that can happen to you than not getting married." She said it many times in the years I knew her. I believed her then; I believe her now.

Speaking of marriage is one thing. I do know of loneliness and of the aching, nearly debilitating desire to leap giddily, eyes afire, into bed with someone who would love me and never think of getting out. On some occasions, I have taken my comfort where I could find it, only to be gripped by a debilitating guilt stronger than the sexual desire that catalyzed the whole thing. And I've been in situations where the chemistry has been too strong, the passion unabated and all-consuming. I've finally learned to run like mad in the other direction when I get such a case of "chemicals." I do have many friends, though. I am lucky to have them in abundance and I know they'll be around for the duration. They are what counts for me; I've learned to live without romance.

There is more to all of this. Rose quotes Alice Schwarzer's *After "The Second Sex": Conversations with Simone de Beauvoir*, written before de Beauvoir's death:

> Simone de Beauvoir has led an extraordinary life and she knows it. Despite her intellectual commitment to solidarity with other women, at a deep level she does not seem to feel it. A calm sense of privilege, an air of exemption from the human lot, pervades everything she says. She is certain she has used her intelligence to live better than the rest of us. As a result, we may look up to her, but it's hard to love her. At one point, Schwarzer invites de Beauvoir to identify with other women: "I know quite a few women who have been made to pay for insisting on the right to show their intelligence and strength of character. People around them make them feel: so you are 'as good as any man,' are you? Well, then 'you are

not desirable' as a woman! Have you come up against that?"
Simone de Beauvoir's answer? "No."

Lucky Simone. I have found — without thinking about myself
in terms of masculine values and *sans* Simone's levels, but with
a modicum of intellect and some strength of character — the
answer to be profoundly and loudly yes. I am far from being
alone in this situation, and it is exacerbated for black women.
As my friend Freda once said to me, "Once a woman hits her
late twenties and on, all the men left are either gay, interested
only in white women, in prison, on drugs, or such duds that
you wouldn't want to go near them. The rest are dead or married, black or white." Or, in a more scholarly vein, Gloria
Naylor wrote in the "Hers" column of the *New York Times* in
February 1986:

> We are a minority community overrepresented in the pools
> of the unemployed, the poorly educated and those subsisting
> below the poverty line, which will concomitantly insure over-
> representation in teenage pregnancy, drug abuse and prison
> populations. In short, there just aren't enough viable mates
> out there for black women and bleak prospects of a greater
> percentage being born.

Naylor notes that, by definition, the black family histori-
cally "looked upon as assets assertive, self-directed women."
But, she says, widespread assimilation of the values of white
America into the black community somehow changed their
position: "The concept is relatively new for us that a woman
who insists on equal (or even superior) weight being given to
her opinions, her salary and her decision-making ability in
the home is 'threatening' to black manhood."

The shape of black women's self-identification and expectations changed with the dream of entering the middle class
and leaving the penury and desolation of slavery, indentured
serfdom, and their post-manumission cousins behind. Entire
generations of well-educated and exciting black women
looked forward to making the term Black Woman into some-

thing new, something different from the various names we've
been called—names like Negress, bitch, Sapphire, Mamma,
and Monkey Woman. Since before the turn of the century,
black women were at the forefront of the fight against racism
in all its forms, defining themselves not as would-be white
women, but as black, female, and determined. In a culture
where women have often been viewed, at best, as prizes, black
women could easily recognize the inutility of an "ornamental"—to use Naylor's word—designation. In the course of the
twentieth century the least favored of women in America
worked to find a new meaning of *woman* that would retain the
sensual and nurturing, and add the bold and self-confident.
Naturally there were exceptions; there always are. But I have
come to believe, quite firmly, that the most admirable women
I know have redefined *woman* and taken it to a place where I
am happy to live.

According to all outward, categorical definitions, the
women in my family were not particularly different or "liberated." My grandmothers held various jobs in the broad ter-
rain of housewifery (never mind the work they did outside the
home)—they cooked and cleaned and raised children, and
were the center of life in the home. They were occasionally
abused and sometimes abusive. Until I was a teenager my
mother stayed at home, ironing, cooking, cleaning, nurturing, watching "The Late Show." A few days after his death,
Mother could say in all honesty that she did not know whether
my father had life insurance or not. And after days of rummaging through piles of papers, check stubs, letters, nega-
tives, and clippings in drawers, boxes, shopping bags, and
suitcases, we rightly concluded that he hadn't. The marriage
had been "traditional."

Yet in spite of what I can now understand as the rather un-
liberated quality of the lives of the women of my family, I also
know that I never announced defiantly to myself that my life
would be better than theirs or that I would never put up with
what they did. And that is because what they did, in its rela-

tionship to who they were and what, I assumed, they thought, caused me no confusion. They were independent of spirit, mind, opinion, belief, and emotion. And I don't believe any of them actually bought much of the romantic chunk of the middle-class dream, certainly not Nana.

"It goes a long way back, some twenty years," is the way the first chapter of *Invisible Man* begins. I was a freshman in college when Ralph Ellison came to deliver a talk at my school. The talk and the reception were disrupted by some black young men who had joined the "let's misread *Invisible Man*" bandwagon that was so popular in the late 1960s. I had recently read the book for the first time and found it wonderful, even though I insufficiently understood what Twain calls "the subtleties of the American joke," which are rife in the novel. I witnessed what seemed to me then a ritual taunting of Ellison, and I was ashamed of myself for being merely aghast. They jeered at him, told him he was a "shameless chitterling eater," evoking the line the fantasizing Invisible Man of the novel yells at a preacher he mistakes for the dreadful president of an all-black college. I wanted to have the authority of a literary critic in defusing the nebulous arguments and attacks against the man. I was several years too young and under-read to take on the battle.

I recall that Ellison himself was graceful under attack — wistful, yet, it seemed to me, having a parent's indulgence toward an obstreperous, hungry, and tired child. He listened as if he had heard it all before, until the male chorus of Young Turks turned on their heels and stalked, as one, out of the heated encounter. The only other time I saw Ellison was at a small dinner party given by the chairman of the undergraduate English department during my early years as a teacher. I was still writing my thesis — one third of it devoted to Ellison — and I was eager to see him in less contentious circumstances. I had such a dreadful cold that evening that all I can recall from it was a frantic and concentrated desire on

my part to keep my nose from running onto my dinner plate.
Every piece of Kleenex I'd brought had been used, so I tried
to take surreptitious swipes at my nose with my napkin. I am
sure that if Ellison remembers the evening or me at all, I
would be that drooping, wheezing Afro-head who sat down
the table and had absolutely nothing to say. My ears were so
stopped up I don't remember hearing anything either.

The young men back in 1967 felt that Ellison's unnamed
hero in *Invisible Man*, whom the reader leaves underground
"in a building . . . in a section of the basement that was shut
off and forgotten during the nineteenth century," failed. They
saw this Invisible Man as someone who had, as they put it,
"copped out," "gone on cloud nine," chosen passivity when the
times demanded concerted action — even violence, if necessary. It was obvious then, and it is even more obvious now,
nearly forty years since it appeared, that the novel is anything
but a cop-out. *Invisible Man* is, among other things, a dramatic
battle — with comic overtones — between the ritualistic struc-
tures of a redefined black folklore and the political meanings
of American life. It is an ironic history of the irony of black
American history. And it challenges its black readers to understand the paradoxical and chaotic nature of that history so
that they may effectively improvise and form an identity
shorn of the degradation of the past, to create something that
is entirely new. In the Epilogue, the protagonist says:

> With Louis Armstrong one half of me says, "Open the win-
> dow and let the foul air out," while the other says, "It was good
> green corn before the harvest." Of course Louis was kidding,
> he wouldn't have thrown old Bad Air out, because it would
> have broken up the music and the dance, when it was the
> good music that came from the bell of old Bad Air's horn
> that counted.

The atmosphere and the world are not changed by wishing.
Something new and lively and artful can be made with old,
stale, bad air.

Invisible Man is Ellison's declaration of independence from an outside world that does not see him. And Ellison is not to be faulted for failing to provide the exact, new definition of *black* when that can only be accomplished by a collectivity of black people living, not writing.

The young men back in 1967 responded to *Invisible Man* as nonfiction, as sociology and public relations, but not as literature that was filled with subtlety, humor, and high seriousness. Black literature, for them, was good when it detailed the horrors of black existence, the blighted lives of black people and their all-consuming anger at the white world. Black literature, for them, was either a catharsis or a call to arms for its black readers. Black writers, for them, were implicitly spokesmen, town criers, muckrakers, tacticians. For them, black literature was a "weapon" — the word is Richard Wright's — and it had to be naturalistic, microscopically and doctrinally correct. *Invisible Man* is the artist's rejection of just those claims — of naturalism, of any attendant political and social assumptions made for the black writer by someone else. The novel, if it can be said to be philosophically derivative at all, owes much to Du Bois and his dream: "I want the colored people to have the right to develop according to their capacity and I certainly would be disappointed if they did not develop much higher things than the white race." *Invisible Man* suggests that one vital part of black liberation is in the development of a self-identification that has no precedents and does not mimic the identities, real or imagined, of either the white Western world or a romanticized African one.

My thoughts about *Invisible Man* of late have been spurred by recent debates involving the fiction of black female writers. Much like the young men at Ellison's talk, black men have blasted the writing of Alice Walker, Ntozake Shange, Paule Marshall, Toni Morrison, and others, charging them with creating negative images and stereotypes of black male characters. The men have said that these images are dangerous, unfair, demeaning, and wrong — the language of their charges sometimes ironically underscores the veracity of the portraits. In some cases, black women have joined the chorus, declaring that images of black men as violent, abusive, insensitive, and murderous only reinforce stereotypes cherished by white America. Apart from the fact that this sort of logic flows from a "blaming the victim" mentality, it recycles the tired notion that black writing is a literal, reflexive, prescriptive arm of civil rights agitation and public relations. It is not surprising, then, that much critical response by blacks to the literature produced by other blacks is interesting only as an exercise in interpreting the social, economic, and sexual politics of the critic.

It is so hard to talk about these things, particularly because critical judgments become measurements of how one has either accepted or rejected new readings and new methods of criticism. I don't deny the validity of extraliterary concerns that attend the reading of black writers. I ask, are the historical references and metaphors in the fictions true, plausible, believable? Is the message of the book merely agitprop, or is it viable political theory in the guise of fiction? But I can't go much further than that. Those who criticize in terms of public relations and sociology run the risk of becoming censors — a filthy avocation, and particularly dangerous to anyone who belongs to a minority group. I recall a story a colleague once told me. It might be apocryphal but he insisted on its truth, and it certainly is plausible. It seems a well-established black personality, a woman, tried to have Toni Morrison's *Song of Solomon* removed from the public libraries of a city because she didn't approve of the "image" of black people in the novel. Her plan didn't work, thank goodness. For readers to have been denied the lyricism, the drive, the depth, the truth, and the raw intelligence of the novel would have been an obscene tragedy.

And who can forget the hoopla surrounding *The Color Purple* by Alice Walker? A few years ago I talked to a woman who told me that she'd just returned from a conference where the gathered scholars had been told not teach it. I asked what the reason was. She said, "Because it reinforces negative stereotypes"—one of the early reactions to the novel. When the woman asked for my opinion I told her that I didn't believe in censorship. Later, after the novel had been layered with so much extraliterary baggage that it was smothered, and the movie version had made of many a thinking person a mumbling idiot, I realized that it was nearly impossible to give a reasoned opinion of it in public; the only safe place to speak of it at all was to whisper something in the shower.

Yet the appeal of fiction that affirms the more unpleasant realities of black life is compelling to many people, and even defines what black fiction is supposed to be. If this were not the case that creative strategy might have died out by now. It would be ridiculous for me to think that stories of the effects of black oppression should not be told. My problem with these detailed stories of degradation—what I call naturalism—is not due to any aesthetic, moral, or ethical revulsion on my part. And my feelings have nothing to do with matters of propinquity. Quite simply I find naturalism to be on one side of a very thin coin, with sentimentality and romanticism on the flip side. My response to the granddaddy of all black naturalistic fictions, *Native Son*, is that Richard Wright went so far in trying to make the novel tough, to avoid writing "a book which even bankers' daughters could read and weep over and feel good about," that his protagonist, Bigger Thomas, isn't a human character at all. Wright succeeded in one way—one might weep about *Native Son* but no one weeps over it—and failed in another; there is nothing more to learn from it than the obvious social fact that dehumanized human beings often commit dehumanized acts. The fact remains that Bigger Thomas is not a person, but a thing—whether I am weeping because tragedy has struck some sentimentalized, romanticized portrait of black humanity, or left cold and disgusted by the details of a blighted life and his epiphany just before he walks to his death in the electric chair. There is no new place to go at the end of such fiction.

In more sophisticated attempts to organize writing by black Americans, *Native Son* is often considered in relationship to *Invisible Man*, which is, among other things, a comic *Native Son*. The materialistic philosophy of the Communist Party, voiced in *Native Son* by Jan and Max, becomes in *Invisible Man* an ironic satire on the way both capitalists and communists treat blacks. Bigger Thomas falls from the roof of a building into the whiteness of the snow and eventually to his death; the Invisible Man scurries off the roof of a building into a white underworld of leftist politics that symbolically kills and buries him, although he later reaches the point where he can end his hibernation. There are other parallels: Mary Dalton, in *Native Son*, says to Bigger, "I didn't know I was sho drunk," minutes before she is to be accidentally suffocated by Bigger, who is terrified of being caught and charged with rape; Sybil, a white woman, asks the Invisible Man, "D'you do it, boo-'ful?"—she is too drunk to remember, but she hopes the rape took place. Two white women, two black men; no rapes, but the axiomatic assumption that they must have occurred.

Influences and anxieties are the bread and butter of writing and criticism, whether consciously recognized or not. *Tar Baby*, by Toni Morrison, pays tribute to Zora Neale Hurston's *Their Eyes Were Watching God*. Though ostensibly more a romance on the surface than *The Color Purple*, *Tar Baby* takes the reader deeper, and beyond the romantically symbolic, focusing on three pairs of men and women in various stages of confusion about the nature of love. The novel reminds us that love is a primitive emotion, one that is anything but tidy, not to be controlled or contained cerebrally. Hurston's Janie and Tea Cake, in their folk world, know this. Morrison's Jadine and Son feel it but cannot control it; the white Valerian and the Principal Beauty of Maine, a white couple, cannot understand it. And in the center are the black Ondine and Sidney, Jadine's aunt and uncle, who are of an older generation of

"Philadelphia Negroes," but who nevertheless know what love sometimes makes people do. This couple lends a credibility and weight to the novel because they come from the very real, concrete place of "Philadelphia Negroes," not from the exotic and polar worlds of Eloe, rural Maine, and the Main Line.

Not only is the source of love elemental—so, too, is the blackness. No matter how much Jadine defines herself as part of a white, international set, she feels a power within her when she sees Son, with his "uncivilized, reform-school hair. Mau Mau, Attica, chain-gang hair." And an image she recalls from a supermarket in Paris disrupts her dreams:

> The vision itself was a woman much too tall. Under her long canary dress Jadine knew there was too much hip, too much bust. The agency would laugh her out of the lobby, so why was she and everybody else in the store transfixed? The height? The skin like tar against the canary yellow dress? The woman walked down the aisle as though her many-colored sandals were pressing gold tracks on the floor. Two upside-down V's were scored into each of her cheeks, her hair was wrapped in a gelee as yellow as her dress. The people in the aisles watched her without embarrassment, with full glances instead of sly ones. . . .
>
> She would deny it now, but along with everybody else in the market, Jadine gasped. Just a little. Just a sudden intake of air. Just a quick snatch of breath before that woman's woman—that mother/sister/she; that unphotographable beauty—took it all away.

The image sticks, remaining with Jade in ways she cannot articulate: "The woman made her feel lonely in a way. Lonely and inauthentic."

Son's love for Jade is elemental and, he hopes, redemptive:

> He loved to watch her eyes when she was not watching his. And to listen to the four/four time of her heels. Son sat there wagging his knees back and forth like a schoolboy. Not thinking most of the important things there were to think about: What would they do? Where would they live? How would he

103

earn money to take care of her and, later, their children? He smiled at the vigor of his own heartbeat at the thought of her having his baby. Watch her. He would watch her stomach while she slept just the way he had when he'd lived like an animal around the house and spent the hind part of the night at her bedside pressing his dreams into hers. Now those dreams embarrassed him. The musings of an adolescent brutalized by the loneliness for a world he thought he would never see again.

There was a future. A reason for hauling ass in the morning. No more moment to moment play-it-as-it-comes existence. That stomach required planning. Thinking through a move long before it was made. What would he name his son? Son of Son?

All the love between Son and Jade cannot be controlled. Certainly not in New York City, a place which brings "sorrow" to Son. The city is a force out of sync with Son; its relentless sounds, poses, and energy offer no real guides for his need to "make it." And Jade cannot survive in Eloe, the godforsaken Florida town that Son takes her to visit, where she finds nothing to do. The balance is askew in their love.

Hurston's Janie and Tea Cake thrive until other kinds of Florida elements — a flood and racism and a rabid dog — end their reverie. But after Tea Cake is dead, after Janie has been forced to shoot his rabies-infested body, he still lives with her in spirit:

> Then Tea Cake came prancing around her where she was and the song of the sigh flew out of the window and lit in the top of the pine trees. Tea Cake, with the sun for a shawl. Of course he wasn't dead. He could never be dead until she herself had finished feeling and thinking. This kiss of his memory made pictures of love and light against the wall. Here was peace. She pulled her horizon like a great fish-net. Pulled it from around the waist of the world and draped it over her shoulder. So much of life in its meshes! She called in her soul to come and see.

The memory of love abides with Son and Jade, as they go in opposite directions — she returns to the international world of Paris, he is converted into one of the mythic blind horsemen of the primitive *Isle des Chevaliers*, intent on someday finding her. Jade and Son suffer from conflicting romantic notions about what the other means. Jade's brand of conformity — a color-less middle-class ethic — has no role in it for Son. Son's real home — the American primitive Eloe and its inertia — is no home for Jade. Each has needed a part of the other's world; neither has known how to forge it into a reality.

I had dinner once with a black female academic, an active scholar in the field of black American writing, who said that Morrison's politics in *Tar Baby* — I assumed she meant sexual politics — were "off," wrong. I didn't have much to say to her because I thought the comment was profoundly off the point. I thought her reading literal; it ignored the texture and wealth of imagery that supports the major and minor tragedies of the intriguing narrative. I should have defended the text as I saw it, but somehow I lacked the energy to do it. I changed the subject. I thought about the novel and how it says that all we want, we black people, is some middle ground where we can live, some place where the appeal and physical beauty of the Western Hemisphere can coexist with our joyful non-Western difference, an *Isle des Chevaliers* that we forge out of love. *Tar Baby* reinforces for us, in case we have forgotten, the enormous force of love and the price we pay for trying to make it something other than what it is. And because the novel's characters are so complex, they are more believable in the simple meanings their lives offer us — more so than some other novels that try only to make the point that simple lives can have meaning.

Everything can be reduced to politics, I suppose, but *Tar Baby* defies the facile projections of sexual politics we would create for it. The novel's politics are broader, grander, more spiritual; they do not function as a primer for those looking to encase fiction in doctrine. *Tar Baby* is about forgiveness and our need to understand it, a need as great as our need to love.

I went to hear Toni Morrison give a reading at the Ninety-second Street Y in New York one night. I remember being amused and slightly confounded by some of the people in the audience. Quite a few women came dressed as storm troopers (missing what seems to me the irony of women dressing in the clothes of men who love to rape them); others were in various costumes also designed to reveal particulars of sexual or class preferences, practices, and prejudices. These women were posing 1980s style. They differed from Ellison's Young Turks because they appreciated Morrison's work, but were strangely alike in their rush to stage a public self-revelation. I wondered what Morrison thought about it all, if she wondered what these women could have read in her books that made them want to dress in these ways for her reading. Would they be strong enough to accept the elegant and simple meanings of her novels, their pessimism, their rejection of mindsets that need a prescriptive politics to announce how and what to say, and what to wear when saying it? And what, I also wondered, would Nana have thought of all this?

At moments like these I muse to myself, in an uncharacteristic, collective voice, about some issue or other that seems to be misunderstood, off the point. And I wondered at the Y whether we had forgiven our oppressors more than we were willing to forgive ourselves our oppression. Had we learned to love them as we were unwilling to love ourselves? Could our own feelings of loneliness and inauthenticity be assuaged by our willingness to dare to love and to forgive each other?

I remember one sunny June day; perhaps it was 1964. My parents were at work, Papa was taking a long walk through the neighborhood, my sister was at a summer job, and I — too young yet for summer employment, for which there were few opportunities anyway — I was hanging around the house, doing nothing. I was filled with that quality of self-importance that only a fifteen-year-old honor student who belongs to a club called Les Élus could possibly display. Nana was in the den, reading the newspaper and desultorily watching television.

At noon we watched the news together. Douglas Edwards gave information on Indochina and the new commitments the Johnson administration was taking to secure the area, particularly South Vietnam, from the communist threat from the North. Nana shook her head from one side to the other, and spoke of the stupidity of it all. Noticing her disapproval — I was standing in the doorway giving that scholarly look, leaning against the jamb, my hands in my pockets — I announced to her that the United States had to protect the world for democracy. Nana looked up at me with a look of pure incredulity written on her face. She hee-heed. I had never seen it quite like that before; I never saw it quite the same way again. I swallowed hard and mumbled something incoherent and inaudible and left the house. I knew that she was right — that all global belligerence had its source in some kind of stupidity or another — and that I sounded like a fool, parroting words that were euphemisms for much of the power and bloodlust of the latter half of the twentieth century.

I think about that afternoon from time to time, knowing now that Nana both loved me and forgave me, as she doubtless loved and forgave Papa and all the rest of the human folly that strode across the stage of her long life. I never thought to ask her how she felt about many things: "What was it like," I should have asked, "to discover your mother and grandmother as numbers on a government roll, created to compensate for the genocide and land requisition of the Cherokee Indians?" But then, perhaps even to have asked the question would have begged for her look of incredulity. It might have suggested that the $14,789,476.15 was an equitable figure.

Inner Lives

I AM WARY of long-distance calls that come in the middle of a weekday afternoon. Like most people, I'm not too pleased with those that come in the early morning or in the middle of the night, communicating doom or drunkenness, but the afternoon calls usually bring highly significant, if not disastrous, tidings. I can't remember one that was in any way pleasant.

I developed this aversion to afternoon calls during my last year of college. It was March, and I was sitting at my tiny desk, in a tiny room that had formerly been a maid's closet but now was a double, reading *Great Expectations* for a novel course exam. More likely I was cramming *Great Expectations*, since I never developed good study habits and only recently have shown signs of any useful academic discipline. At about 1:30 the telephone rang. I was tempted not to answer it because almost all calls that came in were for my roommate, who had what one could call a social life. But I answered the call anyway.

A man's voice, from far away, was on the other end, asking for me. I admitted to being the person he sought, and he introduced himself as the chairman of a prominent graduate department of English at a southern university. He was calling to encourage me to enroll in his university's Ph.D. program.

The call took me by surprise, but it was not completely bizarre. I had recently won a paid four-year fellowship to any graduate school that would admit me, and the awarding foundation doubtless had sent press releases to departments throughout the country announcing the winners — who were all black, and who, the foundation hoped, would become the first of a new wave of well-educated and degreed blacks ready to teach in America's universities and colleges.

The gentleman asked me several questions about my fields of interest, my feelings about life in a large university. They were relatively benign questions and I gave him equally benign answers.

Then came the pitch. He offered to fly me down to visit the campus, meet with the department, and talk to the students. He could easily arrange my flights and since my spring break did not coincide with that of his university, I might have a reasonably decent visit without losing any class time. Furthermore, he explained to me, I might find the trip educational and enlightening. He was certain that it would be enlightening for the white students at the university — I can only imagine how few blacks were there in 1969 — because he was sure that none of them had ever heard a nigra speak as well as I did and that my visit might help reform some of their opinions as we moved from the racially perilous sixties into a new decade of hope.

I can't say that I dropped the phone or slammed it down or quietly murmured obscenities in his ear. I wasn't so forthcoming at the age of twenty. And I'm not sure that I should have; I would have agonized over not getting whatever I said right. I sighed, thanked him for his interest, and told him that I would get in touch if I thought I would make my visit. Naturally, I never called him.

The call from the southern literary scholar contained important realities, and in some ways it was just as well that he reminded me of them. I was raised with the ethic that black individual expression was simultaneously a representation of both itself and a collective whole. This was Du Boisian double-consciousness at work: individual acts were seen by the white world as representative emblems of blackness. Hence, the beliefs inculcated from post-infancy on were that one had to work twice as hard and be twice as smart as the whites, individually or collectively, to have any chance for success. Hence the sorrow that my grandmothers would express on hearing that a murderer or rapist was "the Negro suspect." In some real and tangible way, they knew that with violence, either overt and physical or subtle and psychological, some unsuspecting black person or persons — unrelated to the crime or the criminal — would pay for it too.

The reverse of all this is not true. Individual black expressions and exercises of grace, taste, discovery, ingenuity, and so forth are never seen as representative of all blacks; they remain remarkable and singular. So, had I traveled to Dixie to enroll in the gentleman's graduate English program, I might have found myself in the peculiar position of being viewed — by all those whites who never heard a nigra speak like I did before — as a singular, northern black, enlightening few and representing nothing but the need for the white South to maintain its supremacy and call all the shots in interracial dealings. That was a battle I was unwilling to enter.

I finished college in three years. I say this not to boast; I desperately needed another year's worth of emotional, intellectual, and psychological maturing, and I have often thought that a part of me was stunted by leaving college too soon. I mention it to suggest the mind-set of a twenty year old in the middle of what she thought was a junior year, but which the transfer office credited as a senior year. I became nervous about my future, a future that was coming on faster than anything I'd ever seen before. My family wondered what I would do too. There was no question of my returning home; at least I didn't think so. Except for Christmas visits, I had left home for good — give or take an odd summer — when I was seventeen.

I wasn't crazy about Kansas City, anyway. Maybe I would go to New York. But what would I do there, or anyplace else? I could work for the telephone company, or take the Civil Service examination to work at the P.O., or take practice teaching courses in order to be certified to teach high school. None of these options seemed plausible at all, and everyone in my family thought them completely out of sync with my character. I never seriously thought about law school — it would have been a great time to go. MBAs were not the coveted pieces of paper they are now, and nothing about the business world appealed to me in the least, not even advertising. We were all stumped. Without any likely options, I applied to go to graduate school in literature. In those days — before people deferred admission to discover important things about themselves, or to make a little money — a lot of seniors, like me, went to graduate school to do the thinking and planning for the future that time otherwise had not allowed. My parents had no money to send me, so I applied for full financial aid, grants, and fellowships.

One rainy Thursday morning during the November before the southern gentleman's call, I went to see my Chaucer teacher, to hand in a paper and to explain why I would not be in class for two days of the following week. I had hit pay dirt with a fellowship and was flying to New York City for an interview. I liked my Chaucer teacher and I did well in his course. I sought from him words of wisdom and comfort.

He was an assistant professor, probably on his first job. I saw him as seasoned, professorial, wise. He had agreed, with no coaxing, to write a recommendation on my behalf for the fellowship and for graduate schools. I had been very pleased, particularly since I had transferred to the university and knew only a few teachers. He had encouraged my efforts, but also had warned me to avoid considering what he called the "high-falutin' graduate schools." He thought I should go to a department with a flexible American literature program, one that could contain my occasionally eclectic style and that would rid me of my excesses without emptying me of my originality. I paid no attention to this seasoned, professorial, wise man and applied for admission only to highfalutin' schools, except Yale, whose application for admission even I found offensive. I wanted his approval and encouragement nevertheless, the day I went to see him.

"What do you want to see in New York?" he asked me.

"Harlem. I want to see Harlem," I said, thinking about Langston Hughes as representative outlander in *The Big Sea*, rushing out of the subway into the bright light of 135th Street and exclaiming, "Harlem!"

My professor looked at me curiously, and with some condescension in a voice tight and firm, and revealing (it seemed to me for the first time) a southern twinge, said, "I thought you'd want to go to Harlem. I know you've probably heard all about it. Kids from your background, who haven't been exposed to much, always want to go to Harlem."

I have rarely shed tears of anger and frustration. The last time was in a First Interstate Bank branch in Los Angeles (I blow it up in my dreams); another time was when a friend continued to chide me about my slow progress on my dissertation long after the point had been made. The time before that was at the reception following my father's funeral, when I almost strangled an old family friend who did a "tsk, tsk, tsk" monologue about long-suffering fathers and their disrespectful children. The time before that was in my Chaucer professor's office.

I can't remember what I said, nor am I able to deliver a reasonable facsimile here. All I remember is that I said words to the effect that I didn't know what background he was referring to, but that mine was just fine, educated and advanced, and that everyone in my family would doubtless have found conversation with his family a new low in their experience, and that Harlem, to those who knew anything about it, was not so much a place as a state of mind I had craved to experience all my life.

Whatever I said, my professor blanched, apologized, and wished me well. I left his office, throwing my raincoat over my shoulders, and rushed out into the rain, not even caring to cover my newly washed and pressed hair. Later that day I had it cut into an Afro style, and not one drop of heat or one chemical has touched it since.

I pounded my fist into my thigh and cursed as I headed toward my dorm. "A kid from my background," I muttered. "Finer than his, I'm sure." I cried, too, knowing that a timid outlander like me wouldn't know what to do with Harlem if you set her in the middle of it. That was the real pain: a joy of belonging, a fear of not knowing how to. And I resented the implication that my background must have been undisciplined, blighted, and dull. I reasoned that had that been the case, after having listened to him I might have recalled more than just his mother and family to him. I felt both haughty and small.

The incident, like the call from the South — which incidentally came from the alma mater of my Chaucer professor — was educational. I stored it to protect me from the world and to save me from myself, in case I began to forget too much. Ultimately, I let my professor off the hook — he merely was a kind of representative white professor for me as I was a representative black student for him. Very little on that score changed for as long as I was a student; living with it goes with the territory. He had thought me a bright girl from a dull, impoverished background and — after a while — that was just fine.

I think of him when I think of the black father of an old acquaintance of mine. Once when I was visiting my friend's home, something prompted her father to ask me what church I'd been raised in — a telltale red flag question if I've ever heard one. I told him that I had been raised an Episcopalian. He said, "It figures." I bit my tongue and suppressed an epithet. I thought his self-satisfaction at being "blacker" than I was obscene, particularly since he had a white wife with whom he was well pleased, and lovely mulatto children who, I am sure, he dreamed would brighten his later years. He saw my frozen North manners and my speech and decided that I was what we used to call hincty. And, perhaps because the nastiest fighting occurs within the home, I loathe him now as I never could my Chaucer professor. Another memory hits me the same way. I recall running into a black graduate school acquaintance of mine who had just returned from the movies, where some rowdy black youths had "acted out." She spat out the words, "Those dirty little niggers were screaming in the aisles and carrying on like thugs outside the theater." I avoided her from that moment on and started trying to learn to live as invisibly among blacks as I already did among whites.

One day in May of the year I received my afternoon call from the South, I was studying for final exams, and preparing to take the three courses I'd need for graduation in August during the summer session. I had stacked all of the novels I'd previously failed to read for my course in my upper bunk and I was in the middle of my cramming blitz. This was an outrageously inefficient way to study, but the results were good for me; I got a fine grade.

At about 2:00 P.M. that day I received another afternoon phone call, this one from my aunt, my father's sister. She was dying of cancer and I had not seen her for some time. She called, her voice quite weak, to offer me a deal. If I got rid of my Afro — which she had never seen — she said she would will me five hundred dollars and a diamond ring. Again, I don't remember what I said; it couldn't have been much: words to the effect of "no" and jumbled phrases, matching, perhaps, what I thought was the incoherence of her request. After she'd hung up I immediately called my father and, angered to tears, asked him to please get his sister off my back. I found out later that day that my sister, who'd worn an unseen-by-the-aunt Afro longer than I had, got the same bribe. And because she had more experience with my aunt, had loved her as I never learned to, she had calmly told her that money wasn't buying love. Neither my sister nor I have ever regretted our stand; neither of us owns one knick-knack, glass, or doily from my aunt's well-stocked home. The only valuables handed down were a few photographs. I felt sorry for my father after vulturish cousins lit upon my aunt's house and cleaned the place out because there were things belonging to his grandmother that I knew he wanted to have.

My aunt died during the first week of August, four days before my graduation. On a Thursday afternoon, I took a slow Greyhound bus from school to Dayton, a city that was filled with so many mixed memories for me: of integrating a school, of learning to live with Grandma and her husband Half-Wit, of playing baseball and worshipping Willie Mays, of church. It was hot, and my best clothes—clothes that would be appropriate for a funeral —were all winter items. I had no dresses, and my only skirts were brightly floral. I arrived exhausted after seven hours of riding scrunched against the bus window by a garlic chewing woman with a thick eastern European accent, who told me about the wonderful things she had heard about the colored people. I arrived at 2:00 A.M. in blue jeans.

My sister had come in from Chicago, my parents and Nana from Missouri. The scene was obviously one of profound sadness as I walked into my aunt's house, saw my uncle—who was understandably devastated—and worried about my lack of proper attire. For the funeral I borrowed a dark green skirt from my sister, who is six inches shorter than I am, and I sat self-consciously and uncomfortably looking at my aunt's draped coffin as the organist played "Jesu, Joy of Man's Desiring," and heard the minister, my aunt's good friend, call her name slowly, three times, like the bells rung with the Prayer of Consecration at Holy Communion, reinforcing the finality of the Lord's Supper there and the end of my aunt here.

After so many years away I was back in the church where my most pleasant memories of Dayton still reside. For there, singing in the junior choir, or hearing the minister preach — his sermons were passionate and stirring, emotional and yet cerebral — I could forget about the playground spit and glares, old men with shotguns, and the two houses, Grandma's and my aunt's, that were filled with chairs not to be sat in, tables not to be touched, and floors not to be walked on. Sitting there at the funeral and counting the memories of my aunt, my family, the church, the music, filled me with an intense anxiety that only strong air and stronger spirits could quell. My uncle thought my clothing inappropriate, which it was, but he was more offended at my failure to convulse with grief. The reception following the funeral remains fuzzy, noisy, endless in my memory. I can only recall waking the next day to a hard, driving, turbulent rain and a two-stop flight back to the university, with an inordinate and inappropriate number of members of my family on the plane: my sister, my mother, my grandmother, and me. My father stayed behind to travel with the coffin to Iowa for interment, and therefore missed my college graduation.

I have known several people — both men and women — who have such clean houses that even their bathroom sinks and tubs are sparkling and dry. That is, they wash the porcelain until it is spotless and then dry it so that there is never a hint of film, bubble, or water to be seen. On confronting one of these sinks, I invariably become less clean and opt not to wash my hands or face, or do anything that would mar the perfection. On the few occasions where I could not resist the sink, I have been known to delay flushing the toilet while I wash my hands and sometimes my face, and dry the now offensive sink with toilet paper, which I also use for my hands and face, preferring not to touch the monogrammed, expensive "guest towels" at my "disposal." I then toss the now considerable blob of paper into the toilet and flush, probably doing the plumbing some very real and accountable evil. I love a clean bathroom, but if a sponge can't do the job well enough, too bad.

My aunt was one such person. Her whole house was like her bathroom sink: pristine, shining, and resisting touch.

Children are universal receivers. They pick up language, gestures, habits, and prejudices with the voraciousness of a new Electrolux. As a very young child I developed a habit, spawned by my shy and brooding nature — for I hated to be seen or heard — of watching the world around me. With discretion, because I was raised well, but with hawkish intensity nevertheless, I sought to capture and hold the revelation of character through word, gesture, and nuance of everyone I saw. My passion for movies and books is the symptom; the ailment is, if you will, a comfort in being outside of myself most of the time. Only at rare times have I shortened this distance created between the world and me and participated with my whole self. And usually then, as in the times I've been in love, I have seemed disastrously out of place among sometimes preposterous partners, generic actors pulled, indiscriminately it would seem, from Central Casting. Though I love a number of people and, to my chagrin, am still *in* love with one or two, the only love songs I have to sing are to my family.

I watched my aunt when I was a child. I looked for the words that would tell me why she was, to me, unapproachable, and tried to discover why she would spend so much time making something that was already clean, cleaner. I wondered why she never said "I" to me, but only "your aunt," when speaking about herself, and why her bulging eyes were windows with the curtains drawn. As I sat looking at her coffin the day of her funeral I wondered why love was something conditional to her, something she thought she had to buy. I wanted to love her as I loved all the other members of my family, flaws and all, but there was a resistance, and there were no answers for my questions. She remained to me an object, an idea, an incarnation of a person who seemed not to like me without my knowing why. And thus I did not ascribe to her, because I did not know how, an inner life. I was able to see some of her actions as a result of cause and effect, but beyond that, there was nothing. She was a flat surface that I grew to dislike because that seemed the only reasonable response. She had a powerful cameo role in the movie of my young life; who she really was and why she was there formed a mystery.

Recently I saw a photograph—a school picture, sepia-toned—of my aunt, taken when she was just a little girl. It is a bad likeness of a rather homely child. The features that would soften in adulthood are raw; the eyes bulge out of a too-high forehead; the lower lip dangles, held up by neither determination, courage, nor spite. She looks profoundly and agonizingly sad.

With the photo is a companion piece—one of my father. He was three years older than she, but that difference is reversed in these pictures. She is an old child; he is young, bright, a beautiful little boy, grinning eagerly at the camera, self-assured, bold. His bulging eyes light up his face; his lower lip is taut, set, and ready to take on all comers.

When I saw these photographs for the first time, long after both of their deaths, I was shocked, precisely because they so visibly confirm what acceptance and rejection do to a child's face, a person's life. I have seen the faces of many black children who look like my aunt, some of them smiling, some not, who have been yanked from childhood—not destroyed, but merely robbed of all that we thought we'd ever have: hope.

My father and grandmother called my aunt "Sister," which was the only verbal archaism (Mother called it "southern") that had any expression in my family. Grandma did not call my father "Son" or "Brother" and she certainly did not address her husband as "Mister." But "Sister" stuck, and I never heard either my father or grandmother call her anything but that, even when they spoke of her in the third person. She internalized this and called herself "Aunt," pronouncing it "ant" in contrast to how my mother's family said it. I think now of "Sister" as old-fashioned, but more important, within the context of my family, it was a verbal reinforcement of her lesser position. I wish they had called her by her first name, or by a nickname, or anything endearing. It might have helped me see her as a flawed human being, like all the rest of us, rather than as a fussy, two-dimensional creature who favored my sister over me.

In a family of singers, with resonant, melodious voices, my aunt had a high, thin, scratchy voice. I hear better than I see; I trust my hearing far more than any other sense. I am attracted to people with dulcet tones, wary and hesitant of those without them. When I think of my aunt I hear that voice calling for "my pet," which was her name for my sister. I think of myself as the second-born, a girl, sitting in her den, wanting to touch the globe lamp and lemon-oiled table, saying very little and feeling uncomfortable in Sunday clothes and not being spoken to at all.

Her kitchen floor was white linoleum; she washed it daily, with waxings on Saturdays. I remember she had a fit one autumn day after my sister and I, in our new penny-loafers with rubber heels, left stubborn black marks on it. We were careful to remove our shoes before we hit the kitchen after that. My aunt would stop to pick up a tiny piece of lint of the floor, and it baffles my mother to this day that a woman so particular would have had a dog. But she did, a miniature dachshund.

My aunt, like Grandma, was a great cook. And although I can't say that I was comfortable around my father's family, to this day I carry with me terrible fat cells born at their tables. Eating was highly ritualized for them and it became my hobby. I consumed hot buttered rolls and highly seasoned green beans with lightning speed. Grandma was the great pie-baker, my aunt the cake-maker. She would serve light, moist white cake with mounds of expensive, hand-packed ice cream. At her table I didn't mind not being one of her pets.

Both before and after we moved away from Ohio, my sister and I would eagerly await our Christmas presents from my aunt. They were always wonderful. She would send us clothes — expensive wool skirts and blouses and sweaters to match. They were of the finest cloth available and were easily the best clothes either of us had growing up. They were always tasteful, always fit, and I thought them worthy of only the most significant occasions. But although her house was no more than two miles away when we lived in Dayton, I never wandered over for a visit. All such excursions had an air of formality to them, from the ritual Sunday dinners after church to picnics and the odd Saturday evening potluck. I would never have thought to tell her anything about my personal life, and although I liked my uncle, I had nothing to say to him either. I spent most of my time trying not to transgress while on their turf by sitting in the wrong chair, or walking, in shoes, on the thick-piled, pure white wool carpeting that ran from her living and dining rooms up the stairs to the bedrooms. Children know when they are being watched; when conversing adults turn their heads, just slightly, and move their eyes to the farthest corner to maintain control. The look is not so much seen by the child as felt, and although I was an easily controlled child, my skin bristled from surveillance at my aunt's house.

I look at the photograph of the child again. I try to hear and remember the minister's remarks, entitled "Sunshine," and I try to give my aunt the inner life that would humanize her for me, that would make her for me — as she so obviously was for her friends — the delightful and caring woman they loved. Susan Sontag writes in *On Photography*:

> Strictly speaking, one never understands anything from a photograph. Of course, photographs fill in blanks in our mental picture of the present and the past. . . . Nevertheless,

the camera's rendering of reality must always hide more than it discloses. . . . Only that which narrates can make us understand.

I think Sontag is right about images we see of events that are foreign or that depict a quality of life that we have never seen before and don't know. And because our lives in the 1990s are being held hostage by a sentimentality on TV, radio, newspapers, magazines, and often movies — where the banal and the significant share the same caption — photographs function as a kind of cultural Rorschach test. We're normal if we see the same thing and create the same narration as everyone else. That battered sepia-toned picture reveals a sad child to anyone with eyes.

The photograph of my aunt does allow me to understand some things — just as I can feel myself present at events that preceded my birth — because a bloodline is working here, and because the face in the picture so confused me when it matured. And I want desperately to have it narrate a story to me so that I might love it. But there are too many blanks.

As a young woman my aunt did not travel to Minnesota to go to college, as her brother did, but stayed in Iowa and went to a local college there. I doubt very much that she had the chance to go to the universities there. After graduation there was nothing else for her to do but go south, where, like hundreds of other young black people, she taught school. There she met and married a tall, soft-spoken Alabaman, and they returned to the North to Dayton. She was a very smart woman, and worked for the federal government, at what I was often reminded was a very high GS level for a black person in those days. She could have been a hit in Washington, D.C. Her husband found his best employment opportunity as a bartender in an exclusive white country club, even though he, too, had a college degree. They had no children and, to my child's eyes, seemed not to regret it. My uncle was as fussy as my aunt about the house, and although she worried, in the cause-effect ways I could discern, that he drank too much and not well, they seemed outwardly compatible, happy to be cleaning and making spotless their very beautiful house. As far as I knew, everyone in the family had been pleased when Grandma moved to Dayton to be near her. Another homestead was being forged; we were not to be scattered all over the country, without a center. I am trying to remember more, to make more sense of her.

My aunt was a superb dresser. She was short and pear-shaped, and, like her mother, never wore a brassiere. She dressed to highlight her attributes and downplay the rest. I never saw her in slacks or shorts because she was hippy and slightly steatopygic. (My mother taught me that word, and oh, how I loved it: "That woman's got stee-otta-pa-gee-uh!") She adored spectator pumps and had tons of them; I never saw her in sneakers. She wore printed dresses and linen suits and hats bought at a milliner's — wool, blocked, flapper-style, hugging her head and lopping to the right or left side to a bow or a low brim. She had lovely hands, with long fingers and long nails which she painted bright red, always leaving the half-moon untouched. And her stockings were seamed, highlighting her well-turned ankles and legs. I recall seeing her run once. We were at a picnic and someone had turned to wander off. With her scratchy voice calling the man's name, she ran past me, breasts swinging like small pendulums from side to side, her legs making half circles with each stride — a dainty, if knock-kneed, lady's run. I stopped chewing to look. She caught up with the man, and on tiptoes said something to him. She often went on tiptoes, not because she had to — she wasn't that short — but to force the issue of being diminutive and a woman, with just a touch of the coquette. I found her use of makeup curious. She wore base powder, just a touch on the light side, and red rouge that formed huge circles on her cheeks. I never understood the use; I chalk it up to the same impulses that had her rise on her toes.

On the other hand, she loved to drink beer and watch

prizefights, and I remember her elation when Sugar Ray beat Gene Fullmer for the title in 1957. Once, at one of her couple club's parties that included the kids, I saw her, with all of the mothers and teenagers, learn the Madison, a popular line dance. I was surprised to see her there. She learned it well.

But my feelings didn't change. I can't ever remember my aunt talking to me at all, short of that afternoon phone call, although she must have often. I didn't begrudge my sister the affection my aunt showed her. My sister was the closest thing my aunt ever had to a child of her own. They had spent time together when my sister was quite small, and my aunt had been a classic black mother to her: stern, yet loving, getting Kirk's Castile Soap in my sister's eyes as she washed her hair in near-scalding hot water, and beating her on the legs and behind with a switch plucked from a backyard tree. My blood chilled at the thought of either experience. I suspect, too, that my sister was an underdog in my aunt's eyes: a child struggling with a brown skin and a marring eczema, and unadored, as she was, by Grandma. I didn't begrudge my aunt her affection for my sister either. It just seemed to me that we were all underdogs; the inequities of love merely reinforced that.

I have tried to let the photograph narrate. It can't. I fear my aunt was desperately unhappy and felt unloved. I fear that her presents and her generosity to others and her house and her tiptoes were compensatory and conditional, a part of the kind of deal timid children make with bullies: if I do this will you leave me alone, will you like me? She might or might not have understood that, apart from what Afros meant to other people — the vaunted political significance — I cut my hair in anger and frustration, stemming from self-pity; I don't know. I learned very quickly, within days, that in the process I had liberated myself from chemicals and hot irons, from the scalp burns and ear burns attending them; that I didn't have to run away from the rain or avoid swimming pools (on the odd chance that I might learn to swim). I think that my aunt saw the haircut as deliberate self-mutilation, an uglifying that for someone of her sensibilities and sorrows was the most absurd thing a black woman could possibly do. To her it was throwing in the towel and cutting off all hope of love, success, and acceptability. But she couldn't tell me that on the phone. I still would have resisted, but I would have understood her better. She just had a deal to make, and I'm not sure whether I was hurt most by the thought that she didn't understand me, or by the idea that she thought I was so venal that I would see the five hundred dollars and a ring as an offer I couldn't refuse.

I recently saw someone I had loved a long time ago. I have often regretted that affair, but I suppose regrettability is one of the functions of affairs. I had been in my early twenties, inexperienced, and eager to awaken the sexual energy that occasionally made me jumpy and accounted for what seemed to me an increasingly lurid tone to my fantasies. But after about five minutes of our reunion my jittery nerves became quite placid and I was able to spend several hours in good conversation, filling up some of the gaps in time with information, leaving others empty — it being inappropriate and quite off the point to talk about loneliness and unhappiness to an old lover.

I came home and drank a little bourbon and thought about memory. I am a great fan of memory, and in my teaching I encourage my students to recognize that literature tells us much about the dangers lurking everywhere for characters who have lost theirs. I tell them about Flannery O'Connor's "A Good Man is Hard to Find," where lapses and distortions in the grandmother's memory, and complete blanks in the Misfit's, have fatal repercussions. I tell them that without memory we are liable to become worse than Sisyphean, repeating tortured and tortuous mistakes without any sense of meaning, or, more to the point, of absurdity.

But there are real dangers in memory too, especially when we film our private histories through the culture's lens, displacing the images and sounds that are ours with prepackaged scenarios and montages that seem — but only seem — to make them clearer, more understandable, more immediate. My encounter with my old lover suggested to me that memories, replayed too many times, can become warped and begin to lie. The lobster scene in everybody's favorite, Woody Allen's *Annie Hall*, would have been more exact about memory — and just as dynamic — had the dinner with the new girlfriend, designed to reenact the one with the lost Annie, been successful, a perfect rendition. It would have revealed more comically and poignantly that memories are not fantasies, are not filmed scenes with actors open to the possibilities of reinterpretation by new casts — that in fact they are both. And when I have avoided the things I should think about, I have wondered whether the lobster scene has anything to say about failed second marriages.

Those few hours of conversation with my old lover finally ended years of worthless and dangerous remembering about a time when I was young, inexperienced, depressed, and clumsy. I sipped my bourbon and watched an albatross fly away.

It isn't that easy with the memory of my aunt, though. A different kind of feeling and remembrance, neither sexual nor romantic but familial, requires a different tactic to reorder. So much depends on time, place, age, other members of the family, and the entire family relationship. I have filled my aunt's story with speculation born of my desire to create motives for her actions. The exercise can only go so far. I can't pay her a visit and spend a few hours talking to her about safe topics. My struggle to remember her has made her more to me than the flat photograph that disturbed me. But I am not purged, nor can I understand her in the way that I would like to.

My memory of her remains like her bathroom, resistant to touch, and now fragmented and totally inaccessible. Does anyone live there? Is her memory useless, except perhaps only to induce anxiety when a voice on the other end of the line comes from far away and it is between noon and six on a weekday afternoon?

Yet, another part of me refuses to take all the blame for my failure to "find" her. Is it not just as likely that the bathroom and its resistance are symbolic of my aunt's desire to keep me and those like me at bay, because, as either David or Lisa in the movie said, "touch kills"? Is it as likely that my failures of memory and the erstwhile lies of my memory are only phantoms, as ersatz as store-bought images, and that the understanding that refuses to yield itself up from the tattered photograph is in the hands of the sad, old child in control, who is determined, in the face of my readings, to keep me and all narrative mongers the hell out of her life?

I Light Out for
the Territory

ON A CHILLY, thick-clouded San Francisco early spring day in 1983, I paid my money and rode the sightseeing ferry around the Bay. I am fond of boats, but this tourist activity was not so much a pleasure cruise as a quest to test my guts. One Saturday evening in 1958, I had stayed up to watch the "granddaddy of them all," as *TV Guide* called it: *San Francisco*, starring Clark Gable, Jeanette MacDonald, and Spencer Tracy. By the age of ten I had already developed a strong appreciation of Tracy and Gable; *Boom Town* was one of my favorites. It was only natural that I would be excited at the prospect of seeing them together again in this old movie. I watched it alone, lying on a couch in the den. My parents were off at a church raffle — they actually won something, I believe the only prize any member of our family ever won that was useful: some stainless steel cutlery — and my sister was God knows where, but she certainly wasn't watching television with her little sister.

In those days I had "opinions" about California. It was stupid to live there, I thought, because an earthquake was bound to come and kill you. I had experienced a slight quake one summer while visiting Nana and Papa. I was not eager to feel the real thing. And living in Tornado Alley — a wide band that cuts across the country and includes Missouri — had bred in me a morbidity about natural disaster that, when added to my terror of airplanes, was plainly pathological. All of these partially formed fears grew worse after my evening of watching *San Francisco*. The primitive but effective footage of the huge quake at the end of the film, with Jeanette MacDonald standing on Nob Hill, looking over the ruins and singing, and singing, caused me to become ill.

My parents returned home from their raffle, excited over their spoils and baffled at the sight of their youngest, who claimed severe illness, *sans* source, *sans* symptoms. And, at ten, I was old enough to be too ashamed to admit the catalyst of my "disease," so I kept my mouth shut and milked as much human kindness as I could. Psychosomania at its best. It took me three days to recover and I vowed never to set foot in that place, regardless of what anyone said about its wonders or food. San Francisco, to me, meant the same thing as willingly boarding the *Titanic* or booking a flight on June 30, 1956 on either the TWA Super-Constellation or the United DC-7 that collided over the Grand Canyon.

On this 1983 spring day I listened to the guide explain that the huge clock we were looking at straight on, as we were smack dab in the middle of the Bay and as far from the Oakland side as we were from that of San Francisco, froze at 5:13 A.M. on April 18, 1906. The boat pitched. I looked at the San Francisco waterfront, with its old gray buildings that reminded me of New York, and the huge sign for Ghirardelli Square off to the right, and Fisherman's Wharf, and I realized that I had made peace with my fear. Had a massive earthquake struck at that moment (not a remote possibility in my mind) I would have been content. I would have been satisfied to go under. I joined the five or ten other brave passengers on the deck, held onto the railing as we pitched, photographed some seagulls suspended in midair by the power of the wind, and looked hard at the base of the Golden Gate Bridge that friends told me was being eaten away by sea urchins. The salt water sprayed in my face; I looked out toward the Pacific and back to the city by the Bay and longed only for a friend to be with me, to hear all the things I was ready to say in the face of my triumph over my neurosis. Had I had more money I would have shipped out on the next trip as soon as we reached the harbor.

The next time I was in San Francisco happened to be the day the cable cars came back after a long stint in the repair and refurbishing shops. I was in the densest crowd I've ever stood in, as thousands of balloons rose to the sky, ragtime bands played, people dressed in Barbary Coast circa 1906 outfits roamed through the crowd, and the clanging bells announced the return of the norm. I didn't think once about earthquakes or Jeanette MacDonald.

I learned to love the sea as only a landlocked person can, during the summer of 1965. I was between my junior and senior years in high school, working in Kansas City, Missouri. Somewhere, in what used to be a locked diary but probably now is decomposing at the bottom of a garbage pit, are the names of the women with whom I worked that summer at the Hallmark Card Company. I was a miscellaneous handworker, paid the minimum wage, involved in the final quality control inspection of one part of Hallmark's 1965 Christmas line. I stood on one end of a conveyor belt, a co-worker at the other, as we checked the quality of the printing on 1966 cat calendars. A vividly photographed cute kitty, posed in some humanly pleasing position, graced each month of the year. The pictures suggested nothing of the more sinister aspects of cats; these whites and tabbys were designed to melt the hearts of even the most ardent cat-haters, like me. I was in charge of checking July through December, and occasionally I had to pull photographs where the color had bled or the kitty was out of focus. I did this all day.

Twice a day a coffee-break truck rolled by, filled with cookies, doughnuts, and hot and cold drinks, and people fled their posts to gather around it for ten minutes. Lunch was inexpensive (although too pricey for my pay), but I occasionally ate some of the fine fresh and delicious vegetables harvested, I was told, from the company's own farm. People were friendly enough, though short on conversation beyond the standard birth, death, adultery, marriage, and baby fare. I remember going to a good-bye celebration for a raw-boned, tall Kansas girl who was about to enter the WACs. I hadn't known they existed outside of the context of World War II and the movies.

I hated every single minute of my miscellaneous handworking. I played mental games, attempting to beat the clock, and lost. Time crept so slowly that I was a bundle of frayed nerves at the end of each day, and a disconsolate teenager when I received my weekly paycheck. That experience, from over twenty years ago, made a great impression on me. I still find cats loathsome, although I have made a separate peace here and there with a few that sensed my feelings about their species and rushed to jump in my lap. I have, as yet, been unable to bring myself to purchase any Hallmark products, though. I don't blame the company, it's just a visceral resistance I obey.

I worked there for three weeks.

My sister was out of college that year, student teaching; she had even taught in my own French class for a few weeks. She recalled that my friends and I lacked a certain amount of respect toward her ("Bonjour, Mademoiselle, ha, ha"). Nevertheless I found her accessible that summer, perhaps because she felt sorry for me. She had been a miscellaneous handworker herself some few years before, and when she would come to pick me up at the factory doors I thought I heard and saw sympathy in the midst of her standard sisterly sarcasm and criticism. Daddy had set us up for the Hallmark jobs, using his own children for this particular mitzvah. Not many years prior to our handworking, blacks could only find work there as janitors; employment opportunities ran that way in Kansas

City. He thought he could instill some extra motivation in us to want to excel in college if we spent summers working at the alternative. This, both my sister and I thought, sniveling, was a rather naive psychological stunt since from the womb we knew we were going to college; it was simply a part of the expectations of growing up. We were quite blasé about the whole thing. Handworking only convinced us that we'd never care enough to send the very best.

July 14, 1965, Bastille Day, was a blazing hot one, as so many are in Kansas City. High humidity, higher temperatures, and a laughing sun baked streets and brains alike. I wandered out of the air-conditioning and paused to catch my breath as I entered the oven of the outdoors. I saw my sister coming in a queue of cars and realized that I was too tired to ask her for a driving lesson. She had promised to teach me to drive a stick shift that summer. As I shut the door of the car she began a bizarre conversation.

"Adlai Stevenson died today," she said.

"Oh, that's too bad," I said. "I always liked his head."

"He died in London," she said.

"Oh?"

"That's a great place to die," she added.

"What? That's stupid," I whined. "What makes one place better than any other if you're dead?"

"London's just a good place to die in, that's all." She was looking at me out of the corner of her eye as she drove.

"I think you're crazy," I said, and slumped further into the bench seat.

Our house wasn't very far away, but throughout the short trip she kept babbling on about London and Adlai Stevenson. I failed to make a connection. I knew that my parents had resisted both Stevenson-Dixiecrat tickets in '52 and '56. And Illinois had no meaningful connection to England that I could see. I thought about Abraham Lincoln and came up short.

We pulled into the driveway. I lumbered out of the car, my clothes sticking to the seat, and walked into the house, where my mother and father stood in the living room, looking as peculiar as my sister's conversation had been. No one said anything to me and I felt that my parents were struggling to figure out what kind of expressions to put on their faces. I began to worry.

After a couple of agonizingly long minutes — worse than any I'd spent all day with my kitties — my mother handed me a thick packet addressed to me, sent Special Delivery, from the American Field Service. Inside the envelope already opened, and presumably read, was all the information I needed to know. Within six weeks I would be sailing across the Atlantic to become a foreign exchange student. I would live with a family in a town called Queensbury. (We looked on a map; it was nowhere near London, but in the North, in the West Riding of Yorkshire.) The force of the shock temporarily numbed me, and I suppose that our foursome, locked in curious poses, resembled a Madame Tussaud ensemble — inanimate, with dumb expressions on our faces, our heads tilted just slightly to the right or left.

After a few minutes I became ecstatic. No more Hallmark, no more Kansas City. I wouldn't even have to learn a foreign language. I was going to England, to a girls' school with uniforms; I would meet the Queen and the Beatles. My sister and I marched, briefly, around the living room humming "Rule Britannia," American-style, with a limping fifer and a drummer.

My parents worried about money. Just before my birthday, two weeks before, they had bought me a watch and a madras suit, to make up for the fact that I was not going to be selected as an exchange student. We had received a letter from AFS saying that I was qualified, etc., but that finding host families for black students was difficult. I was so naive, I didn't even think how ironic this was for an organization promoting world unity. And, although the cost to my parents was not astronomical in current currency terms — under a thousand dollars — in 1965, with my father's relatively low salary and six people under one roof, it might as well have been ten thousand. He took out another loan.

My sister and I attended the same high school — Central, Casey Stengel's alma mater — although she was in her third year of college before I crossed the school's threshold. Much had changed in a short time at Central. In her days, from 1958 to 1960, it was becoming integrated peaceably — without the traditional fire hoses and dogs — but temporarily. White students from the surrounding neighborhoods were joined by those bussed in from Harry Truman's hometown of Independence, and blacks were moving into the immediate school area. By the time Truman High School was built the area was nearly completely resegregated, in what had to have been one of the fastest white flights in history. I recall only three whites in my freshman class of well over 350 in 1962.

I look at my sister's yearbooks and see only a few blacks here and there. All of the "literary" societies (fraternities and sororities), nearly all of the academic clubs, and most of the honor societies are all-white. The pre-vocational clubs like Future Teachers of America and ROTC have a bit more black presence, as do the sports teams. My sister befriended one of the Little Rock Nine, who had "escaped" to high school in Kansas City. And she joined one of the most active NAACP youth groups in the country, mortifying the family one day when she called from jail because she had been arrested for picketing the segregated Fairyland Park, Kansas City's answer to Disneyland.

The five years that separate my sister and me seemed like a lifetime then. In Dayton, I and one or two other blacks had integrated a school over a period of two years. I was driven to and from school during the first year by two white mothers, who, knowing the attitudes of their neighbors, sought to keep me off the streets. I was alone when I steadfastly refused to leave the Little League bleachers as adults threatened to chase me away. While I experienced all of this in isolation, people my sister's age were on the threshold of organized activity that would find them billy-clubbed and jailed for their passive resistance. They would soon belong to organizations like SNCC, CORE, and the NAACP.

When we moved back to Kansas City I was too young to understand my mother's sarcasm on discovering that I would be attending D. A. Holmes, named after a black preacher, the same school — the former all-white Benton School — that my sister had been unable to attend years before. I knew that lunch counters, swimming pools, restaurants, and public johns were segregated. But I was not a part of the protest that helped change the policy for some of them. My private life did not resonate with public issues of desegregation and activism the way my sister's did. I was part of a second wave, with a different agenda in place, by the time I entered Central Senior High School.

My friends and I reaped the immediate benefits of the work my sister's generation had done. There had been few recruiters from white colleges interested in black students when my sister was a high school junior and senior. Expectations were different, more limited; family tradition and the existence of a network of family and friends dictated that her choice would be the University of Minnesota. By the time my friends and I were high school sophomores, we were already debating the merits of Ivy or Independent, single-sex or coed — choices that we knew would be forthcoming. Central, in my day, was a powerhouse of academic self-confidence and athletic prowess. We knew we were good; we knew we would make it. And although there were other black and integrated schools in the city, we felt that we were in the best of all possible places. We went so far as to avoid those teachers who we thought weren't good enough for our college plans. And we must have been some of the smarmiest, most arrogant little twerps on earth. Perhaps that was a requirement for the times, for although I have not kept up with my classmates, I believe a great number of them graduated from colleges and universities all over the country, and some from places my sister and her friends could only dream of attending.

I remember sometime in my junior year, our college-track class held a two-day exchange with a Catholic high school on the Kansas side, in the vicinity of the Shawnee Mission schools that were so highly touted nationally then. The English class we visited was reading Thomas de Quincey, and although I suspect that none of us had ever heard of de Quincey, we thought the class inferior to our own, and looked upon the whole scene of being dark children walking the halls and sitting in classes with uniformed white Kansans an interesting sociological exercise that left us craving nothing. To us, Central was better.

Central even had a chapter of the American Field Service, quite an oddity for all-black schools. In previous years we had sent two students abroad and several families had hosted foreign students in their homes. Once I decided to apply for the coveted, year-long Americans Abroad Program, my counselor quickly made adjustments in my classes so that I would have all the basic requirements for graduation after my junior year.

Central had a chess club, foreign language societies, math, camera, and pre-vocational clubs. We had winning sports teams. In 1992 we would have been an uplifting filler on the evening news, but in the early 1960s we considered ourselves doing the obvious — trying to excel with grace and occasionally, as a friend of mine was eager to note, "all lips and teeth." From time to time I come across a blurb in the national press about Kansas City schools; the obvious news is that things are worse.

But on July 14, all I could think about was getting away, expanding my horizons beyond even those I shared with my friends, and getting out of America.

On August 10, 1965 my father and I boarded the Santa Fe Chief, eastbound to Chicago. From there we were scheduled to take the Broadway Limited to New York, where I would sail for Europe. My father had suggested we fly, but I had too many NBC bulletins announcing the latest crash of one jet-liner or another ringing in my head to go along with the idea. My mind, not to mention my stomach, could not fathom the trip. Outside of Streator, Illinois, our train stopped, and remained motionless for five hours—long enough to miss our connection and a planned backup. We ended up taking a milk train, some night-owl Pennsylvania Railroad creeper that had one single, stuffy coach loaded with marginal types whose collective smells, soiled clothing, and alcohol breath suggested that they were more likely candidates for being put off a train than riding one. I was uncomfortable and self-conscious, fearful that the slowness of the train might necessitate our transferring to a plane somewhere around Pittsburgh. But we arrived safely, if smelling soiled and feeling queasy.

I had never been to Manhattan before, and it was as advertised—honking taxis, pedestrians everywhere, the sights and sounds of the opening montages of countless A and B movies from Hollywood. My father took me to the automat; it was too late in the day and I missed the chance to wave to my family at home from the huge windows outside of Rockefeller Center as the "Today Show" was broadcast. New York was noisy, brassy, fast, and—to my surprise and delight—bright, with a blue sky and colors everywhere. We went to the top of the Empire State Building and I took pictures. The afternoon of the eleventh we strolled along Fifth Avenue, went to the Park, and as dusk turned to night, ambled along Forty-second Street; it was an age, a time, perhaps just a moment, when my modest father saw nothing so lurid or filthy on the marquees or standing on the corners as to be worth hiding from his seventeen-year-old daughter.

Early the next morning we were off to the West Side Terminal, standouts among the hundreds of people in the cavernous room, on tiptoes, bending, squatting, turning to view the small freighter, *Groote Beer*, which a large group of Americans Abroad were about to board. I looked at the ship, remembered Barbara Stanwyck and Clifton Webb in *The Titanic*, swallowed hard, thought further about John Wayne and Robert Stack in *The High and the Mighty* and breathed easier, and walked with my group up the gangplank to begin a year as a real foreigner in another country.

My father had been humming the Sam Lewis and Fred Coots standard, "For All We Know," as we stood together looking out at the ship and the Hudson. The first line of that song, "For all we know, we may never meet again," made me realize — as if I hadn't known it all along — that my father was just as great a fatalist as I. I heard from a boy from Baltimore, through an unlikely exchange of postcards that zigzagged across Europe and America a year later, that his parents had seen my father weep as the ship pulled out of the docks.

August 12 was a sunny though hazy day. The Statue of Liberty was gray as we chugged toward the Atlantic. We all cheered. I was excited but calm as I tugged the back of my madras jacket, making sure it didn't creep too high on my rear end, and headed toward my appointed cabin just at waterline, where I would spend my nine-day voyage with three other girls. We were on our way to Holland; from there we would take the ferry to Great Britain.

There wasn't much to explore on the ship. The boatload of American students quickly found the dining room, the swimming pool, and gazed at the A-deck, off-limits to us and reserved for seventeen passengers: one very worldly woman, who reminded me of Ava Gardner in *Mogambo*, and sixteen young Europeans who spent most of the trip going from one state of dishabille to another. We peeked into the lifeboats, prepared for the required evacuation drill (I nearly fainted at the sound of the horns), and surveyed each other's name tags for clues to identity and destination.

That first evening we were assigned dining tables for the entire trip. We met our waiter and tried to figure out which of the two entrées, written in French, would be the best. Our combined years — probably several hundred — of high school French were of little help in the face of the menu, so we guessed, and were always pleased with what came out of the kitchen.

Later that evening, the first edition of our ship's newsletter and information sheet carried news of the raging Watts riot that had begun the night before. Several of my shipmates sought me out and asked me to explain what was going on. I said I didn't know — I hadn't heard anything — and I walked around the ship, holding tightly to the railing, breathing an air I had never smelled before, gazing at constellations whose names I did not know, leaving behind all that I had ever loved and hated. News of Watts left me emotionally and psychologically drained. The reasons for rioting were obvious enough; I couldn't understand why rioters always hurt themselves. But I was glad to be gone, glad to be on my way to I didn't care what.

I did not see or speak to a single black American from August 14, 1965 — when the only other black student on our ship, a good-looking boy from California, rather begrudgingly acknowledged me with his first and last "Hi" — until August 19, 1966, when I left Ozark Airlines Flight 499, which had just slightly overshot the runway at Kansas City Municipal Airport, and walked the long distance to the terminal to greet my parents. The only people of color I had seen for a year were West Indians when I was briefly in London, and Pakistanis and Indians whom I would glimpse fleetingly in Bradford as I rode the bus or walked through the downtown area. Getting off the boat at Rotterdam I felt jerked back to a time before my birth, to sights that reminded me of World War II documentaries: gray baroque and rococo buildings, plazas with cobblestones, french fry stands with mayonnaise as a condiment instead of ketchup. I bought a raw herring from a wizened, babushkaed old lady who had her stand in the middle of a plaza. Our troop of six, four girls and two boys on our way to the United Kingdom, walked around the city all day, amazed at the canals, at the speed of the automobiles on the streets, at the real Van Goghs and Rembrandts in the museum, before we caught the night ferry from Hoek van Holland to Harwich.

After years of riding coach on the Santa Fe and the Union Pacific, the coaches of the British Rail train that took us to London made me feel that I had stepped into one of those old documentaries. Everything was different. I recalled that my German-born French teacher in high school said she had not slept for weeks on arriving in the U.S. because our sirens reminded her of air-raid signals during the war. I heard a London siren — different from American ones — and my stomach dropped because the only other time I had heard the sound was in the theater, seeing *The Diary of Anne Frank*, when the Nazis found her hiding place and came to take her and the others away. Next to the terror I experienced in that theater, the San Francisco quake was nothing.

I laughed at the "Keep Left" traffic signs, appreciating their sentiment, and made a mental note that I'd have to relearn techniques of crossing the street. I saw double-decker busses, a pub in Ealing with the gear of eighteenth-century pirates everywhere on the walls and ceiling, Buckingham Palace lit up at night; I was living the whole travelogue. I had hoped to travel to Bradford alone, to organize my thoughts and compose myself before I met my hosting family, but instead I was met by my host "mother" and one "sister" and we left King's Cross, riding second class, at high speed north toward York-shire. I peered out the window, turned down a cigarette — I didn't smoke — didn't say much, and tugged at my madras suit top. On the way I discovered the uses of the fish fillet knife, drank a cup of what was perhaps Typhoo tea, ate trifle, and tried to understand what was being said to me. I had only heard royal and movie British, and although my host family did not speak broad Yorkshire, I still was deaf to much of what they said. It took two weeks for my ear to accustom itself to the many accents I heard. By the time I next saw a black American I was incapable of mimicking any American accent; I couldn't hear one anymore.

The wanderlust hit me one day in the summer of 1974. I cajoled my friend Kathy into driving west with me, on what turned out to be rather limited funds. But we got as far as Yellowstone Park before turning back east. We took a northeast exit out of the park, headed toward Billings and then Miles City, Montana. The road looked perfectly normal in the atlas, but it turned out to be something quite different: we drove into the mountains and over the highest pass I've ever seen — straight up, higher and higher. Peaks seemed to be all around us. The two-lane road was well plowed and dry, even though the snow at the roadside was very deep. There were only ornamental guardrails all the way up to something like eleven thousand feet. I was not driving, and I knew as soon as we started climbing that I would not have been able to. I sat in the passenger seat, looking out the window, and had a cosmic experience. The sight of the mountains was just too much for me. I felt as insignificant as the flakes of snow that occasionally blew up against the windshield. I found myself trying to reckon with the universe and failing fast; I was experiencing an existential terror.

When I lived in Oregon I used to look for Mount Hood every morning. It loomed like a huge deity over the city of Portland, and for some reason I had to try to see it, to arrange my mind for its existence. If I didn't seek it out I would be caught off-guard; it would suddenly appear in my rearview mirror and shock me with its magnificence. I would be frustrated on cloudy days, knowing the mountain was there but beyond my sight. Once or twice I would drive out to the airport, where it was possible to get a panoramic view of the mountains all around Portland, or up to Washington Park, where I would gaze down at the city and over to Mount Saint Helens, Mount

Hood, and other peaks. Living in the City of Roses convinced me that I couldn't handle the scale of the West; the mountains were just too massive, too powerful. They were only for the wanderings of the gods, not for human me. I admire mountain-climbers more for their mental balance than their physical skills. Were I to come upon Mount Everest I would doubtless commit suicide.

Living in England reversed the scale for me. Everything seemed smaller: the houses, the automobiles, the streets, the stores. The people were normal size, but not their environment. Riding in an Austin Minor was at best microcosmic. Time was different too. A large number of my friends had no telephone at home, so activities outside of school were organized through the mails: "Why don't you come for tea," they'd write, "on Thursday at 4?" The rhythms of life, along with the attitudes and the food, were completely different from anything I'd experienced before.

I think of the school — Bradford Girls' Grammar School, 1875, Hoc Age 1662 — and the prayers and hymns in the morning before class, the school song to the music of "Personent Hodie," one of the most glorious of all Christmas carols. And I see the school mistresses, oozing erudition; many of them were single, being of a generation that lost too many of its finest, and its ordinary, in the world war bloodbaths of the first half of the century. I was assigned to the lower sixth form, taking classes in French, English, history, and German with students whose sophistication in those subjects made the levels of Central and de Quincey in Kansas seem downright primitive. I have mixed feelings on the differences between English and American education; I believe in American-style liberal arts and the smorgasbord effect of course choices in college, even though I know the English system encourages students to know subjects well at the secondary school level, giving them more than just rudimentary skills. I only wished that I had been as well primed for their courses as my English classmates obviously were. I recall Miss Armstrong, the German mistress who was so kind and patient with me in a subject I never learned, nor, I suspect, cared to learn very well. And I recall my feeble attempts at English literature — ironically my weakest subject in England, though it turned out to be the field of my Ph.D. — and the summer examination that required four essays on Greek, Elizabethan, and Shakespearean tragedy in two and a half hours.

But the major education of my year in England was not in school. It was in finding out how to live in another culture, to live intimately with strangers, and to live with a self I had had no opportunity to know in the confines of an American Middle West where race and habit retarded a teenager's discovery of her own character and mettle. I will never forget my first day at B.G.G.S., when a girl who later became a fairly good friend asked me to define and defend U.S. policy in Vietnam. I knew better than to say we were protecting the world against communism, but other than that, I could come up with nothing intelligent at all. I was embarrassed and shocked at my ignorance, at my failure of intellectual curiosity and citizenship. And from my first school day there until I took as many pictures as I could on my last and waved good-bye, I was estranged from my country. All the mental and physical reflexes I had learned in order to survive each single day in the United States had disappeared. And from my first day at school, and that difficult question, I began to realize that one of racism's aims is to keep black people intellectual and emotional provincials. The necessity of concentrating on surviving in black skins saps the energies; not only does it keep real political and social power in the hands of whites, but it makes the self no more than a sociological fact, dancing, marionette-style, to a degrading tune.

One of the most chilling things about the Fugard, Kani, and Ntshona play, *Sizwe Bansi is Dead*, is that all the characters' energies are exhausted in making sure that South African identity papers are in order. They have no energy, or time, left for any more rewarding pursuits. This mental provincialism showed itself a few years ago in a letter to the Chicago *Scene*, a South Shore weekly newspaper, written in outraged tone and language, demanding to know why the paper had run an article on U.S. foreign policy; blacks, said the writer, had no right to say anything on the subject.

When I arrived in England I came from a mental ghetto as well as an environmental one. Shortly before I left I wrote home, in a detached, eighteen-year-old's style, "The greater independence and necessary calm and coolness of a person unattached to any tight strings gave me a chance to think about what I had previously done (or as the case often was, had been done for me automatically). Therefore, had this year only given me strength of character — which it has done — the year's experience would have been worth it."

I have never gone back to England. Any of my friends can attest to the fact that I am the one guaranteed pauper of their lot. But, more than that, I've always known that what happened to me could never be repeated — no lobster scene for me. Wearing the school uniform of the most prestigious girls' school in the city of Bradford protected me from all sorts of things, from overt displays of racism and the condescension of mother-countryists eager to deny the worth of any "colonial." But I'm no Anglophile; I know England has long been one of the most racist countries on earth. I might have gone anywhere that year and had the same reactions, but I didn't. Because I was an exchange student and a guest for some, and a human being and a friend to others, I felt free for the first and only time in my life. My friend Maurice, when he wants to get my goat, sometimes calls me "Miss Episcopalian." This happens after I've delivered some rapid-fire, ten-dollar-word tirade about poor manners. What I found in England was a freedom to discover myself, to grow.

At seventeen, I lit out for the only territory where everything could have happened so fast, where language was no real barrier: to an old, English-speaking world. There was no more room in the U.S. for that sort of a journey, for a black female like me, if there ever had been. I've never been quite the same for the experience. Back in my own country, I have remained estranged ever since from much around me. I wouldn't have it any other way.

My sister said the same thing happened to her when she spent a summer in France once. She returned and changed the whole focus of her life: dumped a husband, changed a career, bought some property. Getting out made it possible to come back to find a self-defined place to live.

My year in England was far from perfect; I changed homes midyear, the mixture of personalities poor in the first, better in the second. I suffered from mild bouts of depression at the idea of returning to the U.S. While I felt no racial barbs aimed at me, I did get a taste of antisemitism that seemed to abound everywhere; it added a dimension to my understanding of European history. I developed acne and suffer with it to this day.

But there are wonderful memories: of learning to plunk elementary chords on a guitar; of drinking beer in neighborhood pubs (unbeknownst to the AFS authorities); of finding that the most pleasurable moments in life could be spent in silence among friends; of finding Millie and Harry Park, whose daughter was on the same exchange in the U.S., and who became two of the six or seven most important people in my life; of knowing what real fish and chips are supposed to taste like from the only place in the world where they are made right: Yorkshire; of towns with histories and graveyards with markers going back so far it stunned me; of school plays and hijinks that seemed so corny and were so much fun; and of days in the Lake District and at Culloden in Scotland that made more sense of Wordsworth and Bonnie Prince Charlie than a hundred classroom explications ever could; of seeing Vanessa Redgrave on stage in London in *The Prime of Miss Jean Brodie*, and Diana Rigg in *Twelfth Night* at Stratford, with David Warner and Ian Holm and the rest of the Royal Shakespeare Company cast ad-libbing to screams of appreciation from the audience; of having parties thrown for me, and on my birthday standing on a chair to take a picture of my cake and feeling the legs go and my head taking dead aim at the icing spelling my name; of sitting straight through three showings of *Help!*; of waiting for a ride after seeing *Alfie* and being accosted by a prostitute who yelled at me, "Gear uff ma pitch"; of arguing that the Beatles were better than the Rolling Stones and occasionally losing; of being shown around Oxford by a Rhodes scholar; of going to the Proms and hearing Sir Malcolm Sargent conduct Elgar and Vaughan Williams; and of seeing the Parks on the day I left England — catching the ferry train to Rotterdam and boarding the M/S *Seven Seas* for the trip back to the United States and, I feared, the status quo.

The Americans Abroad students who'd been in the United Kingdom and Holland sailed home with the next year's group of Europeans. I don't believe I was the only depressed one of the group. The first night out there was a blind-date dance. All of the girls on ship put their names on pieces of paper in a fishbowl and these were drawn out by the boys. Two hours of primping and fantasizing were followed by the presumed gentlemen knocking at stateroom doors for their dates. The person who drew my name — a slight Italian, who may have had some tutoring on how to live in America — came to the room that I shared with the three other girls who had been in the United Kingdom. I answered the door and he screamed and ran off at breakneck speed, probably up to the A-deck, there, perhaps to vomit. Judging from his reaction to my face, he might well have dispatched himself to Davy Jones. He had obviously seen something that frightened him, and all pretenses to civilization (and here of course I mean the civilization he would have said he had a hand in perpetuating) disappeared.

I was surprised at the violence of his reaction. My cabin mates expressed pity and spread the word, so that within a short period of time the drop-dead-handsome Swede who was one of the ship's chaperones escorted me to the dance where

I watched several hundred Europeans and a handful of Americans swim and frug to an endless string of Beach Boys songs. I remember leaving the festivities and going out to the railing on the deck and wishing the boat would turn around.

We were on it for many days. I still have copies of the news dispatches from the wire services:

August 12, 1966:

Washington: President Johnson asserted that the United States would remain firm against communist aggression in Southeast Asia. He added that the United States stood ready to assist in the peaceful development of the area once the forces of communism put away their weapons.

Honolulu: Gen. William Westmoreland, commander of U.S. forces in Vietnam, said American troops would have to be augmented in the Vietnam war, but he declined to speculate on the number that ultimately would be required.

Grenada, Miss.: State troopers broke up knots of heckling whites who gathered near the Negro section to taunt 250 civil rights demonstrators.

August 13, 1966:

Manila: A partial withdrawal of U.S. troops from South Vietnam may be possible in two years, South Vietnamese Premier Ky predicted.

Jackson, Miss.: Dr. Martin Luther King decried the black power movement and reaffirmed the effectiveness of nonviolent protest in his closing to the annual convention of the Southern Christian Leadership Conference.

Chicago: Repentant Beatle John Lennon said he was sorry he compared the popularity of the singing group with Jesus Christ but insisted it was true that the Beatles were more popular.

The boat docked in New York on August 18, 1966, as an airline strike crippled the nation. On August 19 I was one of the lucky ones to get home quickly, since American Airlines and Ozark were the only carriers flying. I flew first class on American to Chicago, circling over a picture-book Manhattan basking in bright sunlight, and from Chicago to Kansas City on Ozark 499, making stops at the Quad Cities and someplace else — I forget — on the way home.

Hart Crane began "Chaplinesque" with these lines:

> We make our meek adjustments,
> Contented with such random consolations
> As the wind deposits
> In slithered and too ample pockets.

Somewhere between the moment on August 12, 1965 when a night wind off the Atlantic pounded against my face and a ghetto adjacent to Los Angeles called Watts was burning, and another moment nearly 365 days later, when a different night wind off the same Atlantic whispered, "Welcome home" as I sought refuge from a dance at sea, I had made my meek adjustments too. I came back no more mature than expected. On the contrary, I have always been a late bloomer, struggling — and sometimes failing — to believe in the self I thought I had discovered away from America and its particular kinds of miseries and illusions. An alien abroad, I returned knowing that I would always be an alien at home, and that my excursion into the territory proved that from then on I'd have to make my own.

PART TWO

Professor Dearest

> You see, Mrs. Higgins, apart from the
> things one can pick up (the dressing and the
> proper way of speaking and so on), the differ-
> ence between a lady and a flower girl is not
> how she behaves, but how she is treated.
> GEORGE BERNARD SHAW

I HAD JUST turned twenty-five when I got my first full-time
teaching position. I was one of five young and eager teachers
who were new to the English department that year. It was an
uneasy time in America: the first oil crisis, the fall of Saigon,
the revving up for the Watergate scandals. The department's
politics mirrored the outside world: lawsuits for sexual and racial discrimination and the constant, egomaniacal, interne-
cine fighting that characterizes most departments on college
faculties, but in my experience is particularly rife in English,
foreign languages, classics, music, art, philosophy, religion,
history, chemistry, biology, physics, sociology, anthropol-
ogy, and physical education.

That first year was a difficult one for us all. In view of the
equally pervasive institutionalized sexism, racism, and antisemitism, the five of us — three white women, a Jewish man,
and I — despaired from time to time over the environment in
which we'd chosen to start our professional careers. I suppose
my despair was the strongest; I left that school after a year.
The man left the next year and became a successful lawyer.
To the best of my knowledge, the three white women are still

there, having made, presumably, whatever adjustments were necessary to find a place, to make a home.

I am sure I am not the only person in the world who ever sprained her ankle getting out of a swivel chair, but I may be the first to admit it. Such an act of supreme gracelessness occurred one morning during the beginning of the spring term. I was in great pain when a student happened by my office with a friend of hers who luckily was one of those rare people who can drive a standard-shift transmission, so I got a ride home in my own car. I wrapped my ankle and returned to school, since I had classes that afternoon and I hold tenaciously to my theory that one should only cancel classes for a good reason — like unspeakable dread at the prospect of facing a class on a given day — not for mere temporary physical infirmity. I hobbled toward the faculty dining room and, since I was unable to spot any friends from other fields, I sat down with various members of my department.

English departments throughout America thrive on clever phrase-turners and quoters, people who have spent the larger portion of their lives reading and remembering, and who, probably from the cradle, have practiced the pun and the put-down. Our department contained one such man, whom I had heard described as someone whose greatest torment was having to live with himself. I have heard this exact line spoken about a number of the more unpleasant people with whom I've worked over the years. Curiously, it's usually said by friends or sycophantic underlings. The line doesn't appeal to me much; my ideas of the means of proper retribution and torment are centered somewhere outside of a victimizer's own self-consciousness.

I have very slender wrists and ankles, as it happens. My fingers are thin and long; my feet are unremarkable, rather corny, and I tend to walk on their outside edges. These physical attributes stand out, to those who are capable of noticing them, and seem out of place with the rest of me, which is rather endomorphic and highly resistant to change, no matter how much I starve or how far I jog.

Perhaps I should have changed into pants, but I didn't. I wore a skirt, making the Ace bandage appear absurdly large wrapped around my ankle. My older colleague said nothing to me during lunch, but later remarked to someone else that on seeing my ankles he was overwhelmed at their delicacy, and found himself at pains to create a symmetry from so peculiar an image as mine.

I am reminded that once upon a time it was scandalous for a lady to show an ankle. The sight of this part of her anatomy was to be withheld, like the rest of her physical delights, from the gaze of the rabble, or from any gentleman short of her husband. And the ankle became a means of measuring the quality of breeding, a kind of human-equine scale of merit in the same league as "Make sure you see the grandparents before you marry her: the kids will look like them," or "Check out the teeth; did God or the orthodontist straighten them and are they real?" This particular spring day was not once upon a time, though, and I suspect that the gentleman was incapable of seeing me as a lady. When I heard what he said, I thought wouldn't it be lovely if my beautiful ankle were a lovely big hoof, that could kick solidly through his tormented head and end his and everyone else's misery.

That was not the first time I had been made to feel other than human — more like a cow than a thoroughbred — but in all fairness, I should add that this man did see me as the female of some species: he remarked, to yet another colleague at another time, that my breasts frightened him.

Richard Wright is quoted in Simone de Beauvoir's *America Day by Day* (dedicated to Wright and his wife Ellen) as having said:

> . . . there is not a single minute in the life of a Negro that is not penetrated by a social consciousness; from the cradle

to the grave, whether working, eating, loving, walking, dancing or praying, he can never forget that he is black; and this makes him conscious every minute of a white man's world whence the word "black" derives its meaning.

This is not an overstatement; it is just right. One does indeed have a penetrating consciousness of oneself in a white world, and those black people I know who don't believe it I deem insane. Make the world an academic one and this sense can be heightened to levels worthy of the house of Usher, and, in too many cases, with the same results. The only white people I have met who consistently display a familiarity with this quality of self-consciousness are white southerners. This is no surprise. Dozens of southern generations have understood themselves as white in a way that northerners have only been learning to do in the last fifty years or so. I speak only of the United States in this; the expressions of racial and cultural identity in other countries both share and do not share the quality I mean.

The interplay between black and white southerners resonates with talmudic intricacy and highly ritualized form. This too is not news; capable sociologists and anthropologists have charted this region in ways I cannot.

During that same first year of teaching — a year that taught me more than I wanted to know about the profession, but which steeled me against many of its disappointments — I found myself acting out a ritual drama with a senior member of my department. He was an old-school southerner, which, I suppose, is a convenient way of saying that he saw himself neither as Tom Wicker nor as Lester Maddox, but as a representative of a class descended directly from Mr. Jefferson, with old and firm ideas of social decorum and racial and cultural superiority. In short, he was a southern gentleman. My presence as a colleague doubtless struck him as the utmost absurdity, an implicit challenge to and a mockery of the very definition of an English department — white and male.

There is a reverse side to this coin, that is, the northern

side. A male friend of mine, a black Ivy Leaguer, tells me that he avoids sherry hours and wine sips with his older colleagues because the men there tend to smile at him patronizingly, congratulating themselves for having made him what he is. They are proud to have given him the opportunity to display what they see as his occasionally profound, but always quaint and inchoate literary gifts. Northern men have done this to me as well. It reveals itself not in a smile, however, but in the particular way they begin calling me by my first name seconds after having met me.

I never had a conversation with my southern senior colleague, but we communicated. Because he saw himself as a gentleman, he could not bring himself to completely ignore me, as northerners can and do with appalling ease. So, when a situation arose, such as passing each other in a hallway or arriving at a faculty meeting at the same time, he would bow slightly, casting his eyes down to make sure they did not catch mine (with an exaggerated flourish worthy of Sir Walter Raleigh throwing his cloak over the mud so that ladies might safely pass), and with the hint of a question he would sigh, slowly, "Miz Pemberton . . . ?" And I would reply in kind, with the hint of a curtsy, also averting my eyes and inclining my head: "Mr. So-and-So . . . ?" uttering the last syllable of his name also as a question. I never thought much about what the answer to the question was or, for that matter, what the question was. Our encounters never went beyond this, and when I think of him I don't see his full face, but merely an image of a graying, brown-haired pate and an imaginary wide-brimmed, feathered hat sweeping across the front of a long black doublet.

There was a veneer of civility in our ritualized exchange — a rarity, I'm sure, when old-school southern gentleman meets northern black lady.

I understand ritual. All of those years of processions and recessions and incense and bells in church, graduate school hurdles ("Ms. Pemberton, there is no intrinsic meaning in this act; it is designed to gauge your commitment to serious literary study"), and coded messages in everyday life ("That's the bell for the last round," "What can I do to get a better grade?" "What a lovely home you have!") have given me an appreciation of the complexities surrounding the behavior between the sexes and between the races. And I've seen just how much ritual is involved. I think of my great-grandmother, Carrie Roberts, and the only two items I've seen with her imprint on them (since she was dead before I was born): the scrapbook she kept with clippings of any story she could find about the "colored" — evictions, murders, transgressions of racial lines, and (mostly) lynchings — and an annotated cookbook. I wonder at her ritualized cutting and pasting; and if I were at all mystical, I would ascribe the meaning of her work to the necessity of my finding it and writing of it now. Her world was so proscribed and burdened with the immediate issues of how to feed and clothe her children. There was meaning in her ritual work, though, clear to see: the cutting and pasting was a kind of self-expression and communication, a black woman simply saving, in lieu of her own chronicle, a smattering of cultural history for anyone who might find it.

Carrie's daughter, Grandma, worked for over twenty-five years as a ballroom matron in Sioux City. So she knew something about behavior, ritual and otherwise: from the filth of all sorts she was expected to remove and from which she developed hard and fast notions about who was clean and who wasn't, to the dances themselves, where men would pay ten cents to mostly misstep around a floor with girls who were girls no longer and whose hard luck it was to have to make their living that way — these same talkative girls who always told Grandma more than she ever wanted to hear.

Much extended verbal exchange between white and black women tends to reveal a strangely romanticized, and mostly middle-class, idea that black women are born to be confidantes — a curious mistress-to-maid mentality on the part of white women who have never seen a servant outside of a movie. Women born to the manor tend to shut up when the servants are around to keep them from hearing intimate information; women born elsewhere see a potential confidante in every black woman they meet. My sister and I have traded stories for years about true confessions we've had to endure from white strangers; I have become so wary of it that I've stopped asking white women questions about anything remotely personal, to the extent that once I was invited to dine with a woman I was sure was a shy loner, only to meet a happy family of three children and a handsome, attentive husband when I arrived.

I remember sitting at a lunch table with several female colleagues once. We were recounting the various nonacademic jobs we'd held between terms during our student days. One woman said, "Well, of course, we've all been waitresses." All the rest nodded. I said, "Well, no, as a matter of fact, I never was a waitress." My colleagues seemed surprised. I asked them how many black waitresses they'd seen who looked as if they were working themselves through college or graduate school, or, for that matter, just black waitresses period, ruling out lunch-counters in business districts and all-black neighborhoods. Our group could come up with only five or six instances in a collective memory spanning over one hundred years, and four of those instances were mine.

There is probably no area of life filled with more kinds of ritual than that surrounding the preparation and consumption of food. In those high-quality restaurants where there are waitresses — there being other assumptions about service and protocol in places where there are only waiters — I have never seen a black waitress. The game in these restaurants revolves around sexual innuendo from man to woman, with look-but-don't-touch rules, more or less explicit depending on whether alcohol is served, and as such it is clearly reserved for whites only. The most highly ritualized and absurd manifestation of this can be observed at the Playboy Club. Judging from what I've been able to see of this game, a considerable amount of hostility often reveals itself on both sides. Naturally, the historic interplay of use and abuse by the master of his female servant comes to mind. And if patron and waitress are black different meanings, different assumptions are usually at play. The celebrated and, I think, very real sassiness of black women also militates against their being involved too much in the look-but-don't-touch game. On the whole they are much less likely than their white counterparts to put up with the verbal abuse or physical entreaty that is at the core of the waitress-diner relationship. But — and this has something to do with some distinctive qualities of black American life — this sassiness is the hallmark of a good waitress in all-black establishments, where more than hash is being slung during the repartee. Tips are bound to be lower for the silent types.

The game between white waitresses and black male diners is something else, too. My father was a great kidder, and he encouraged, in a way quite discernible by the look on his face, sarcasm and sass. I had dinner with him once at Durgin Park, a restaurant known for its sassy waitresses, in Boston, a city where black people do not generally relish their dining escapades. He and a strapping Irish waitress had each other near tears wise-cracking at each other. He later remembered the restaurant fondly, not only because, as he said, "they knew what a meal was," but because the waitress was one of the best he'd ever seen. He joked with waitresses whenever they were at all amenable, knowing full well that twenty years earlier he might have become a clipping in Carrie's scrapbook because of it. Forget the twenty years; he might have been one any time. This taboo has fine lines, tempting lines, that are crossed daily in society when it comes to black men and white women; there is a predisposition on each side to like the other, to stick out tongues and chant, "Nyah-nyah," at the rest of the world.

Rituals and food, racism and sexism. I have eaten at a

Woolworth's counter once — when I was ravenous somewhere in the West as I was driving across country and my only alternative was a bar with a confederate flag in the window — but now that I can, I generally prefer not to. Similarly, I have never entered a White Castle fast-food restaurant and never will. There used to be one such establishment on my way to school in Kansas City. Several of my friends and I used to stop at the window and look in at the scattering of whites still left in our rapidly resegregating neighborhood. There were so few whites left that the White Castle must have been going broke, but they were damned if they were going to let us in. So at the age of eleven I became convinced that racism was stronger than the profit motive. And I began my lifelong boycott of "sliders."

During my early years as a college teacher several of my junior faculty colleagues and I would gather on Friday afternoons over pitchers of dreadful beer and recount the week's absurdities, slurs, and mini-dramas. Next door to our favorite bar was a pizzeria advertising authentic and delicious Italian food, with waiters from Italy — and an entire kitchen staff of black men who could be glimpsed behind the swinging doors. I looked forward to those Fridays because they seemed to be relatively free of rivalry and self-aggrandizement; we all knew our jobs were temporary, that frozen tenure lines would stay that way, so instead of tripping each other to reach the finish line first, we stayed back and enjoyed each other, even if we didn't like our collective plight. (There were others who jockeyed for a phantom first place, but we didn't go drinking with them.)

One particular afternoon in early spring there were seven of us in the bar, four men and three women. The other two women were white, as were all the men. We had begun our regular rehash of the week when, after the first round, the two other women got up from the table and went to the water closet (that's really what it was, an all-purpose water closet, damp, stinking, with a chain-pull toilet). I stayed at the table.

Seconds after they were out of earshot, the men began talking about the pulchritude of these women. Innuendo turned to concrete fantasy. The language became rougher, the pitch faster. All they needed were some towels and jockstraps to snap at each other.

I froze, unable to form even a harrumph in my throat, and I felt my heart sink in a way it never has since that day. I began thinking hard about the way I had been treated all of my professional life, and I understood then that I had no real sexual identity to them, who doubtless considered themselves gentlemen. To them I was neutered; far from being a lady, I was not even a flower girl. I realized that black women in white institutions are either vamps or mammies, and I was clearly not the vamping type. I have rarely felt so alone.

I should have remembered that sex and the academy are usually a funny mix. Once, several years ago, I was sitting at a bar in the Palmer House in Chicago with my friend Maurice during a Modern Language Association convention. We were having a few drinks, talking about mendacity and illusion, while we waited for a mutual friend to join us for dinner. After a while Maurice noticed some ladies of the evening who were sitting across the horseshoe-shaped bar. Pretending to continue our own conversation, we turned all ears to theirs. It seemed one of the women was a veteran of MLA conventions, and she was giving some advice to her fledgling companion:

"First of all, just drink ginger ale. They'll keep buying you drinks all night if you let them and you'll be drunk as shit in a few hours, and that's all, with nothing else to show for it," the older one warned.

"Really?" said the fledgling.

"Damn straight, honey." The veteran was looking very serious. "The whole town is crawling with these professors, but I'll lay you ten-to-one there ain't a girl in Shy-town gettin' more than drinks from 'em. This is a good time to take a fuckin' vacation."

The pattern hasn't changed much since my assistant professor days. Now that I am aware of how I'm seen, I still suffer, but not nearly so much as I might. After all, in a peculiar kind of way I'm saved from the kinds of sexual abuse and harrassment I've seen directed toward white women by white men. I'm robbed of my essence, flattened by this horrible combination of racism and sexism, but in order to live I consider my neutering a kind of freeing that has allowed me to observe, unscathed, the tortuous and stupid relations between white men and women. My experience with the few black men in the academic world has been roughly the same, except that the misogynists among them are nastier and the neat guys rarer.

It remains peculiar, and not as demoralizing as one might think, that a gasp at my ankles and a Raleighesque flourish mark the high points of being a woman in my business. I once did have a colleague who saw me differently, but nothing happened beyond my fantasies and I moved on before I could find out whether I had imagined the whole thing.

The Zen of
Bigger Thomas

"WE LEAD SUCH dramatic lives," my friend Luke said to me on the phone some time back. We are old friends. We only manage to see each other once every five years or so; in between, we talk on the phone. It's always a long and expensive call. We seem to have developed a similar sensibility; both of us try to view the world with the same highly focused, stark realism. In other words, we ache inside and we like to think we can't be fooled.

By "we," Luke didn't mean himself and me. He meant black people — all of us.

Luke said that something lately had reminded him of a cocktail party we had attended in the seventies, where a tragedy had recently struck the host's family. "Do you remember the So-and-Sos' party?" he asked me. How could I have forgotten it? I had been visiting him, taking part of a spring break to leave the frozen climes of New England to head south, and we went to the home of a late-middle-aged black couple he knew who were throwing a bash to celebrate the opening of a black art exhibit. They had signed on for the gala and were carrying out their pledge completely, in spite of their tragedy.

Their home sprawled on the inside, lending a depth to its only slightly-larger-than-normal Georgian exterior. The hundred or so guests roamed through a large living room, done in tasteful Oriental design. There was a patio, terracottaed to death, where rattan and wrought iron peacefully, if uneasily, coexisted.

The host was a dapper man with a slight limp. He had chestnut brown skin, smooth and ageless. His hair was completely gray, worn short; his mustache was salt and pepper, and full. His eyebrows arched and his forehead formed deep lines when he spoke, but when he smiled his face relaxed, melted, so that he looked almost like another person. He had on a three-piece gabardine suit of a deep rich gray. I remember how perfectly it fit him. And the surprise was that he tended his very well-stocked bar himself, with a generosity that bordered on the absurd. He poured such mean drinks. Several people asked him why he was working his own party, and he joked, saying he liked to avoid both "*pre*tense and *ex*-pense." He said he also hoped people would slow down a little with him at the bar. He didn't mind people drinking their fill, he said, but they tended to lose perspective at the sight of free premium liquors. I reasoned that standing in one place and moving in only a small space was probably less painful to him than working the crowd. After all, sooner or later, everyone would be by to see him.

His wife was tall, perhaps five feet ten or so. They looked alike, for she too had smooth, burnished chestnut brown skin, gray hair — with just a little black streak. It was styled in a soft wave that ended on the right side of her face, just slightly covering an oval, sparkling diamond earring. She circulated through the crowd gracefully, and I remember noticing that when she extended her hand, catching the hand or elbow of the person to whom she was talking, she held on tightly, as if to keep herself balanced. She wore a long blue dress of African design and incredible beauty. Her voice was low, a liquid southern Atlantic coast accent that immediately reassured one. I spoke to her only briefly; I liked her.

I did not know my hosts' story. I didn't know it until after I found a slightly staggering Luke motioning me to join him on a loveseat in a corner of the library. He had two drinks: one for me, one for himself. We sat down and he said: "I have to tell you this. I don't know where to start. It's horrible."

I said, "So, Whimper got tenure, did he?"

He said, "No, just shut up and listen."

Not a week before the party, our hosts' only daughter and son-in-law had been shot to death as they went to a grocery store. There had been no discernible motive — no drugs, no bad blood, no trouble — no reason other than that they were in a particular spot when two young men fired Magnum 357s. The couple died instantly and so did their unborn child. There was no robbery; their car was not taken. The murderers fled on foot, and by the time of the party had not been caught. Descriptions of them were sketchy. They were both black, between five feet ten and six feet tall. They wore high-top basketball shoes, black chino pants. One had an Adidas sweatshirt on; the other's said Nike. They swore. Everyone in the vicinity of the shooting had ducked at the first shots, so, beyond that, they had little to recall. The white owners of the grocery store had refused to come out to the parking lot to see the carnage. A bent, elderly black woman, with knee-high stockings folded down over her ankles, was found lying near the couple. She had collapsed, a heart attack, her much used paper shopping bag having spilled its contents of reduced-for-quick-sale fruit and a box of Tide. A passerby tried to revive her as the ambulance came. Her left shoe had come off when her ankle twisted in the fall. The shoe had been stuffed with newspaper. The old woman died and remained unclaimed at the morgue until a local church gave her a decent, if anonymous, burial.

Luke said that he had begun the party the same way as I had — drinking champagne that was being served by a liveried waiter. But when he was cornered by an old friend of his and told the story, he made a beeline for the bar. Finding our host there, Luke asked him to join him in a nice, long, serious martini, and engaged him in conversation about tuck-pointing. Luke told me that he couldn't think of anything else at that moment, and that our host seemed to warm to the topic. After four more drinks — and after Luke's already skimpy knowledge of tuck-pointing had been exhausted — he came and found me, and we sat down.

At 3:00 A.M. on a frigid Chicago morning a few years after that party, the telephone rang in my sister's apartment. I was sharing it with her, trying to undo bad financial times and save a little money. On the other end of the line was the Kansas City Police Department. The officer told my sister that our mother was in the hospital after having been attacked by an intruder in her home. He had no other information, but suggested we call the homicide division for further details. The homicide officer could only tell us that Mother had been stabbed several times and that there was a lead in the case. She was in intensive care. He didn't tell us whether she was expected to live or not.

We threw clothes into bags, grabbed the dog, made a quick thermos of coffee, and ran from the apartment to my car and drove, in icy silence and terror, the five hundred miles. Halfway there, my sister called the hospital to check on Mother's condition. She was told that the surgery was over, but that Mother remained in intensive care and could not speak. We had no idea of the nature of her wounds. I thought, and then suppressed saying, that maybe she couldn't speak because her throat had been cut or that she had become catatonic. Two hundred miles from the city we imposed radio silence for fear that we would hear of her death during the on-the-hour news wrap-up.

When we got to the hospital we were greeted by family friends who wanted to know where we had been. We explained that psychologically we couldn't have handled the wait for a morning flight, so we drove. We found out that Mother had been stabbed with shards of glass from a leaded window bordering the front door, and that surgery to repair her abdominal wounds had resulted in the removal of her gall bladder. She had not been stabbed in the face or neck. She had dragged herself to the telephone after the attack and called the police. She had not been raped, a disappointment to those who asked that first and then thought we were lying when we said no.

Mother lived alone in the only house she and my father had ever owned. They bought it in 1958 — really a shell of a house that whispered to you when you entered, "I need more money. Fix me." It never stopped whispering that, despite countless good and bad repairs over the years designed to make it more structurally sound and aesthetically pleasing. But my father loved it: it was his castle. And after he died, Mother — who had never shared his fondness for it — clung to it as a measure of her independence, as space and furnishings and dry rot and memories of love.

It was after midnight. The attacker broke in, demanded money, which Mother did not have, and started stabbing her before she could possibly have gone for money anyway. She probably would have been murdered had she not surprised her attacker by being up at that hour. Her notorious night-owl ways, for which my sister and I have chided her for years, helped save her life. There she was, eating dinner at nearly 1:00 A.M., watching "The Late, Late Show," when the attacker entered. He was wearing high-top basketball shoes, black chino pants, and a sweatshirt, cut off at the sleeves, that said Puma.

I was afraid to go into the intensive care room to see her, but I did. I wanted her to be someone else, but I also feared that she might be now, suddenly, an old lady who had been attacked by a thug, and not the vibrant mother I'd always known. I looked at her swollen face, which seemed to have

166

aged a century in just a few hours; the tubes in her mouth, in her nose; the bandages everywhere. She was groggy, but she recognized us and she gestured, weakly, for a pen and paper. We gave her the back of an envelope and she wrote, her flawless Palmer-method hand now shaky and nearly unreadable: "Have they caught the bastard yet?"

"No," we said.

She shook her fist weakly, but her eyes were on fire. I relaxed a little.

Mother recovered. We were all lucky. My sister had a severe attack of eczema for several weeks, and I have attributed some bizarre behavior on my part two years later to a quiet nervous breakdown caused by the event. Mother's assailant was caught and jailed. But she never slept another night in her home. Instead, we packed her up and moved her to my sister's. She has remained physically and psychologically sound since that night — when, she told us, the police had been so surprised at her calm that they thought she couldn't possibly have been seriously injured. One of them had even asked her if she thought she needed an ambulance.

I remembered all of that when Luke called me. Remembering that party reminded me, as if I really needed reminding, of just how certain kinds of dreadful possibilities — nay, likelihoods — go hand-in-hand with our more hopeful cultural expectations. This drama, as it were, delivers nothing new.

I think I'll pour myself a long, serious one, and think about the tuck-pointing on the building outside my window.

Marianne Moore writes, in "Picking and Choosing":

Literature is a phase of life. If one is afraid of it,
the situation is irremediable; if one approaches it familiarly,
what one says of it is worthless.

I have spent a good portion of my lifetime with literature, being a partial professional — reading and teaching it. Full professionalism — writing about it — I've chosen to avoid, even though that hasn't helped my career. It's just that about eighty percent of what I read by full professionals, some of whom obviously are afraid of literature, some of whom are far too familiar with it, is more a competition in the repetition of the obvious, in old or new jargons, than enlightening scholarship. I admire the energy and talent of those who create the twenty percent of the really good stuff. Something — I don't believe it's fear; perhaps it is — has kept me from trying to join their ranks.

On days when only tuck-pointing and a bourbon will do I've wondered about this extra layer of marginality I've imposed on myself; of being a more and more questionable hire as one scholarly fallow year follows another. The only answer I can find is that there is a relationship between American literature and my life that is so organic, so fundamental and alive, I don't want to detach myself from it long enough to take on the supposedly objective eye of the critic. Literature defines a familiar world that ever remains mysterious; and much American writing provides me with a mirror with which to try to see myself as a black woman. All I see reflected is an interesting kaleidoscope of images moving just over the shoulder of the image of myself I have drawn on the mirror. As Invisible Man's Professor Woodridge told his students, "We create the race by creating ourselves and then to our great astonishment we will have created something far more important: We will have created a culture." I see that the self I have drawn does and does not look a part of the kaleidoscope over my shoulder. I keep peering, wondering what to make of the entire scene.

I seek a narrative, a fiction, to order days like the one I spent several years ago, on a gray June Saturday in Chicago, when I took a roller-coaster ride on the bell curve of my experience. The husband of one of my favorite students of all time had thrown her a graduation party. She was a "special" student, which in this case meant older. She made a Faulkner seminar a joy to teach, with her insight, her willingness to argue, and her expansive, adult humor. Her husband was obviously not a poor man; they lived on Chicago's Gold Coast. I asked the elevator man which apartment was theirs; when he said, simply, "Four," I got the picture; they lived on the entire fourth floor. (Later, on the way out, I overheard some women chortle that they'd asked, "Which apartment number?" "Rubes," I thought to myself.)

It was a lovely party. I had put on a brightly colored, sprightly dress. I congratulated the graduate, and spent the afternoon drinking martinis, something I rarely do because gin is a very dangerous spirit. I made my rounds through the group, the only black there. I listened to a terribly well-dressed woman describe her new interior design business. I talked to another woman — a delightful sixty year old who easily could have passed for forty — who obviously had been blessed with "three squares a day and no worries," as my father used to say. We discussed thirties literature. There was nothing out of the ordinary. I was a professor enjoying myself at a party held by a recent graduate. Everyone in the room had impeccable manners, straight teeth, and enough experience in life to be interesting. Some, like my student, were sincerely committed to social change. Others doubtless would die first.

After two or three hours I left the party and drove to my sister's apartment in South Shore to help her with some late afternoon Saturday chores. We took Mother shopping, bought groceries, ate more a snack than dinner, and then launched into one of my sister's furniture moving projects for the rest of the night. At about 1:00 A.M. we finished, and, famished, decided to eat a late dinner. We thought we deserved a treat, so I drove to our favorite barbecue place, Thomas's, not far from the apartment. There, at about 1:30, I stood in a line about ten people deep, waiting to place my order through the bulletproof plexiglass window, and watched as three or four young men on the other side, with gauze-like caps and soiled aprons, scampered around a tiny space, lifting slabs of ribs out of the smoker, chopping them into short ends, large ends, and tips, and placing them on bread in a light cardboard server with a handful of french fries and maybe a carton of coleslaw, looking up to ask, "Mild or hot?" for the sauce. It was a typical late Saturday, early Sunday crowd: people with alcohol or marijuana hunger; some, like a skinny little girl with hollow eyes, about six, exhausted, in torn clothes, perhaps with mere hunger. We stood against the wall like suspects in a lineup, awaiting our orders. A young man edged into the shop, through the narrow space between our line and the counter; he walked to the back, opened a cooler and pulled out orange, grape, cola, and cherry soda pops. After paying for them he yelled at us that he would be the only person alive on earth within a year; with that, he left. I half-smiled with the rest of the line, some of us no doubt thinking, as I did, that it might serve the fellow right — one man joked that the shortage of beds in mental hospitals was putting a strain on the community — and all of us laughed, only to resume our uneasy silence, punctuated by murmurs, as we waited. I got my order, walked out, and said no to an incense seller hawking his wares.

In some ways it had been an uncanny twelve hours of extremes, yet it also had not felt much out of the ordinary. Bemused, I put my thoughts on a back burner, sure that few people in Chicago that day could one-up me, as I saw a skewed total image of the kaleidoscope and me.

Click.

A black man is running across an apartment house roof. It is nighttime; snow is on the ground. It is winter and the place is Chicago. His name is Bigger Thomas of *Native Son*, and he is soon to be caught by police and jailed for the murder of Mary Dalton. While Bigger awaits the inquest, Richard Wright narrates:

And regulating his attitude toward death was the fact that he was black, unequal, and despised. Passively, he hungered for another orbit between two poles that would let him live again; for a new mode of life that would catch him up with the tension of hate and love. There would have to hover above him, like the stars in a full sky, a vast configuration of images and symbols whose magic and power could lift him up and make him live so intensely that the dread of being black and unequal would be forgotten; that even death would not matter, that it would have to be born in him, a humility springing from a new identification forming the basis for a new hope that would function in him as pride and dignity.

Click.

A black man is running across an apartment house roof. It is daytime; flurries are in the air. It is winter and the place is Harlem. He has no other name but that of the novel's title, *Invisible Man*. When he has come to the end of his tale, preparing to end his literal underground hibernation and reenter the world, he says:

> Here I've set out to throw my anger into the world's face, but now that I've tried to put it all down the old fascination with playing a role returns, and I'm drawn upward again. So that even before I finish I've failed (maybe my anger is too heavy; perhaps, being a talker, I've used too many words). But I've failed. The very act of trying to put it all down has confused me and negated some of the anger and some of the bitterness. So it is that now I denounce and defend, or feel prepared to defend. I condemn and affirm, say no and say yes, say yes and say no. I denounce because though implicated and partially responsible, I have been hurt to the point of abysmal pain, hurt to the point of invisibility. And I defend because in spite of all I find that I love. In order to get some of it down I have to love. I sell you no phony forgiveness, I'm a desperate man — but too much of your life will be lost, its meaning lost, unless you approach it as much through love as through hate. So I approach it through division. So I denounce and I defend and I hate and I love.

Sometimes I wonder why I keep brooding about *Native Son* and *Invisible Man*, but I do, rereading them (along with a few other novels) again and again, halfway expecting them to render some truth that will help me better reckon with my world. And I know my fascination has to do with the fact that to me they are so similar. Bigger Thomas and Invisible Man are a kind of Castor and Pollux, black Dioscuri living in twin urban worlds, dying or surviving, it would seem, by the will of the gods, with *Native Son* functioning as a comic tragedy and *Invisible Man* as a tragic comedy.

There is something about the murderers of the young couple and of the teenager who attacked my mother — and of the umpteenth street-smart, fearsome black male image in the movies and television — that renewed my thinking about the novels again recently. I began to see these black men as latter-day Biggers, the ghastly but not unexpected fulfillment of the implicit and explicit warnings of *Native Son*. For Bigger Thomas white people are his nightmare; he can find no role to play but in a nightmare of theirs. In his Manichean universe Bigger's own existence is an affront to the world around him. And his "epiphany" just before his death — that he killed for some deep-seated, inchoate sense of self-affirmation — is really the revelation of a self created through store-bought images. Instead of finding another "orbit" through which he can live, he dies a victim, turned victimizer, of the earthly polarities called white and black. Bigger is indeed a man of half-understanding, ruled by illusions and carrying out their furthest conclusions.

Invisible Man makes a joke of Bigger's illusions. The unnamed protagonist, through a series of symbolic deaths and rebirths, slowly peels away the veils of illusion, only to find the same absurdities lurking on the other side. Having literally cast himself underground — a movement approximating the Zen idea that "the only way to get saved is to throw oneself right down into a bottomless abyss" — Invisible Man seeks some adjustment, some middle ground between the polarities where he says no and yes, where he affirms and condemns, where he loves and hates.

For Bigger Thomas what lies on the other side of illusion is Elysian; for Invisible Man it is only more illusion. To mangle Wallace Stevens, Richard Wright asks with Bigger Thomas: What is life, "if it can come/Only in silent shadows and in dreams" and only, if at all, in a vague recognition of self through acts of violence? His answer is that it is death. Ironically, Wright, a spiritually pessimistic man, becomes eschatologist. Ralph Ellison, as Zen master, believes, using Stevens' words again, "We live in an old chaos of the sun" and always will — and that salvation comes in making ourselves something entirely new.

I like Ellison's version better, but Wright's seems more enduring. Did the young men find their lives or consciousnesses as they pulled the triggers of their Magnums? Did the teenager witness his own birth as he gouged away at the flesh of my septuagenarian mother? Did they all laugh? Or — more likely — are my questions themselves also a part of the veils of illusion, as are any answers I could provide? And as long as the world creates Bigger Thomases they will heed the call to the *danse macabre*, just as Invisible Man and I see in the mirror the kaleidoscope of illusion over the shoulders of our real and imagined reflections.

Toni Morrison said to Dick Cavett in an interview, "Imagine something," in answer to his question about the nature of her father's experiences growing up in Jim Crow Georgia. She refused to go into detail about them, "imagine something" being both sufficient and correct. Make something up; it happened. Cavett didn't press the point. He understood her.

Years ago, when I was relatively new to the academic game, I went to a conference on feminism and literature. It was held in New York City, always an exciting place for such gatherings, and there were some fairly famous, heady people there. I listened to all sorts of papers and panels, took notes, mingled. At the requisite cocktail party after the first day's proceedings I looked up over the edge of my glass at a woman who was coming toward me, a clipper ship in full sail with me as port. Several inches short of my still raised glass — I was stalling for time — she held out her hand to shake mine. Pumping away with real strength, as my ring began to recess into the flesh of a sister finger, she looked me square in the face and demanded, "Tell me about your pain."

I paused. Then I told her, "Since the surgery, thank you, my left knee is working much better and it doesn't seem to react to the weather as much now as it did in the past. But it still creaks when I walk up stairs." Her hand went limp, her face lost its color and she backed off, wearing a most peculiar expression on her face.

When I was a sophomore in college a famous American novelist came to my campus to talk. He had published, not many years before, a highly successful novel — black humor, a campus favorite. For some reason, I honestly don't know why, during the Q-and-A session I asked him if he didn't think that most black novels might as well be written as nonfiction essays, and specifically that James Baldwin should stop with the novels and keep the nonfiction rolling. I had read a column in a newspaper that had made the point and I had violently disagreed with it. The author said he agreed. Later that afternoon, he approached a junior, who looked nothing like me at all, and told her he didn't like the loaded, catch-22 question. She told him that she hadn't asked it. "He mumbled something," she told me later.

The bourbon glass is empty, and it's too dark to see the mortar on the building across the way. Like Invisible Man in the Epilogue, I've ended an exercise in condemnation and affirmation, this time with the aid of alcohol. Thinking about literature and my life has helped me reckon with my world. The Zen of Bigger Thomas is illusory and mechanistic, not really Zen at all. It is possible and downright satisfying to de-

nounce and defend, to live contentedly in the paradox. Toni
Morrison writes wonderful novels that say yes and no. I
haven't been to any feminist conferences lately, but I regularly read some of the good stuff coming from feminist critics.
And I occasionally teach that campus favorite by the famous
novelist, a fine, sarcastic book about cultural idiocy and how
to survive it.

Waiting for Godot on Jeffery Boulevard

REGARDLESS OF THE kind of working schedule I've had, Saturday mornings are reserved for two things: cartoons and chores — a habit fixed in me as a child that I find very hard to break. I must admit that in recent years the cartoons have been missing, not because I feel that I'm too old to watch them, but because the current vintage lacks the startling, clever, and expensive animation that left room for the imagination in the classic ones produced by Warner Brothers and sometimes others. Also, cartoons provide insights into the past; the early ones reinforce images of blacks as animalistic and stupid, as barnyard aberrations and King Kongs. Bonding with the underdog Wile E. Coyote, I want him, just once, to capture the Road Runner. Occasionally, I've found reruns of "The Bullwinkle Show" in the odd city where I've lived for a spell, and animation be damned, I delight in the puns and sardonic humor that were lost on me when I was young. Watching "Bullwinkle" also allows me to practice my very rusty Hollywood Slavic accent, à la Boris and Natasha, that hearkens back to Oscar Homolka and Maria Ouspenskaya. If cartoons aren't available "The Three Stooges" will do. One reason why I left the West Coast was that my sense of reality was disturbed when college basketball games would come on at ten or eleven o'clock in the morning, preempting my cartoon hours.

Saturday chores are Saturday chores: grocery shopping, dusting, vacuuming, picking up newspaper and clothing piles, emptying trash, doing laundry, going to the cleaners — and shining shoes. As my father hoped I would (he said the condition of the shoes was the first thing he noticed in a job applicant), I try to take good care of my shoes, particularly keeping the heels repaired, since I have a tendency to walk on the outer edges of my soles. I have rubber heel plates put on to retard the inevitable erosion, and I otherwise maintain clean and shined leather uppers. As a child I bargained for ten cents per pair of shoes to shine. Once or twice a year I could make a couple of dollars by rummaging through my parents' closets, reshining those that hadn't been worn in twenty years along with the current batch. As an adolescent I lost my interest in this activity, but the difficulty of finding comfortable, wearable shoes reignited it in adulthood. I have to take care of the shoes I have because I can't afford to replace them.

One Chicago morning, I gathered up a pair of my trustiest work shoes — a pair that a student of mine once said made me look schoolmarmish and dowdy, to which I replied, "So find me some that are *au courant*, reasonable, and won't cripple me" — noticed their failing heels and went directly to a shoe repair shop. I had been clearing the last of my things out of my sister's apartment in anticipation of Mother's arrival. After she had been stabbed in her home we had spent weeks sorting out the effects of three generations' worth of living, finding minor treasures of letters, photographs, and books belonging to my grandparents, my parents, my sister, and me. My sister was in Kansas City for the final leg, helping Mother with the paperwork to sell the house, engaging the movers.

The gray was bright, the sun poked through clouds, an early spring snowstorm was being rapidly thawed by late spring temperatures. I decided to walk, to think about the move and hope that Mother would withstand the aftershocks as well as she had the major earthquake that had so brutally changed the course of her life. I also wanted to try to get some of the sand and rock-salt and fear out of my body and brain, to move my joints freely again. I was on my way to Jeffery Boulevard, a relatively short artery that cuts off Lake Shore Drive, about twenty blocks south of the Museum of Science and Industry, the University of Chicago, and Hyde Park.

Jeffery Boulevard is a main drag of South Shore, lined with the kinds of businesses that define black communities throughout the country. I walked along Seventy-first Street to get there. I passed empty storefronts with gated doorways — the modern portcullis effect — with rusting metal, Master and Yale locks still in place, piles of mud, newspapers, torn lottery tickets, half-pints of Old Blind Boy, and dog manure holding tight against the woven metal. Urban tumbleweed. There was a minuscule automobile body shop; a bakery still in business; a couple of gutted buildings; small grocery stores advertising soda, cigarettes, liquor, and potato chips, one or two run by Middle Easterners, some by blacks, some too filthy to enter. Groups of men stood talking to each other outside of the stores, as little children scampered in with greenbacks crumpled in their hands, often accompanied by handwritten notes, buying a candy bar, two packs of Kools, a loaf of bread, and a gallon of milk. I ambled: past the half-dozen liquor stores that I recall seeing closed only in the wee hours of the morning; a currency exchange, where for a percentage of the total a paycheck can be cashed, money orders bought, telephone bills paid; a dry-cleaners; the remnants of three failed restaurants at one site; a fish house; an Armed Forces recruiting station; a drugstore; and a few clothing and shoe stores hanging on in the face of the lower overhead and lower prices the large Loop chains could offer.

It seemed I saw only men and boys that morning, boys from about five years of age through preadolescence in various stages of outrage at each other, some fighting, some grumbling; teenagers gesturing at each other threateningly, or laughing, or snarling, tugging at their genitals every few minutes or so, making sure their manhood was intact. Quite a few of the little boys, teenagers, and men wore plastic bags on their heads — clear or opaque shower caps they seemed, in the chemical-setting stage of the latter-day conk called a curl or jeri-curl. The older men used their hands only to highlight their speech. A few of them had bloodshot eyes; they wore old shoes and clothes, dingy stingy brims, lusterless pinkie rings.

I reached Jeffery Boulevard just as the sun broke free, making my neck hot as I crossed the threshold of the shoe repair shop.

It was a standard shoe shop: smells of polish and machine oil, piles of bagged and unbagged shoes tagged behind the counter, a few posters advertising dances and cabarets, an outdated calendar from a local church, cans of Kiwi and Esquire, bottles of Shinola, some dusty packages of shoestrings, a deposit-for-work-necessary sign. Under the glass counter, a couple of handmade purses — consignment sales — and some used, but repaired and shined out-of-style pumps and slingbacks for sale.

Three men were in the shop; one, the proprietor, had on a work apron, the other two sat on stools in coats. They didn't stop their conversation as I entered, nor did they look my way. The proprietor was making a serious point:

"I say it's the truth. The Bible don't lie. If it's in the Bible then it's true."

"Yeah," said the first man, nodding his head.

"Isn't that the truth?" said the second.

"Genesis is true. The Lord God made the world in six days and rested on the seventh," preached the proprietor.

"Lawd, that's true," said the first man.

"Uh-huh," from the second.

"And Noah put animals, two by two, on the Ark, and everything else died in the flood," opined the proprietor.

"Ain't that the truth."

"Yes."

"And God created Eve from the rib of Adam," he slapped his left hand into his right palm.

"That's sure 'nuff true."

"That's what it says, the Bible is true."

I bounced from one foot to another, my old dowdies resting on the counter. I looked at the men. They all seemed able-bodied, in a middle-middle age. I was getting angry, but I bit my tongue before I could snarl something about Eve coming before the Ark. I unzipped my jacket to alleviate the heat, and only after about four more minutes, bringing to an end what seemed my eternity of waiting, did the proprietor allow himself to recognize the existence of trade. He kept talking about Genesis, walked behind the counter as the other men nodded and verbally assented to his words. He asked me what I wanted, took out a piece of chalk and put two X's on the heels, tore off a ticket, took my two-dollar deposit, and resumed his place in the trinity of holy men.

I walked out of the shop, getting bumped to the side by three young teenagers, two with plastic bags on their heads, who were running in and out among pedestrians, yelling obscenities. I was sorry I'd walked. I took my now stiff legs on an alternate route back, via residential streets, where I looked at houses and remembered my childhood. I have never been able to afford a house and the only one I knew intimately, which had been the scene of family triumphs and recent disaster, was being sold that weekend.

I was angry with the men in the shoe shop, not because I wanted them to stop their ritual or to leave their temple of shoe shop or barber shop and the rites they had reserved for themselves there. But just outside the door was desolation and death, and somehow the everlasting quest to verify the physical origins of the earth was, to me, a greater blasphemy than my uncharitable thoughts. I wanted them to act in the face of all the ironies of black American life, to leave Genesis and the *fait accompli* of the Earth's formation behind, to stop preaching to the converted and get out in the streets to do some small thing, like suggesting to young men that obsession with one's genitals stunts one's growth and that curls, though no doubt pleasing to their wearers, look like conked, greasy Afros to a whole lot of people — potential employers, for instance.

My father died before I received my Ph.D. It had taken me a long time to finish my dissertation, or rather, a dissertation, because the first one I'd chosen to write turned out to be unworkable. The first one was going to deal with the behind-the-scenes activity of black writers on the Federal Writers' Project of the WPA, and how the government provided a forum for them to write. My adviser had recommended the topic to me and I became enthusiastic about it. I decided to read anything and everything germane to the period and I wrote several large boxes' worth of file cards that would have provided the research basis for several theses. But behind-the-scenes scholarship doesn't come from libraries, it means interviews. Jerre Mangione, who wrote *The Dream and the Deal* — a history of the Federal Writers' Project — talked to me for a couple of hours, as did Herbert Aptheker, whose many history books on black America have all the information the mainstream ones leave out and whose commitment to change hasn't wavered in decades. But after that I ran into stone walls. None of the surviving black writers I contacted wanted to talk. One or two said they wanted to forget those hard years, when they had to work at subsistence levels. Two were in exile in Europe and I didn't have the funds to go a-traveling; not that it would have made much difference, since one of them was quite unpleasant about the whole business and launched into an unprovoked tirade about Richard Wright ultimately getting what he deserved. I assumed he meant that Richard Wright died, which from all accounts is going to happen to that writer too, but I didn't write him back.

I was teaching while trying to write a dissertation, which meant that I really didn't have much time to spend on it anyway. And after three years of getting nowhere I knew that I had to find another topic. I spent one summer looking at the thousands of file cards I'd made from library work and vowed to get a thesis out of them if it killed me. I found one, and four months of solid writing produced a huge tome on the effect of the political Left on Langston Hughes, Richard Wright, and Ralph Ellison, as it appears in their work. What all my research had shown me was that for a while many American writers believed that leftist politics could reorder the world, that writers should and could divorce themselves from the institutions and much of the ethos of America. For black writers this could mean an opportunity to redefine blackness, getting rid of the degraded connotations of black pinned on it by a white and Christian America. I enjoyed writing the thesis and came to the thundering conclusion that the organized Left had very little effect on these three writers' work, even though Wright was, for a time, a member of the Communist Party and Hughes and Ellison, like many writers of the period, went through various fellow-traveling phases. I concluded that a native radicalism, with its sources homegrown in the nature of the black experience, was quite sufficient to catalyze the putative protest aspects of their writing, and that (for Wright in particular) Marxism, vulgar or not, was more a word than a coherent theory. What was most outstanding in all three of the writers was their effort to suggest, create, reveal a black soul free of institutionalized definition and control.

While doing my research I was struck by a quote from Benjamin J. Davis, a prominent black Communist, who wrote in 1947:

> As a Negro American, I want to be free. I want equal opportunities, equal rights; I want to be accorded the same dignity as a human being and the same status as a citizen as any other American. This is my constitutional right. I want first-class, unconditional citizenship. I want it, and I am entitled to it, now. . . . Out of my personal experiences as a Negro American, and in quest of the liberty, freedom and equal

rights proclaimed in the Constitution, the Bill of Rights, and the Declaration of Independence, I, like thousands of other Negroes — and white citizens — joined the Communist Party.

The irony is poignant and telling, ultimately suggesting that in order for blacks to gain true freedom they must become ideologically adversarial to a government that exists, ostensibly, because of its belief in freedom. I suspect Davis caught the irony and that it made sense for him to turn left to get right.

I spent no time writing about Paul Robeson, but I found his experiences in America paradigmatic of these ironies of being black and leftist. Robeson was also a man burdened by layers and layers of images of himself — to those who had seen and heard him, an idea born of an either threatening and vile, or exciting and bold image. Shortly after his death in 1976 I saw a TV documentary about his life that concentrated on the failed efforts of his family and friends to have him belatedly and posthumously honored in the College Football Hall of Fame. In addition to his achievements in the fields of law, music, theater, and civil rights, Robeson had excelled on the literal field as well, as a varsity football player at Rutgers. Dorothy Butler Gilliam, one of Robeson's biographers, notes in *Paul Robeson: All American*:

> In the century and a half of its existence Rutgers had had only two black students. The realization that he would be its third and, for four years, probably its sole black, was undoubtedly a lonely and bewildering prospect for Paul when he arrived on campus in the fall of 1915.

Du Bois had even written a couple of paragraphs about him in the *Crisis* in 1918.

Robeson suffered through countless indignities from white Saturday gridiron heroes, who sought to maim his body or his spirit, or both. And he prevailed over — perhaps transcended — these weekly obscenities to become "All American." But later, after Rutgers, both before and after the bloody riot in 1949 at Peekskill, New York, his presence, his candor, his versatility, and probably his innocence, too, were anathema to those protecting the fragile crucible of American freedom. And, among other things, Robeson was not allowed to join the ranks of those who reviled him — who wouldn't even take the field to play against a black adversary — in the hallowed hall of fame.

I was between thesis topics when Robeson died. Had I been more enterprising — especially after I found a copy of *Can You Hear Their Voices?* autographed by Hallie Flannigan to Whittaker Chambers sitting quietly and alone on a shelf in the stacks of Columbia University's Butler Library — I would have used my index cards and then studied the behind-the-scenes world of the Federal Theater Project. Even though Robeson wasn't a part of it he helped define the times. But I didn't, and other people have since done a good job on the topic. Robeson had been ill for several years; he might not have been able to speak to me anyway. But the least I can do the next time I'm near Hartsdale, New York is to take a look at his grave and the inscription: "The artist must elect to fight for freedom or for slavery. I have made my choice. I had no alternative." There was no passivity here, no waiting for things to "just change." Robeson had caught the ironies and looked left to try to get right.

Recently two black men I knew died. They were both in what is often referred to as the prime of life: one was forty-three, the other, thirty-nine. One, whom I'll call Walter, died of AIDS, the other — I'll call him Kenny — died of inertia and alcohol.

Walter was, quite simply, the most elegant man I've ever met. He was not a natty dresser, or highly affected; it was his natural grace and decency that gave one pause. I did not know him well, but I enjoyed his company whenever we were together. When I needed a lift or a laugh I knew I could get one by ambling down to his office doorway and bantering with him. He liked me too, and writing on my behalf after I'd moved on, he recommended my "mordant sense of humor." I appreciated that.

I can't imagine how anyone could have felt uncomfortable around Walter. He appeared so relaxed and calm that his mood was contagious. He also would run interference without being asked. As far as I was concerned his gayness was his private business. I saw him dressed to go to the bars one day, and I hoped that he resisted becoming stereotypical and anonymous in that world because he was extraordinary and unique in the world we shared. But, again, that was his business.

I called him the summer before he died. I didn't know he was ill and he didn't mention it. We had a grand old talk about mendacity and illusion. One of the prices of my quest has been that, ever moving on, I too often let ties drop. I had forgotten how much fun it was to talk to Walter because it was never necessary to explain anything to him. He naturally and immediately understood the irony, humor, or seriousness of any circumstance and worked from there. His bespectacled eyes took in the world completely.

I will always regret my vacillation after I heard he was in the hospital. I didn't know what the reason was, and I castigated myself for thinking that he probably had AIDS. When I blew through the town he lived in one Christmas, I didn't think of him; I was busy and forgot to remember to call. When I did remember it was too late, and I missed the chance to banter again with him, finding out — again too late — that some of his friends had sought out people whom he might remember, who might break through the ravages of his dementia to say good-bye.

I met Kenny when I was in college and spending the odd weekend with my sister in Chicago. We would sometimes go visit a good friend of hers, Kenny's sister, a lawyer now, who lived with her parents and most of her eleven siblings in a house on the South Side. We always had a wonderful time there, as only children from a painfully small family could. We would look on, astounded, at how everyone managed to eat, sleep, and function, with distinct personalities and drives, in this one house that to our minds might have accommodated no more than two parents and four children. What's more, there were always cousins and aunts and uncles, friends, and an occasional grandparent, on the scene.

It was not an idealized, television sitcom setting, although some scenarios were familiar. A few of the boys had problems with the law, with street gangs, with drugs. The girls could see few options awaiting them except the perpetuation of the status quo of motherhood. But they were a tenacious and strong family, and to me, looking in from the outside, they seemed to rise above most of their distress with extraordinary grace.

Kenny was the next in line from my sister's friend, and about my age. I liked him the first time I met him because he was dry, relaxed, funny. He was always cooking: vats of spaghetti, frying chicken after chicken, barbecuing ribs and Polish sausages. And he knew what he was doing because his food was delicious. Whenever I was at his house I thought that it might be fun to go out with him. But I no more knew how to get that desire across than I could read whether or not the interest was mutual. In those college days, when my sister would let me "run" with her, everything was exciting and a raucous night spent listening to music, playing cards, and drinking beer with Kenny and the others made the social emptiness of my campus life much easier to bear.

I remember asking my sister, shortly after I met him, what Kenny did. She said he just "was" — that is, he lived at home and did not work, and although some members of the family thought him the smartest and most talented of the lot, he had no plans. Whatever his dreams were and how they had been dashed remained a mystery. He was part of a lost generation of black men my age, their blood in inordinate amounts shed in Vietnam, in gang warfare on the streets — all that vaunted "possibility" of the sixties rotting away in the cell of a grave or a prison.

Over nearly twenty years I saw Kenny no more than ten times; the last time was a Labor Day picnic several years before his death. Always thin, he had deteriorated from too much alcohol. He looked gaunt and brittle. He was irritated because the night before he had gone out to help rescue a distant cousin from some unpleasant altercation in the Loop and had gotten his glasses broken for his pains. Worse, he said, nobody liked the cousin at all, but with family "you have to respond."

Three years later what was left of him was quietly eased into a grave.

On dry days, and chilly November ones of the soul too, I sometimes find myself thinking about Walter and Kenny, the scourges of AIDS and hopelessness in many black lives. Not only to ease the pain and sadness, but also to be hard and cynical with myself, I repeat T. S. Eliot's refrain from "The Hollow Men":

> *This is the way the world ends*
> *This is the way the world ends*
> *This is the way the world ends*
> *Not with a bang but a whimper.*

But it doesn't last, which is good. If I am to think about Eliot at all, it is better to consider:

> What we call the beginning is often the end
> And to make an end is to make a beginning.
> The end is where we start from.

Nothing can bring back Walter or Kenny, or other Walters or Kennys. To see their ends as a beginning, in one way, is to despair, to concede to the triumph of death-in-life, of disease and desolation. But, in another, it is possible to have hope that AIDS, at least, will be seen as the disease it is, and not as some "asked for" scarlet *A* or retributive product of homosexuality, drug addiction, or, increasingly, promiscuity and bad luck. Perhaps enough time and enough money will save enough Walters.

I don't know what saves the Kennys—certainly not medical laboratories. He had plenty of reasons to stay at home, indoors. I write at a time when a resurgence of overt attacks on black Americans has been featured prominently in the media: a gang of white youths in Queens attacks a group of black men buying a pizza, beats them, and chases one of them into a busy street where he is run over and killed by a car; membership drives for the Ku Klux Klan are publicized, and these robed atavists march through Georgia bearing and burning crosses; white students at many American colleges and universities, even at decorous Seven Sisters and Ivy League schools, taunt and attack black students; and no one seems to know what laws are when somebody riding a subway looking for trouble finds it. I suspect the theories about why these violent events have taken place outnumber the events themselves. I have not been surprised at these news items and, having read my share of the history of the world, and of the twentieth century in particular, I have been profoundly skeptical of the word "progress." Technological progress, yes; human progress, no. Suffice it to say that a surprising number of the most fortunate people in the history of the world—born white, in America, in the twentieth century—are blind to the nearly limitless possibilities that exist for them in their condition, and are thoroughly without charity or a sense of fair play when someone less fortunate is given a chance to improve his or her chances in the game.

When I was young I wanted to believe that my generation would change things; that youth was fired and inspired by the need to see justice done; that the sacrifices others had made, of their bodies, their youth, and sometimes their lives, for me and others like me, would endure always in the hearts and minds of those who came after me; that customs and conventions of intolerance could be shattered, replaced by a respect and appreciation of difference; that the power of black spiritual expression, that electrified the Civil Rights Movement and that sought to make activism synonymous with faith, would overcome the passive fixation with Christian eschatology; and that were I to have children, they would live in a better world than mine. I was skeptical then; I certainly don't believe those things now. We all have had our moments.

Mary Maples Dunn, the president of Smith College, said in response to the racial incidents on her campus: "Clearly sanctions our society has been imposing on racist or ethnocentric behavior are slipping out of place." The strength of racism has survived a short-lived attack of decency, and as Alexis de Tocqueville wrote over 150 years ago in the introduction to *Democracy in America*, reflecting on the travesties of the Old World:

> . . . everybody feels the evil, but no one has courage or energy enough to seek the cure; the desire, the regrets, the sorrows, and the joys of the time produce nothing that is visible or permanent, like the passions of old men which terminate in impotence.

And the watchword of the age is that things never change and attitudes die hard, even as they are so easily reborn.

A graduate school acquaintance of mine once told me, reflecting on her years of teaching, that she could do many things for her students, but she could not civilize them. Unlike Huck Finn, they were not civilized already. I have often wondered what the parents of some of my students have given them in the way of civilization, and I've concluded that it begins and ends with a belief in the power of money to create happiness, sometimes accompanied by a desire to learn and sometimes not. And over the years I've discovered that youth — even occasionally black youth — can be inspired by things like right-wing republicanism, the politics of the dead; that in 1991 there are black children in a number of inner-city schools who do not know who Martin Luther King, Jr., was;

that a white freshman at a prestigious American college wanting to know what all the flak was about in the 1950s and 1960s,
could ask, "How come the blacks didn't just go out and vote?";
that in the preservation of custom and convention many communities noted for their strongly Christian identities harbor
a rabid and trenchant racism; that there are black people who
call themselves "creationists," doubtless unaware of the Social
Darwinistic underpinnings of a "theory" that would have
them exist in some netherworld between dead and slave; that
while some black churches still inspire activism, or at least
consider the feeding and clothing of the poor tactics worth
continuing, others are content to spread the "feel good" word
that things will be better on the "other side"; and that I don't
have to explain my disaffection to my children because they
don't exist.

I don't know that Kenny's blackness in a white world had
everything to do with his despair. But the odds are it did, and
slowly and deliberately he let himself die because he could de-
vise no way to live. If there is a beginning here, it is in the will
of those who have survived him to change the world.

I have never seen a performance of Tom Stoppard's *Rosencrantz and Guildenstern Are Dead*, but I enjoyed reading the play.
What a wonderful idea it creates, giving inner lives to those
walk-ons, those two stooges of *Hamlet*. It makes one wonder
which is worse, being part of an entourage or having one. Here
are Rosencrantz and Guildenstern waiting, in all confusion,
for directions from Claudius or anyone else with authority in
Elsinore to tell them what to do. They are spectators, observers
of life going on around them, powerless to discharge the forces
that are bringing about their own deaths. It is an absurdly
tragic and comic situation with deadly serious implications.
As Guildenstern remarks near the end of the play:

> No . . . no . . . not for us, not like that. Dying is not
> romantic, and death is not a game which will soon be over

. . . Death is not anything . . . death is not . . . It's the
absence of presence, nothing more . . . the endless time of
never coming back . . . a gap you can't see, and when the
wind blows through it, it makes no sound . . .

I never worked my thesis into a book; perhaps I should
have, going back to my literary history like Jack Burden re-
discovering Cass Mastern at the end of *All the King's Men*. I
only regret that my father died before he could read it and
argue with me over parts of it. One summer when he was still
living, I spent a few weeks at home, and for some reason we
became embroiled in the most violent argument we ever had.
He taunted me for my slow progress — I was "between" topics
that year — and we both took out our frustration on each other
at what seemed so promising once, but now appeared
thwarted. It was an instance where, had we owned guns, one
or both of us would have fired, leaving two more senseless
statistics. Perhaps my reasons for letting the tome lie fallow
now are tied up with mourning. But I do recall one important
part of that argument. My father was fond of telling his
daughters not to put any trust in "the great white hope." He
screamed at me not to believe that I could possibly have a future if I thought a savior riding out of the clouds in an academic gown would take my hand and lift me up to a place
where life would be simple. For him redemption and salvation
were self-made conditions; one had to be awake and alive to
possibilities in order to grab them. An awful treadmill
awaited me if I thought otherwise.

"Don't wait for the great white hope, Gayle. Don't wait,"
he would say.

"There must have been a moment, at the beginning, where
we could have said — no. But somehow we missed it." Those
are the last words of Guildenstern. It is dangerous to depend
upon the benignity of great white hopes. The ones at Elsinore
had other things on their minds; Rosencrantz and Guildenstern died.

There must have been a moment when Kenny could have said "no" to the malevolent, dream-bashing world around him and invented a way to live, on terms he could craft for himself. There was humor, intelligence, and calm in him and a soul that could be felt by looking through his thick glasses and into his eyes. But his resistance to life was too strong and he became another stooge in service to Dr. Death and his entourage.

As I neared my sister's building after my trip to the shoe shop, the streets with houses gave way to those with apartment buildings. The sun had disappeared and the beginnings of a stiff breeze off Lake Michigan were blowing debris into puddles, newly formed by the melting black snow. I trudged up the steps and into the apartment, threw my coat on a chair, kicked off my tennis shoes, turned on the television, and lay down on the couch. Whatever was on the screen I couldn't watch it, so I got up and flicked the machine off. My sister's dog, Baron, a quiet and wise old miniature Schnauzer and easily the finest dog in the history of the world, came over to the couch, took one look at me, licked my hand and stretched out on the floor next to me.

I couldn't get those men in the shoe shop out of my mind. I thought about their poses — two on stools, the proprietor in his apron, preaching — and I began to see them as almost cartoon-like, of the current vintage, but not quite. They were strangely animated but not really alive to me. In my visions and revisions I sought to make the three men in the shop something other than members of an entourage waiting for death. I wanted them to be as vigorous and poignant as Gogo and Didi of Beckett's *Waiting for Godot*. Their quest to reaffirm the veracity of Genesis was lifeless compared to the arresting and ritualized determination of Gogo and Didi, in the face of a raw and absurd world, to continue waiting for somebody named Godot. I refused to see the call and response of the proprietor and his friends as a mantra, although it could have been one. They were keeping each other company and waiting for something, some person, some agency, some power to reckon with the bleakness outside the shop's door. Thinking about my father's house, my mother's strength, and that ghastly argument years before, I wanted the men's conception of redemption to change. I wanted them to gather up all that collective spirituality and transform it into some small act on the streets.

I said, "You know, Mr. Baron, I could take the sight of the bandages and the wounds; I even thought I could handle the prospect of a permanently injured mother. But something out there today is too much for me."

I put my head back and cried myself to sleep.

The Anglophile Moment,
Or: You Came a Long
Way From Saint Louis

Calling all cars! Calling all cars! . . .

> Police officers, county or city, all over the state, all over the
> South, should be bending every effort to apprehend and jail
> the labor agents now operating everywhere about us to take
> the best of our negroes North to fill the rapidly widening labor
> breach there . . . We must have the negro in the South.
> The black man is fitted by nature, by centuries of living in it
> to work contentedly, effectively and healthily during the long
> summers of semi-tropical and tropical countries.

So proclaimed an editorial in the Macon, Georgia *Telegraph*
in 1916.

I have a friend, Bette, a woman born and raised in Germany, who married an American and came here to live. Her
husband was the G.I. of the movies who finds the young Ger-
man/English/French/etcetera woman and brings her home to
the folks. Contrary to the movies, however, this was a peace-
time romance. He came back to continue his education; he
was in graduate school at Princeton during their early years
together.

Bette and I were talking, having lunch sitting outside the

building where we both worked; it was a hot, sunny spring day. I mentioned some of the tidbits I'd come across in my research for my dissertation, some of which interested her quite a bit. It seems that Bette had spent many an afternoon having lunch, sitting outdoors on warm spring days, with other graduate student wives and their young offspring. Bette recalled her distress, her inability to say anything back to these women when they chastised her about Nazi atrocities — she was not Jewish and would have been about seven or eight years old at the end of the War. She said the other wives would go on, in deep, musical southern accents, about how horrible those German people were and how the wives knew they surely wouldn't have tolerated such horrible things happening in their own country.

I smirked, commiserated, and then told her that I had some information she might like to have. Bette got very excited and wanted my facts right away even though she was now years beyond Princeton and associated with a less disingenuous, or, perhaps, ingenuous crowd, depending upon how you look at those Princeton mothers. We scampered back to my office where I pulled out a few file cards, turned to a few articles, and she wrote feverishly on a fresh card — which she vowed to keep in her wallet — some American facts. Her favorite was that school systems in Mississippi in the first half of this century routinely excised all references to freedom, liberty, and ephemera like the Bill of Rights and the Declaration of Independence from textbooks allotted to black schools. When she asked me how this was done I said I didn't know, but that theoretically it would be fairly easy since, in Mississippi in those days at least, there was no such thing as integration, so there was no chance of crossover mistakes in textbook shipments. Her eyes caught fire when I gave her some statistics on the Red Summer of 1919 when eighty-three blacks were lynched in the South, some of them still wearing army uniforms from their service in World War I. She quickly filled up her card and promptly put it in her wallet. If she could have gone back in time at that very moment, she said, and been forced to re-live every second of her life between that spring day and all those others, she would have done it gladly. I'm sure she doesn't have the card anymore, but I still would not like to trade places with one of those belles should Bette ever recognize her on the street.

For the last ten years or so I have heard a lot of the phrase, "Let's put it behind us." I first noticed it with Watergate, and I've heard it in reference to the Vietnam War, and, most recently, the Iran-Contra scandal. I still don't know what the phrase means, but I assume it translates roughly into, "Let's pretend it never happened." I don't believe those who say it means "Let's not dwell on the past"; there are good reasons not to do that either, but dwelling presupposes more understanding of the meaning of the past than the purveyors of the phrase ever admit. There are great pitfalls in willfully forgetting the past, but I think the most dangerous is that it becomes difficult, and sometimes impossible, to gauge the present or plan the future with much intelligence. It is important to know the path, the process, through which the present is made. Inducing cultural amnesia runs the risk of reproducing the medical scenario of "the operation was a success but the patient died."

Bette had not "put the Holocaust behind her," but she suspected her Princeton lunch mates had put slavery and *de facto* and *de jure* segregation behind *them*, and she recoiled at their superciliousness. By opening her mouth to speak and revealing her German birth, she was charged with co-conspiring to commit the unspeakable by those whose sense of superiority erased their own complicity in other, American, crimes against humanity. They also had accents.

Standard American education is woefully incomplete when it comes to detailing the nation's historical beginnings. Surveys have shown that a distressing, nay, terrifying number of citizens cannot recognize the differences between the

Constitution, the Gettysburg Address, and the Declaration of Independence — selected lines of which some think are communist propaganda. As bad as that is, the older texts, written by American Puritans, are rarely, if ever, touched in most curricula. I am sure the most popular image of the Puritans is a cross between the Pilgrims eating Thanksgiving dinner with Squanto the Indian and religious mix-ups surrounding Benjamin Franklin as a Quaker. Both Indians and Quakers were persecuted mightily by several sects of Puritans and Ben Franklin was quite skeptical about many a religious notion.

The Puritans were a tough bunch of people, and their writings reveal American beginnings, detailing religious fervor, rampant intolerance, outrageous superiority complexes, intellectual zeal, and fleshly inconsistencies, foibles, and doubts. In June 1630, John Winthrop wrote "A Modell of Christian Charity," one of the most important and interesting of all early Puritan texts. Winthrop, leader of a rather prosperous group of English Puritans and later governor of the Massachusetts Bay Colony, after months aboard the ship *Arbella*, set forth debarkation principles — to wit, we have an enormous charge to carry out and the social status quo must be maintained once we get on land; we are making a new world. The text makes me think of the film *The Admirable Crichton* with Kenneth More and Diane Cilento, where a group of shipwrecked upper-class Britons manage to survive when roles are reversed, when the loyal butler takes over and the "useless" master obeys. Winthrop would have none of that. He wrote:

> First, since the work and end we aim at are extraordinary, we must not content ourselves with usual ordinary means. Whatsoever we did or ought to have done when we lived in England, we must do that and more also wherever we go.

"More also" did not mean changing roles.

Winthrop was very clear about what he envisioned for the colony:

We shall find that the God of Israel is among us, and ten of
us shall be able to resist a thousand of our enemies. The Lord
will make our name a praise and glory, so that men shall say
of succeeding plantations: "The Lord make it like that of New
England." For we must consider that we shall be like a City
upon a Hill; the eyes of all people on us.

Quite a charge, and probably the first "We're number one,
we're number one" documented on American shores. As Sacvan Bercovitch notes in *The Puritan Origins of the American Self*,
the influence of Puritan ideology and rhetoric — the myth of
preordained greatness — has been considerable throughout
U.S. history. He says, "The persistence of the myth is a testa-
ment to the visionary and symbolic power of the American
Puritan imagination." One need only take a look at the back
of a dollar bill to see it — *novus ordo seclorum* (the new order of
the ages) — to get a hint of the zeal behind the formation of the
city upon a hill.

It took time, but some of the Puritan social order that Winthrop so wanted to preserve did fall apart. There was dissen-
sion over religious orthodoxy, political organization, and
social mores. As generations followed, and as Enlightenment
notions took hold, the fabric of society changed, as did people's expectations of what life could be. Nevertheless, that desire to be "like a City upon a Hill" was compelling. Those
Enlightenment men who created the revolution that formed
the country, over one hundred years after Winthrop, were
bound and determined to "form a more perfect union" and to
make the United States a beacon for the rest of the world.

"I told Jesus be all right if he changed my name," begins a
famous black spiritual. Revolutions — religious, political, or
social — must change not only names but people, to make
them into something new. And calculating the worth of the
city upon a hill by the putative religious or racial superiority
of its inhabitants can lead to all sorts of problems. Only sixteen years after Winthrop's *Arbella* speech, Nathaniel Ward

published his *Simple Cobbler of Aggawam*, perhaps another model of Christian charity and a denunciation of what he saw as creeping religious toleration among Cromwellian English-men. He wrote:

> My heart has naturally detested four things: The standing of the Apocrypha in the Bible; foreigners dwelling in my coun-try, to crowd out our native subjects into the corners of the earth; alchemized coins; tolerations of diverse religions, or of one religion in segregant shapes.

Fleeing from what they saw as religious intolerance, Puritan colonists may have created much that was new; but as people they seemed not to have changed at all.

Similarly, the secular city on the hill has very questionable foundations if slave quarters are in the vicinity (slave quarters are not new; they're old hat in the history of the world). Twenty years after Ward denounced religious toleration, laws were enacted in the Virginia colonies—the spawning ground of quite a few Founding Fathers—that give further in-sight into the development of the "new man" of the new world:

> Whereas the only law in force for the punishment of refrac-tory servants resisting their master, mistress, or overseer can-not be inflicted upon Negroes, nor the obstinacy of many of them be suppressed by other than violent means, be it enacted and declared by this Grand Assembly if any slave resists his master (or other by his master's order correcting him) and by the extremity of the correction should chance to die, that his death shall not be accounted a felony, but the master (or that other person appointed by the master to pun-ish him) be acquitted from molestation, since it cannot be presumed that premeditated malice (which alone makes mur-der a felony) should induce any man to destroy his own estate.

Thomas Jefferson, one hundred years later, provided some insight into this quality of thinking. He noted an important difference between Roman and American slavery: Roman slaves "were of the race of whites. It is not [the Roman slaves'] condition then, but nature, which has produced the distinction." Yet even Mr. Jefferson, in his "Query on Manners" in *Notes on the State of Virginia*, was aware of the rather weak supports and threadbare reasoning that lay just below the surface of so many rationalizations for white superiority:

> Indeed I tremble for my country when I reflect that God is just: that his justice cannot sleep for ever: that considering numbers, nature and natural means only, a revolution of the wheel of fortune, an exchange of situation, is among possible events: that it may become probable by supernatural interference!

Part of the rest of the spiritual goes:

> Then He told me,
> He said your father won't know you, child
> If I change your name.
> Yes, He told me,
> Said your mother won't know you, child,
> If I change your name.
> But I told Jesus,
> Said it would be all right,
> If He changed my name.

A good portion of an incompletely understood American past asks, "What's in a name?" And I would counter, "Quite a bit; the revolution isn't over yet." In order to understand where we are now it is important to reckon with the path and do everything but put the past behind us.

I once saw Eubie Blake give a bravura performance of a rag on a public television documentary. At the end, he turned, in anger, away from his piano and nearly shouted, "Black people are the only people who throw away their culture," his long fingers slashing the air in front of his face. During the concert Blake had been reminiscing about his youth, of how he sneaked out of his home and learned music in the bars and brothels of Baltimore much against the wishes of his parents.

He felt that black Americans willingly let slip through their hands the real meanings of their art, their music, their dance and poetry. Scholars for years have noted the "loss" of black culture from the time of the Harlem Renaissance at the end of the twenties. As Saunders Redding observed in *Anger and Beyond*:

> In general the mind of white America fastened upon the bizarre, the exotic and the atavistic elements . . . and turned them into a commercialized fad. . . . Commercialism was the bane of the Negro renaissance. . . . The Charleston, the Black Bottom, the Lindy Hop went down to Broadway and Park Avenue. . . . From being an authentic form, the blues became the torch song popularized by Ruth Etting and Helen Morgan.

And I remember a television program where Billy Taylor was interviewing Branford Marsalis, the superb saxophonist. Marsalis and three other black musicians had done the background work for Sting on the album *The dream of the blue turtles*. Taylor asked Marsalis to discuss the venture, particularly since white rock musicians, he said, feel that blacks cannot play rock. I did a triple take at the television and bunged the side of my head with the heel of my hand, particularly since rock developed from black music. Eubie Blake, with nearly hundred-year-old eyes and ears, having seen so much of it all, believed that black art had been either tossed, stolen, or turned into something with unrecognizable or unrecognized origins.

The problem, of course, has something to do with the internalization of the negation of blackness. To have pride in what one creates when one's being is considered worthless means that the creator must either rise above his or her humanity or accept the freighted and astounded applause of the crowd. After all, most black culture is associated with poverty and the struggle against insurmountable odds. What meaning can that culture have for the upwardly mobile, twentieth-century black?

Blake understood that art is a part of the path, the process, of moving from one place to another. And I suspect he knew quite clearly where he had been, what his end was and how he had reached it. Opting for cultural amnesia for him meant cultural suicide.

Zora Neale Hurston, in *Their Eyes Were Watching God*, writes of a Mrs. Turner, a black woman who hated blackness, whose total internalization of its negative connotations flung her to the extreme, made her a fifth columnist in the fight for equality. Hurston writes:

> Anyone who looked more white folkish than herself was better than she was in her criteria, therefore it was right that they should be cruel to her at times, just as she was cruel to those more Negroid than herself in direct ratio to their Negroness. Like the pecking-order in a chicken yard. Insensate cruelty to those you can whip, and groveling submission to those you can't.

Hurston brilliantly expands the dimensions of Mrs. Turner's hatred and peculiar vanity:

> Once having set up her idols and built altars to them it was inevitable that she would worship there. It was inevitable that she should accept any inconsistency and cruelty from her deity as all good worshippers do from theirs. All gods who receive homage are cruel. Otherwise they would not be worshipped. Through indiscriminate suffering men know fear and fear is the most divine emotion. It is the stones for altars and the beginning of wisdom. Half gods are worshipped in wine and flowers. Real gods require blood.

The Mrs. Turners of the world are eager consumers of the form and content of their own oppression.

I remember, quite vividly, being eight years old, living in Dayton in the house we shared with Grandma. The neighborhood was middle- to lower-middle-class white and the flight was on once we moved in. The parents of two little boys across the street were giving one of them a birthday party, to which I was distinctly and directly uninvited. However, a fair-skinned, beautiful little black boy up the street was invited. There were all the children I knew in the neighborhood, balloons, ice cream, a lot of music, and a photographer from the daily paper — the party made the front page of the next morning's edition. I watched the scene, taking it all in, trying to learn to embroider, as I sat in my front yard until Grandma rescued me from my masochism, took me into the house, and served me up a glass of milk and a piece of rhubarb pie without saying a word. The black boy went to the party and I resented his going, but as I grew older I stopped caring; his attendance integrated the party and formed a particular sort of Pyrrhic victory. Like *Invisible Man*'s paint factory man, Lucius Brockway, who is in charge of putting "a little black dope" into each can of white paint to make it whiter, the black boy turned an event that was slightly pink to a sparkling alabaster.

The elements of the scene are very simple and very complex. The family across the street was self-consciously celebrating its whiteness, but in order to do it most effectively it had to include (traduce? co-opt?) what was literally a more beautiful blackness. Eubie Blake feared black complicity in the loss of a culture and wholesale buying into another that would "put behind it" the revelations and the meanings of the path to now.

I once went to a dinner celebrating a black academic achievement program at a major U.S. university. The room was filled with black Ph.D.s from Ivy League schools — Du Bois's Talented Tenth some eighty years later. Now any room filled with Ph.D.s, regardless of their hues, is likely to be a festival of self-adoration. But this night was a corker. A lorgnette salesman could have made a killing there. The after-dinner address was given by an elderly black academic with a nineteenth-century scholarly sensibility. As he talked about his research I looked around the room at poses so stylized, depicting such extraordinary annoyance and boredom, that they made a Velázquez painting look informal, fluid, and animated. I thought it one of the funniest and most distressing spectacles I'd ever seen, this competition between the old scholar and the young crowd for "lording it over" rights. Du Bois himself had once been a Young Turk, challenging the black brain trust at the turn of the century. But somehow I thought he would have been sad seeing this scene, held in a room where, doubtless, the nigger joke was still imbedded in the walls, passed on from one generation to another. I kept thinking of Du Bois's line, "I want the colored people to have the right to develop according to their capacity and I certainly would be disappointed if they did not develop much higher things than the white race . . ." I wanted to see something new, something different, some combination of "We're happy to see you even though you have passed your prime. No offense. And thanks." I sat with my thesis adviser and we kept looking at each other, astounded. He told me I'd have to write about the evening one day. Well, I have.

I spent the summer before my first full-time job in Chicago, dieting and taking care of my sister, who was recuperating from surgery. I actually lost twenty pounds; I may have shed more than that. Shortly before the school year began I returned to my old haunts back East to help a friend put on a black fund-raiser for the starving in Biafra. She was a good buddy, or so I thought; we had spent many a fine time together, running through real and imaginary money, doing the sorts of wild, in-one's-early-twenties things that one is lucky to survive to remember.

I had been looking forward to the event; I'd even bought a long dress which I thought complimented my reduced figure. My friend was eager to enlist me — and my car. She wanted to impress her new boss, a prosperous black woman who owned a summer home on the island where the festivities were to take place. She was proud to be part of the black community on an island noted for its summer population of rich and powerful whites. It was a good place to have a benefit for the hungry.

Early one morning I gathered up my friend and a coworker of hers whom I hated on sight — an extraordinary reaction that made me a believer in chemicals, both attractive and repellent — and we set off for the ferry. We reached the island and drove up to the boss's house. My friend and her colleague were staying at the house; I was dispatched to my motel to unpack things. Shortly after I got to my room, one of those quaint cabins, damp, with spiders in charge, and designed for the beachcomber to use only for sleep, I got a call to come back to the house as soon as possible. For the next four hours my friend and I drove around this popular summer resort island looking for two motel rooms, in the height of the season, for some politician and his secretary. For the sake of propriety it was necessary that they have separate rooms, but the intention, evidently, was to tryst the night and weekend away. The search was not my idea of island fun, but I didn't complain; things would get better, I was sure.

We were acceptably successful and drove back to the big house and the boss, and I went back to my cabin to await dinner plans. My friend called me early in the evening to say that she was having dinner at the house and that . . . well, I'd understand. It wasn't a special meal, nor was it a preliminary to the affair; the swells hadn't arrived yet. I ate a quiet fried clam take-out dinner in my cabin room, sat on the veranda and watched people walk up and down the street looking at people watching them walk up and down the street, checked the ferry schedule, killed several spiders, and went to bed. Very early the next morning I deposited half of the ferry charge, in change, on the boss's porch and rode away, never turning back, never again seeing or speaking to my friend.

I realized retrospectively that something had been building up, some sense of having been used once too often, of having been too available when the whole scene had been defined outside of myself. And I knew that my response carried just a bit too much drama, but something about the whole scene had begun to bother me and I had to leave. I was suspicious of an enterprise that purported to help feed the hungry when I couldn't get a meal for my labors to help delude the public trust in a politician. Chalk up one for sniveling. But, more than that, it was my fear that the process, the path had been forgotten — that these people were celebrating having arrived somewhere without knowing where it was and what it looked like. It seemed to me an awful conformity to my belief that giving money to someone doesn't change the giver, doesn't alter the system, although I'm sure the Biafrans couldn't have cared less. I was just looking for something new.

One of my most persistent fantasies is to own a radio station that plays my favorite music all day and all night, punctuated, perhaps, with a bit of in-depth news coverage similar to the quality found on National Public Radio. A part of each day's programming would include a half-hour show called "The Anglophile Moment," to satisfy what I assume would be a good portion of my audience. The show would begin with "God Save the Queen" always, in some really drawn-out version — like an Elgar "Pomp and Circumstance" march — that could have them rolling in the aisles. Then an announcer, with the most Mayfair of accents, would hold a brief interview with a famous Briton, or just a person on the street, but preferably someone known for his or her disdain for America and American things. That would be followed by a snippet from John Major's reports to the House of Commons with the backbenchers yelling at him. Perhaps, too, some reruns of an outraged Margaret Thatcher — just for old time's sake. Then a song, something written by Andrew Lloyd Webber or the Beatles. To end the program there would be some dialogue from a Charles Laughton, James Mason, Alec Guinness, Glynis Johns, Lord Olivier, Dirk Bogarde, Anthony Quayle, Richard Attenborough, Ralph Richardson, Deborah Kerr,

John Gielgud, Greer Garson, Michael Redgrave, or Robert Morley movie — one of the World War II films loaded with patriotic sentiments. "The Anglophile Moment" would end with a recording of T. S. Eliot reading anything, followed by a Handelesque trumpet flourish.

My friend Maurice has accused me of having Anglophilia because I like Vaughan Williams and dark beer, but the condition is much more involved than that. In my business, I run across extreme cases of it constantly. Obviously, people who teach English literature have it to some degree or another — from those who have manufactured curious hybrid accents and who claim to love boiled beef and potatoes, to those who rarely miss an opportunity to say something unpleasant about the British, which is a trait I consider yet another manifestation of love.

But even outside the academic ranks, Anglophilia abounds in our culture. During the 1976 bicentennial celebration I drove my friends the Parks to Philadelphia to see the Founding Father sights there. We were standing in a cobblestone plaza near the Liberty Bell when a woman from the Middle West, to judge by her vowels, stopped with her three children and exclaimed: "Look, the Queen was here!" There was a placard on the stones commemorating some visit by Elizabeth II. My friends turned to look at each other and then to me, mimicked the woman's accent, and said, "Ooh, the Queen!" They were making fun, but not in the expected way. They're Yorkshire people; they wouldn't cross the street to see anybody, including Her Majesty.

A British accent in America can open doors and clear space for people. Some Anglophiles assume, on hearing a Briton, that the person is well educated, smarter by leaps and bounds than they are, and directly, if distantly, related to royalty. A friend told me of the astonishing success of an Englishwoman who was a colleague of hers. The British woman was unkempt, rude, and a mediocre scholar, but she marched through her department like Sherman through Georgia, with everyone from the chairman on down handing her the matches. My friend, after introducing me to her said, *sotto voce*, "Just another asshole with an English accent."

Anglophilia reveals more about the adorer than the adored, of course. Having seen a bit of British society I find it difficult to understand the appeal of such a classed society, where the vaunted American social mobility is nipped at birth. And I'm sure there would be cries of foul were the majority of Anglophiles I know subject to the rules of the society they love to love.

I am beginning to think the United States is not a young country at all. The vitality that used to define it in the eyes of the rest of the world is now most visible in Third World immigrants here. Perhaps the nation has progeria. The United Kingdom is verifiably quite old and has learned to live with itself over time. "The Anglophile Moment" would give a concentrated dose of British to the would-be converts, reliably and on shed-ule, where they could daily express their love of a past that isn't theirs — and then for the rest of the day they could concentrate on the processes and paths that form their reality.

Satchel Paige lived right around the corner from me when I was growing up in Kansas City. His daughter Pam was my best buddy — in the real sense of the word. We didn't spend a lot of time talking about baseball; there were few children I knew, even Pam, who cared about it as much as I did. I almost murdered Pam one day when she said Willie Mays had been at her house the night before. Mays was my childhood hero; I would have been content to see him through a window.

The Paiges were everyday people with lots of kids and some notable differences: they had a grand piano, a room brimming with trophies, and a father who was a living legend. Satchel Paige, that cagey, lanky pitcher of the Negro leagues and later the majors, is often quoted; his "Don't look back, somebody might be gaining on you" is part of baseball lore and every announcer's medley when his name is mentioned. I believe that Paige, born in Mobile, Alabama, some guess as early as 1906 — who was denied the opportunity to play in the majors until 1948, when he was past his athletic prime, because of racism — knew all about his present and the processes and paths that got him there. There was irony behind his famous quote; only then could he be so bold as to say, "Don't look back."

O Porgy! O Bess!

MOTHER, NANA, AND I shared a passion for movies, but this is not to say that my father didn't like them. Movies were a vital part of the nine-year-long courtship between my parents — and there is something of the Hollywood ending in the fact that when Mother went to Los Angeles with Nana, Daddy waited for her return to Minnesota, remaining more or less constant, I suppose. It still took three years after she got back for them to marry. In keeping with older traditions, he wanted to be finished with school and to have a job prospect before the marriage. And because he went through college, "studying a term, playing bridge a term, and working a term," as he would say, the process took a good long time. Mother was in no hurry either. All those years of courtship added up to a goodly number of movie dates.

But my father was never at home during my routine movie trivia questioning sessions, plus he was an early-to-bedder, never awake for the late shows, so I rarely thought of him in connection with movie-lust. There were other, more obvious places to go for information. And perhaps because he was away from home for the whole workday and many evenings, he was not in the least interested in taking Mother or the whole family to the movies. This homebody quality of my father's, which became evident to Mother after two children and a couple of relatively lateral job changes, had a direct economic reason: he couldn't afford movies or dinners out. It also had to do with his belief in the culinary superiority and economic common-sense of preparing one's own food — the first time I had dinner in a restaurant with my family I was well past puberty — and in a preference for entertainments available from those two wonderful inventions: the phonograph and the television.

As a result of these habits, it is not hard to recall the movies that he did bother to leave the house to see. One of my sister's favorite stories details the night she and my parents left me alone in my crib, snoring away, to take in *The Foxes of Harrow* and bought ice cream on the way home. I think she liked to tell me that I'd been left alone, defenseless, just months old, to encourage in me retroactive fears of parental indifference, sudden crib death, or invaders. I see it as one of the last gasps of sibling hegemony, when recalling the final good old days of her reign made her feel better.

My first movie recollection is an image of Frances Langford singing in some World War II USO-type show and the entire stage being blown to bits by an air raid. I don't know whether I saw this scene in a theater or on television, but it was probably instrumental in imprinting a certain quality of dread on my personality.

I do remember that while I lived at home, Daddy took Mother to see three movies: *Ben Hur*, *My Fair Lady*, and *Thérèse and Isabelle*, a French movie about two lesbians. Mother was quietly shocked by the whole thing, and felt it sufficient to answer my prurient questions with a rather wide-eyed evocation of: "And, you know, the aggressor was the one with blonde hair! Usually, it's supposed to be the dark one." That answered more questions than I'd asked.

I recall sitting alone with my father watching only three movies on television. One was *No Down Payment* — an interesting one about the trials and tribulations of Korean War era young white marrieds and the meanings of a developing notion called suburbia. I particularly remember the film because Daddy went off to the bathroom during an off-screen rape scene. When he returned to the den he asked me what had happened. I realized that I had never had to form words to reveal to him my knowledge or lack of it concerning sexual violence and I stumbled, and nervously said that the character Cameron Mitchell played had raped the woman next door. He said, "Humph." I continued to watch the rest of it with emotions altered, feeling that somehow I must have disappointed him.

The second was *Love Me or Leave Me*, Doris Day as Ruth Etting, James Cagney as The Gimp. My father and I watched it intently, with my father proclaiming it the best performance Cagney ever gave and the film that proved Doris Day could sing. I am sure it was a combination of the fine period music, the torch songs Etting sang, and the memories of his own youth that had something to do with his love of the movie. I saw it on a late show a few years ago and still thought it was good, all the better for the memories of him it evoked. Say what you will about Doris Day, but when she belts "I'll Never Stop Loving You" I am transfixed and can only hear my father saying, "That gal can sing." That was all the praise necessary.

The third movie we saw together was the 1951 version of *Show Boat* with Kathryn Grayson, Howard Keel, and William Warfield. It was being run on network television for the first time and because the music was so good — Jerome Kern and Oscar Hammerstein — I assumed it would be a full-family affair around the small screen. As the credits began to roll my father began to complain; he said he hated the story and didn't want to see the movie. My mother, always a fan of costumes and beauty, objected and won. But the mood was different. Daddy ran down the plot of *Show Boat* — the necessarily futile love of a mulatto woman for a white man. He said it was drivel. I wondered what part of it he meant: the tragic mulatto love or the film's sentimentality. I assumed both. After seeing it I couldn't disagree with him. Second, he said that if there had to be this damn tragic mulatto theme why wasn't a Negro woman in the part? He had remembered the 1936 version with Helen Morgan—who had done a very popular version of "Bill"—and he wasn't about to feel any better with Ava Gardner in the same role. "At least Morgan was a singer," he said. Third, and most surprising, he said he never liked "Ol' Man River," Paul Robeson in the '36 version notwithstanding. He didn't explain, and I believe it is because, though he could sing it and did at one time, he felt the song reinforced a sentimental quality of white attitudes toward blacks, the tenacity of which astounded him. The combination of make-believe and status quo of the libretto destroyed his ability to disengage and enjoy.

When my sister was sixteen she enrolled in the Columbia Record Club. She had babysitting jobs that could underwrite the expense, and ever since Daddy had come home, two years earlier, with a gizmo called a stereophonic phonograph, we had been dying to get some stereophonic records. Luckily the machine had a seventy-eight RPM setting and my father's collection of seventy-eights and twelve-inchers was amazing—from race records to opera, from ragtime to white and black big bands with lead singers like Sinatra and Whiting, Ivey Anderson and Billy Eckstine, from piano concertos to Broadway reviews. But my sister and I longed for the long-playing record. Prior to her joining the club we still had just the few LP albums my father had bought with the machine: a Lena Horne album, the original Broadway soundtrack to *My Fair Lady*, and a couple of big band recordings, made in an age when big bands were having hard luck in finding recording dates. My sister and I were very excited when the first records arrived: Ella Fitzgerald singing *The George and Ira Gershwin Song Books*, volumes one and two, Leonard Bernstein conducting "Rhapsody in Blue" and "An American in Paris," and Johnny Mathis's *Faithfully*. I was so flattered and pleased that my sister included me in the ownership of the records, writing "The Pems" on the back of each instead of her name only. It was a mutual proprietorship that suggested we were growing up and leaving some of the pettiness of childhood behind.

The records represented our musical tastes in the late 1950s. We knew all the words to every rock and roll song on the radio, but we never could afford to buy forty-fives in the quantity it took to remain *au courant* and perhaps we believed part of the propaganda about the music — that it would die. So we banked on perpetuity, and we played and played and sang along or danced along to our treasured Gershwin. The younger you are the better you learn: we know not only all the lyrics to most of Gershwin's songs, we can even sing you the introductions — and we can do a short-handed but creditable job of "playing" all the solos and taking either the piano or clarinet or brass through "Rhapsody in Blue" and "An American in Paris" in the style of the Mills Brothers. It didn't take long before "The Pems" collection grew, along with that of my father — so by the time I was about thirteen, quite a few long-playing, stereophonic albums were in residence. For several years my father had a talk show on a local black radio station, and he would come home with loads of albums sent to the station which it would never play: singleton recordings by unknown vocalists, early Muzak orchestra renditions of standards guaranteed to undo any of their musical worth, a few comedy albums, and some rock and rhythm and blues surprises — we own Cliff Richards' first American-released album and we had a copy of the Shirelles' *Will You Still Love Me Tomorrow?* long before the single cuts hit the airwaves, which raised my stock immensely among my friends.

Long-playing albums were wonderful because it took more effort to ruin them than it did seventy-eights, of which I destroyed my share. I can still recall the pain and agony on my father's face after I got up from a chair — I was about seven —

and on the cushion, broken into bits, was Sarah Vaughan's "Poor Butterfly." And I wept bitterly after I broke Jose Iturbi playing Chopin's "Polonaise in A-Flat Major" — so much my favorite that I was consumed with it and danced throughout the house, playing it nearly nonstop from about the ages of five to seven. With vinyl albums our only casualties came when we left the curtains open in full sun while records were lying on the top of the machine.

As my father grew older, and as the stresses of his profession became more pronounced — fighting for public accommodation laws, the integration of trade unions and workplaces — his taste in music changed. He seemed less able to listen with relaxed enjoyment to the music that had been so important in his past. Ironically, my sister and I spent more time playing Ella and Sarah and Billie and Count and Duke than he did. Daddy would come home and slump in a chair, turning on a precursor of an "easy listening" station. We would chide him, but it didn't work. He simply couldn't take music that demanded an alert, participatory listener. It takes energy, I suppose, to revel, to become ecstatic, to swoon, and my father didn't have much left after a day at work. Something in this reduced and bowdlerized sound soothed him, though. He went to bed with his radio lulling him to sleep, my mother nightly shutting it off hours later when she would retire.

When I was in graduate school I would occasionally buy my father remastered collections of classic jazz. I think he listened to them only rarely. I do know that he would play a few Billie Holiday songs now and again, for he adored her. He had met her; I haven't found it but I know I once saw a photograph of Holiday autographed on the back, "To Pem, With Love, Billie." Mother hates Billie Holiday and denies any knowledge of the picture; the story never has become any clearer than that.

William Dean Howells wrote one of those "it's not that he can speak so well, but that he can speak at all" introductions to Paul Laurence Dunbar's *Lyrics of Lowly Life*, published in 1896. Dunbar wrote dialect poetry celebrating black folk life, and standard English poetry and novels, from the end of the nineteenth century until 1906, when he died at the age of thirty-four. The introduction from Howells, who was one of the most important American novelists and editors of the time, was good for Dunbar's career. It helped sell his book, and it was one of the earliest examples of white commentary on black writing. Howells says of the dialect poems:

> We call such pieces dialect pieces for want of some closer phrase, but they are really not dialect so much as delightful personal attempts and failures for the written and spoken language. In nothing is his essentially refined and delicate art so well shown as in these pieces, which . . . describe the range between appetite and emotion, with certain lifts far beyond and above it, which is the range of the race. He reveals in these a finely ironical perception of the negro's limitations, with a tenderness for them which I think so very rare as to be almost quite new.

And so forth.

Dunbar's short life was not a particularly happy one. He was a very dark-skinned black when talent and intelligence were thought to be tied to a complex ratio of the parts of white blood to black, the larger doses of the former increasing the abilities. Howells even notes this: "Still, it will legitimately interest those who like to know the causes, or, if these may not be known, the sources, of things, to learn that the father and mother of the first poet of his race in our language were negroes without admixture of white blood." Dunbar was caught in a vise, a stifling double bind. He suffered from both sides: the astounded whites, and the blacks who held on to intraracism with grand wizardly tenacity. But he did achieve a measure of fame in his lifetime, and I wouldn't venture to guess how many black high schools bear his name. Dunbar certainly made out better than Phillis Wheatley, commonly thought of as the first black poet, who lived from around 1753 to 1784. Thomas Jefferson said of her work:

> Among the blacks is misery enough. Their love is ardent, but it kindles the senses only, not the imagination. Religion indeed produced a Phyllis Whately [sic]; but it could not produce a poet. The compositions published under her name are below the dignity of criticism.

Wheatley, so far as my research has led me, never had an opportunity to reply to Jefferson. Dunbar, however, wrote to a friend:

> One critic says a thing and the rest hasten to say the same thing, in many instances using the same identical words. I see now very clearly that Mr. Howells has done me irrevocable harm in the dictum he laid down regarding my dialect verse.

Howells had given a loud and contagious kiss of death to Dunbar by praising the dialect poems over those filled with high seriousness, believing that the only niche for Dunbar was in the evocation of a rural, folk black world. Dunbar himself thought his dialect poems important because they preserved a quality of black life from the past that was rapidly disappearing, a kind of historical, anthropological chronicling. At their finest, the dialect poems demand performance; reading them silently undermines their power and essentially much of their meaning, for Dunbar believed that performance was at the core of the nonliterate folk world he evoked. His dialect poems would mimic the folk tradition by being verbally handed down just as the stories of rural blacks were passed on to their children.

The first Dunbar poem I recall, recited to me of course, was "A Negro Love Song":

> Seen my lady home las' night,
>   Jump back, honey, jump back.
> Hel' huh han' an' sque'z it tight,
>   Jump back, honey, jump back.

> Hyeahd huh sigh a little sigh,
> Seen a light gleam f'om huh eye,
> An' a smile go flittin' by—
>   Jump back, honey, jump back.
>
> Hyeahd de win' blow thoo de pine,
>   Jump back, honey, jump back.
> Mockin'-bird was singin' fine,
>   Jump back, honey, jump back.
> An' my hea't was beatin' so,
> When I reached my lady's do',
> Dat I couldn't ba'to go—
>   Jump back, honey, jump back.
>
> Put my ahm aroun' huh wais',
>   Jump back, honey, jump back.
> Raised huh lips an' took a tase,
>   Jump back, honey, jump back.
> Love me, honey, love me true?
> Love me well ez I love you?
> An' she answe'd, " 'Cose I do"—
>   Jump back, honey, jump back.

It is a masterly job. Only those with severe cases of atonality and arrhythmia could be deaf to its aggressive syncopation, liveliness, and even timbre. It's hard not to dance to it when it is "read" well.

But, oh, such a problem for Dunbar: middle-class blacks didn't like such poems because they reinforced negative images of black people. In Howells' words, "These are divinations and reports of what passes in the hearts and minds of a lowly people whose poetry had hitherto been inarticulately expressed in music, but now finds, for the first time in our tongue, literary interpretation of a very artistic completeness." Whites loved the poems because they thought the same way as Howells, in a fashion that conjured up visions of happy darkies and good old days and other such malarkey. But some blacks liked them because they were good and enjoyable and authentic, and Dunbar was famous because of them. Dunbar

knew that the joy and pain of living in a black skin had histori-
cally expressed itself in many ways, including the rhythmic,
musical, theatrical, and folk. Or, as Toni Morrison writes in
Sula:

> . . . just a neighborhood where on quiet days people in val-
> ley houses could hear singing sometimes, banjos sometimes,
> and, if a valley man happened to have business up in those
> hills — collecting rent or insurance payments — he might see a
> dark woman in a flowered dress doing a bit of cakewalk, a bit
> of black bottom, a bit of "messing around" to the lively notes
> of a mouth organ. Her bare feet would raise the saffron dust
> that floated down on the coveralls and bunion-split shoes of
> the man breathing music in and out of his harmonica. The
> black people watching her would laugh and rub their knees,
> and it would be easy for the valley man to hear the laughter
> and not notice the adult pain that rested somewhere under the
> eyelids, somewhere under their head rags and soft felt hats,
> somewhere in the palm of the hand, somewhere in the sinew's
> curve. . . . the pain would escape him even though the
> laughter was part of the pain.

(Or maybe the pain would escape him *because* the laughter was
part of the pain.)

Dunbar's nondialect poetry is late nineteenth-century,
American romantic work, occasionally stentorian, often lyrical. His work was the first place I went to look after I came
upon Papa's "Beyond the Veil." Papa's poem reminded me of
Dunbar's "Ode to Ethiopia":

> O Mother Race! to thee I bring
>   This pledge of faith unwavering,
>   This tribute to thy glory.
>   I know the pangs which thou didst feel,
> When Slavery crushed thee with its heel,
>   With thy dear blood all gory.
>
>   Go on and up! Our souls and eyes
> Shall follow thy continuous rise;

> Our ears shall list thy story
> From bards who from thy root shall spring,
> And proudly tune their lyres to sing
> Of Ethiopia's glory.

Unhappily for Dunbar, Howells is correct when he says of the nondialect verse:

> Some of these I thought very good, and even more than very good, but not distinctively his contribution to American poetry. What I mean is that several people might have written them; but I do not know any one else at present who could quite have written the dialect pieces.

Indeed, my grandfather was one of those who might have written "Ode to Ethiopia" — black public poetry, didactic, terribly solemn, designed to be declaimed in booming voices, the sort of verse that makes people say they don't like poetry, not so much because of the poetry itself, which is usually mediocre to bad, but because of memories it evokes.

Then there were the dialogue and lyric poems of Dunbar, like this short one called "Retort":

> "Thou art a fool," said my head to my heart,
> "Indeed, the greatest of fools thou art,
>   To be led astray by the trick of a tress,
> By a smiling face or a ribbon smart;"
>   And my heart was in sore distress.
>
> Then Phyllis came by, and her face was fair,
> The light gleamed soft on her raven hair;
>   And her lips were blooming a rosy red.
> Then my heart spoke out with a right bold air:
>   "Thou art worse than a fool, O head!"

The assumptions of this poetic language make it necessary for Phyllis to be fair, with raven hair and rosy red lips that doubtless highlight the whiteness of her face. She is not Wheatley. In no way can this language successfully paint a portrait of black female pulchritude, although the thought and the emotions in the poem are not foreign to the black experience. Dunbar may have recognized that when one buys the form and the tradition one also buys all the racial and social implications of the language of form and tradition, and the price is sometimes expensive.

Dunbar was the first American black poet whose collective work was large enough and expansive enough to reveal the complexities and ironies facing a black poet, even before pen is put to paper. What possible language is there to redeem blackness, to sing of blackness without losing blackness? How does one resist, in Du Bois's words, bleaching the "Negro soul in a flood of white Americanism?" Once pen is put to paper, as Dunbar found, dissatisfaction abounds everywhere: his standard English lyric poetry is too derivative and sounds inauthentic; his dialect poetry sounds authentic but speaks of lowly lives when lowly in American English means worthy of trivialization and degradation. Dunbar's poetry dramatically displays Du Bois's double-consciousness — and his "We Wear the Mask," published before *The Souls of Black Folk*, foreshadows Du Bois's discussion of the veil:

> We wear the mask that grins and lies,
> It hides our cheeks and shades our eyes, —
> This debt we pay to human guile;
> With torn and bleeding hearts we smile,
> And mouth with myriad subtleties.
>
> Why should the world be over-wise,
> In counting all our tears and sighs?
> Nay, let them only see us, while
>   We wear the mask.
>
> We smile, but, O great Christ, our cries
> To thee from tortured souls arise.
> We sing, but oh the clay is vile
> Beneath our feet, and long the mile;

> But let the world dream otherwise,
>   We wear the mask!

It's a better poem than "Ode to Ethiopia" because it is concerned with a painful and sometimes mortifying reality that at its core is absurd, and it is not bothered with romantic visions of a self-proclaimed Ethiopian heritage. Or, to look at it another way: in Psalm 137 the Hebrew captives in Babylon ask, "How shall we sing the Lord's song in a strange land?" Dunbar's poetry is a testimony to the extra ironic layers of the black American dilemma: How do we sing our song at all, when the language we created is a joke and the language we have by necessity acquired denies us? Does anyone hear the pain that is a part of the laughter of "A Negro Love Song"? Does the performance of the poem, from behind the mask, on the other side of the veil, redeem it and its black captives? Black poets, black artists have been asking those questions and testing solutions for over one hundred years.

Good late-night movies are hard to find, harder still if cable isn't available and VCRs cost too much money, or if either has yet to be invented, which was the case when I lived at home and stayed up with my mother. She could last until "The Tonight Show" was over and then pick up the really late movie; she was watching one of those when she was attacked. But I couldn't last; those strong genes obviously are thinning out with me. I do recall a short period when even my father would stay up a little later and we would watch "The Tonight Show" together, first with Steve Allen and then with Johnny Carson.

John Bubbles was a frequent guest with Carson until illness prevented him from performing. My father was a great fan of John Bubbles and told me many times about Buck and Bubbles, the vaudeville team. Something about John Bubbles and that high, scratchy, liquid tenor voice and his soft, smooth tap struck chords of sadness and delight in my father; he would go on to mention Bert Williams, sometimes singing a phrase or two of Williams' famous "Nobody," which Whoopi Gold-berg later included in her stage act. I often wondered, still do sometimes, how it must have felt for the black Williams to sing in blackface a song called "Nobody." And I decided, and sometimes still do, that the redemption was all in the performance — all in the performer knowing something, feeling something quite different from what a white audience saw, and also communicating something else, some quality of solidarity and kinship, to a black audience filled with sadness and delight.

From what I understand of its origins the cakewalk conforms to the multilayered irony of Williamsesque minstrelsy. Dancing the cakewalk was very popular just before the turn of the century and afterward. It had evolved from slavery, when blacks mimicked the formal dances of the whites, sometimes, evidently, to the delight of the slave owners. Clearly, the blacks were doing some subtle things unseen by the whites, who doubtless were amused by these "inferior" blacks attempting their dances. The cakewalk had resilience, however, and toward the end of the century fashionable whites were doing it. So here was a black dance parodying white dance danced by trendy whites. Finally, black dancers, responding to the new popularity of the dance, displayed it, improvised on it, and ended up dancing a black dance parodying white dance danced by whites now danced by blacks. Singing a song in black skin in blackface is part of the same structure; the black dancers are doing something else in their cakewalk, and so is the black singer.

From 1952 to 1956 there was a touring revival of *Porgy and Bess*, Gershwin's American opera which had debuted on Broadway on October 10, 1935. I have a studio recording of "Great Scenes" from the opera, with Leontyne Price, William Warfield, McHenry Boatwright, and John Bubbles. Bubbles was in the original cast and reprised his role as Sportin' Life. I have heard many versions of the opera, but my RCA record is my favorite by a long shot. This opera, this music, is, of course, an American legend, and black singers — operatic and not — have found much success in concert and on wax and vinyl with the likes of "Summertime," "It Ain't Necessarily So," "I Loves You Porgy," and "Bess, You Is My Woman Now."

The liner notes on my album's jacket call this performance "A 'Dream Cast' in the Gershwin Masterpiece," and I concur. I know of only one or two performances of anything that can match Price's in "Gone, Gone, Gone." And John Bubbles is wonderful, satanic, tempting, horrible, as Sportin' Life.

But the album, performances notwithstanding, has also raised questions in my mind for years. How can one sing *Porgy and Bess*? Granted, the music is powerful, beautiful, but the story is pure banal sentimentality, regardless of its potential folk verisimilitude. Does singing the opera magnificently undermine or ironically twist its messages? The opera is based on Du Bose Heyward's 1925 novel, *Porgy*, and the Theatre Guild put on a stage play adapted by Heyward and his wife Dorothy. I found a copy of *Porgy* in a used bookstore several years ago and I read it, curious to know the original story. The novel is a darkie story with pathos and melodrama. To be fair, it resists some of the broader stereotypes of blacks even while it focuses on others. I was driving to the supermarket a few months ago listening to public radio and I heard a woman, a scholar of Gullah, proudly announcing that most people did not realize that the inhabitants of Catfish Row were really Gullah people. I thought her comments were profoundly off the point; I wanted her to answer my question of how one sings *Porgy and Bess*. I sat in the car until the program was over, waiting; she didn't go any further.

I have never asked my question disingenuously. I know that any kind of opera, grand or folk — which is what Gershwin's opera has been called for years by those who don't want it in the same canon with *Aida* or *Turandot* — is not where one goes to get subtlety or serious portrayals. I once heard Joan Sutherland quoted as having said that she found it difficult and tiring singing the roles of madwomen from the grand operatic canon night after night; all the good roles were of a stereotypical hysteric. She said that she looked forward to lighter roles from time to time. But a work of the importance of *Porgy and Bess* must also be judged on grounds larger than those that govern opera simply because the scene is a black one and the intended audience is white; it is not an American version of some European upper class being entertained by the shenanigans of a lower one set on stage and put to music.

And I don't ally myself with those black people who are contemptuous of any black expression they think projects a "negative image." The question has to do with how one performs a work that is so blatantly exploitative of the meanings of the black folk and urban worlds which Harlem Renaissance black authors worked so hard to de-stereotype as they proclaimed them and redeemed them. How does one sing the music, albeit beautiful music, that properly locates America's musical innovation in black artistry but then remakes it? Or, as Serge Koussevitsky said in 1935 of Gershwin and the opera, "His score is for the most part original and unconventional: Gershwin's original spirituals touched the authentic mood." Does touching the authentic mood replace authenticity itself? What are the hidden costs when one buys the language of form and tradition? Or is singing *Porgy and Bess* really the same as doing the cakewalk? And if so, which cakewalk?

On the surface, then — on days when I am thinking and not listening — *Porgy and Bess* gets tangled in a web like that of Dunbar. Howells, as exemplary advocate of Dunbar, was also his detractor; what he said about Dunbar's work was simultaneously right and wrong.

Porgy and Bess is a story of Porgy, a crippled beggar, who finds fleeting love with the worldly, addictive Bess — a kind of Charleston, South Carolina Quasimodo and Esmeralda. There is a pastoral quality straight out of Thomas Nelson Page to the black ghetto of Catfish Row, a tenement that formerly was an aristocratic house on the waterfront. The community survives, vulnerable to nature — there is a climactic hurricane that ravages the area — and to dangerous influences from faraway urban dens like New York. Crown is the virile, wild bad man, capable of surviving in nature, a violent, brutish outlaw who has been Bess's "husband" for five years. His double is the citified sharper and dope peddler, Sportin' Life, who seeks to lure Bess away from Catfish Row with packets of "happy dust." The inhabitants of the Row are a simple people living under capricious white law: one of them, Peter, is arrested and detained for an indefinite period of time for being a witness to a murder committed by Crown and then is released out of the blue by the good white lawyer, Archdale, because "his folks used to belong to my family and I just heard he was in trouble." The people of Catfish Row run the gamut from the pious Serena to the superstitious Clara to the strong and bold Jake and the tough and resolved Maria — a cross-section of saints and sinners.

As an alternative glimpse of lowly life, *Porgy and Bess* obviously has a different perspective from Dunbar's because the writer, the composer, and the lyricist were all white. It is black life viewed from the outside, where personalities and circumstances, as types, are projected onto the milieu. And while there is nothing wrong with a folk opera about the folk — and the black world that forms the basis of the opera, doubtless, is a plausible place filled with plausible people — it is perplexing that the presentation of this world is driven by sentimentality and naturalism. The range of emotions that are elicited from sentimental portrayals rarely go beyond the "amused contempt and pity" of Du Bois's theory of how white looks at black. The portrayal of black life becomes localized and isolated. The opera lies as it tells the truth, advocates as it detracts.

Bess, the unlucky, "bad" woman who almost redeems herself, and Porgy, the handicapped fixture of Charleston's streets, riding through town in his makeshift cart pulled by a goat, are romanticized primitives, served up to satisfy what

H. L. Mencken in 1927, with his own brand of amused contempt and pity, saw as a new age: "Can it be that the Republic, emerging painfully from the Age of Rotary, comes into a Coon Age? For one, I am not above believing it. The colored brother, once so lowly, now bursts into the sunlight all along the line." Ultimately, *Porgy and Bess* becomes social propaganda reinforcing a sentimental idea of blackness — establishing the "recent past" of the setting as archetypical — and perpetuating a musical canon which, along with spirituals, must be part of the repertoire of any aspiring or arrived black operatic singer.

Du Bois was right when he wrote of the "twoness" of black identity, of the black person caught in a "world which yields him no true self-consciousness, but only lets him see himself through the revelation of the other world." But he went further:

> This waste of double aims, this seeking to satisfy two unreconciled ideals, has wrought sad havoc with the courage and faith and deeds of ten thousand thousand people, — has sent them often wooing false gods and invoking false means of salvation, and at times has even seemed to make them ashamed of themselves.

To look at it another way, black people have run the risk of sentimentalizing their own lives by internalizing the white response to the sentimental presentation of black life, such as that found in *Porgy and Bess*. The dangers go beyond the risk of being ashamed of themselves, but also of finding their lives, their beings, pathetic and deserving of degradation. While a white audience of *Porgy and Bess* may respond to the bathetic "I Got Plenty O' Nuttin' " with the detached amusement the song encourages, complete with banjo, a black audience may well be driven to the point of insanity by watching the literally partial black man, Porgy, sing of the simple pleasures of life with Bess.

Various scholars and observers have noted that the

majority of black people in the 1930s and 1940s enjoyed seeing blacks in movies, regardless of the quality of their roles. And while many protested both the predominance of degrading roles and the superficial renderings of black life, it was important for them to see "their kind" on screen. The magic of movies, the putative reality portrayed there, produced some occasionally interesting episodes. For example, Fredi Washington, a light-skinned black woman who actually got to play a light-skinned black woman's role in the 1934 version of *Imitation of Life*, was chastised in real life by people faulting her treatment of her "mother," Louise Beavers, in the film. I am told soap opera stars run similar risks from fans who have projected their television roles onto their beings. Such stories underscore the power of these visual media. Does the black audience of *Porgy and Bess* weep at Porgy's bold determination to go to "New Yawk," cart and goat and all, to find the lost Bess?

Something else happens to me on days when I am listening to and thinking about *Porgy and Bess*. My worn, scratchy RCA album resonates with the pure magic of the performances. A few weeks ago I finally decided to find the answers to my questions, once and for all. So I went to the library, borrowed the original score of the opera, and although I was immediately put off by the silhouette drawing of Porgy on the page opposite the "Index of Scenes" — it is a gross caricature of a black figure riding in his cart drawn by his goat, with crutches showing; he has woolly lumps of hair on his head and lips that protrude to the same plane as the tip of his nose — I kept going and I put my record on to read along with the music. My album conforms to the music and lyrics for the most part; Price does not sing, "With Daddy an' Mammy standin' by" from "Summertime," but rather, "With your Daddy and Momma standin' by" — an updating of language if not sentiment (and not consistently done: Warfield does sing "Mammy" in "A Woman Is a Sometime Thing"). But no one sings "nigger" when it appears. I've seen this changing of negative epithets in older texts to more positive ones before. I remember noticing that Eudora Welty's "Why I Live at the P.O." in its original 1940s version has the line, "There was a nigger girl going along on a little wagon right in front. 'Nigger girl,' I says, 'come help me haul these things down the hill, I'm going to live in the post office.' " In *The Collected Stories of Eudora Welty*, 1980, the line reads, "There was a girl going along on a little wagon right in front. 'Girl,' . . . " I'm not sure whether the updated omission of "nigger" properly preserves the sentiment coming from the character. And Stephen Foster must roll, as on a rotisserie, in his grave with the line, " 'Tis summer and the people are gay" in his old Kentucky home. But such concerns, when I'm listening to *Porgy and Bess*, are mere bagatelles.

Porgy and Bess is filled with stunning duets: "Bess, You Is My Woman," "What You Want Wid Bess?," and "I Loves You, Porgy." While I like all three, "What You Want Wid Bess?" is more complex, more demanding of the singers, Crown and Bess. The setting is Kittiwah Island, where the Catfish Rowers have gone to have a picnic. Porgy has stayed at home, but Bess has joined the rest of the jubilant throng, singing and dancing on the island. Naturally a stereotypically God-fearing lot, the picnickers are going against church orders by behaving in such a fashion — religion is an important ingredient in the entire opera, and there is much prayer-making and hymn-like singing throughout the three acts — and Serena, the ever-pious one, sends them packing back to the boat for carrying on so. Bess runs into Crown, who has been hiding on the island since he murdered Robbins in Act I. Their duet is an enactment of might versus will, as Bess tries to escape Crown's clutches and tell him of her love for Porgy, while Crown insists that she be prepared to go with him when he comes for her back at the Row. He also doesn't want to hear what she has to say: "You tellin' me dat you'd rather have a cripple dan Crown?" Crown's is an ego to respect. Their meeting on the island reminds me of the one Huck and Jim have on Jackson's Island; like Jim, Crown has been surviving on a local menu of birds' eggs and such truck. When the boat leaves Bess behind, the Rowers don't believe she's fallen off and there's no search for her. Crown forces her to stay with him, throwing her into a thicket for starters.

But the duet itself is marvelous, moving through five keys as Bess attempts to resist the powerful and demonic Crown. Bess uses some elementary psychology on Crown by suggesting that she is past her prime and that a fine stud like him deserves better: "What you want wid Bess?" she sings in a bluesy, syncopated solo. The climax of the duet is reached in sections 160 to 162, the musical counterpoint underscoring their competing "readings" of the situation:

Bess: Can' you see
Crown: What I wants wid other woman,

Bess: I'm with Porgy, now an' for ever,
Crown: I gots a woman, yes, An'

Bess: I am his woman, he would die without me,
Crown: dat is you, yes, dat is you, yes,

Bess: Oh, Crown, won't you let me go
Crown: I need you now an' you're mine jus' as long

Bess: to my man, to my man
Crown: as I want you. No cripple goin' take my woman from me.

Bess: He is a cripple an' needs my
Crown: You got a man tonight an' that is

Bess: love, all my love.
Crown: Crown, yes Crown, yes Crown.

Bess: What you want wid Bess?
Crown: You're my woman, Bess,

Bess: Oh, let me go to my man.
Crown: I'm tellin' you, now I'm your man.

This part of the duet is sung in B major and is a tense, dramatic battle that Bess loses because she isn't strong enough to contend with the physical might of Crown. She is determined to sing her love for Porgy as she begins to break physically and emotionally under Crown's pressure, and Price is marvelous dipping under into her chest voice, going low to reinforce her resolve. Boatwright's Crown is pompous, violent, and proud. One afternoon, listening to it, I decided that it represented a wonderful paradigm of white and black relations in America, but I let that go and relaxed, content to listen to some really fine singing.

This time, there was such a difference between what I was seeing on the page and hearing on the record that I wondered how I might articulate it. The thinking through the text and the score was in conflict with the hearing of the rendition. Something was happening through the act of performance that made many of my questions about how one can sing *Porgy and Bess* moot, for this "dream cast" was doing the cakewalk with it. And like my photograph from the March on Washington, where Williams and Young and King and Reuther and Randolph and everyone in the background jump out of the frame and into the entire history of my life and of black life in general, some things — the opera's story, its setting, its assumptions about blackness — were being transcended through the act of good singing. (It's my theory, and Apollo theatergoers' too, that the singing must always be good in a circumstance like this for the transcending to occur.)

By Du Bois's definition of black identity and the double-consciousness at its core, the black cast was perforce implicated in the "amused contempt and pity" and just plain sentimentality at the basis of the story. Merely thinking about *Porgy and Bess*, I could go no further than that. But hearing *Porgy and Bess* made me understand that a triple-consciousness was being revealed through the process of performance. The singers, as representative stereotypes, sang through the stereotypes to transform them, to transcend the art and even an enthusiastic audience's approval, to reveal a truth through lies that breaks the double bind and announces a self-created black identity. As Du Bois describes double-consciousness there is too much room for blacks to sentimentalize their own condition; there can be no movement toward real freedom because they are incapable of changing the ways in which they are seen. Triple-consciousness goes one step further: how one is seen is a given, with variations on the modifiers of both contempt and pity. How one performs the act, in all cognizance of the outside world, becomes a supreme act of individuation that can go beyond Du Bois's "longing" to the attainment of "true self-consciousness," of "merging [the] double self into a better and truer self." The same thing happens when Michael Jordan flies, when Sarah Vaughan blues a note.

I am a bit beyond the "but I know what I like" stage when I comment on music, but I am not a schooled critic. I agree with those who deem Gershwin a master. He was an innovator, a definer of a kind of American music that is a hybrid of black and European. Gershwin took the sounds that run through Aaron Copland back to Prokofiev and Stravinsky and fused them with blues and ragtime — the creations of countless anonymous geniuses of piano, strings, brass, and drums. He had high hopes for *Porgy and Bess* and in one way or another they have been met in revivals over the last fifty-seven years. I think of the opera as consummately American not only because of its music, but also because of its ambiance and the sensibility at its core. An audience brings with it the sum total of the historic black and white American experience as the overture begins.

Not long ago I read a review of a revival at Glyndebourne, in England, which was held in the summer of 1986. Joseph Lelyveld, no stranger to writing about black issues in white-defined settings, reported that the opera was hailed there; it became the highlight of the season. He wrote:

> Instead of becoming an excursion into American folkways, this "Porgy" emerges as a heroic struggle for survival in a set-

ting of deprivation and distress. Scenes that had traditionally been played for laughs or treated as light interludes, were reintegrated into the narrative as Mr. Nunn [who directed the revival] felt sure Heyward and Gershwin meant them to be. Most important, minor stage effects were not allowed to obscure Porgy's own progression from an embittered and isolated cripple to a character of tragic stature.

Porgy's cart and goat, deemed by the director to be "Disneyesque" in their effect, are banished from Glyndebourne's stage.

Lelyveld says the first-night audience, "seeming genuinely stirred . . . responded with a standing ovation, punctuated by stomping and cheers, that lasted nearly ten minutes." And further on in the review he says, "The contrast between Catfish Row and the panorama of privilege that the Glyndebourne gardens present on a summer's evening might have been expected to make an unavoidable, perhaps awkward, statement of its own." Lelyveld seems to suggest that something happened at this revival. Some result of the high seriousness with which the enterprise was undertaken, some peeling away of fifty-one years of American coatings, allowed a British audience to see and hear the universals of *Porgy and Bess* and, perhaps, to witness a transcendent artistic moment, and to be in attendance when a stage full of black people practiced triple-consciousness. I don't know whether such a thing could happen here, whether Joseph Lelyveld could say the same thing if the whole kit and caboodle of Glyndebourne were brought to the Met — if just saying so could undo the "American folkways." I doubt it. I'm sure *Nicholas Nickleby*, another of Mr. Nunn's productions and one revealing some "English folkways, " has culturally different resonances for an American audience than it does for a British one.

In 1967 Langston Hughes published his last volume of poetry, *The Panther and the Lash*. It was the last year of Hughes's life. He dedicated the volume to Rosa Parks, the woman whose refusal to move to the back of a bus ignited the 1955 Montgomery bus boycott. It is a powerful, angry volume of poetry, the work of a man tired of knowing that the "dream" is still "deferred." One of the best poems from the volume is "Cultural Exchange." The stanzas in the poem's center have always intrigued and pleased me:

> In the Quarter of the Negroes
> Where the doorknob lets in Lieder
> More than German ever bore,
> Her yesterday past grandpa—
> Not of her own doing—
> In a pot of collard greens
> Is gently stewing.
>
> Pushcarts fold and unfold
> In a supermarket sea.
> And we better find out, mama,
> Where is the colored laundromat
> Since we moved up to Mount Vernon.
>
> In the pot behind the paper doors
> On the old iron stove what's cooking?
> What's smelling, Leontyne?
> Lieder, lovely Lieder
> And a leaf of collard green.
> Lovely Lieder, Leontyne.
>
> You know, right at Christmas
> They asked me if my blackness,
> Would it rub off?
> I said, *Ask your mama*.

My father had a copy of the book and I remember coming home from college and talking briefly with him about the poems. Daddy loved Hughes, particularly the Simple stories that appeared in the Chicago *Defender*. In 1967 I didn't know how to defend *Invisible Man*, not to mention how to understand the layers of meaning in Langston Hughes's poetry. It took me a long time and considerably more concentration than I had then, to think of Hughes as the poet who started me thinking about triple-consciousness. For throughout his poetry the various personae of his narrators and characters of his poems transcend the merely sentimental and the starkly naturalistic to announce identity and consciousness somewhere else, some place where the veil — perhaps the veil of Maya — is removed and a pure consciousness, a dialectical synthesis of simple consciousness and double-consciousness, shines through the pain and the laughter. It is a place my father had to know, particularly at meetings where he was asked by whites, all bemused and sincere, why black people had so many children; he would answer, using other words, "Ask your mama," and they would applaud.

The "leaf of collard green" in the Lieder of Leontyne of "Cultural Exchange" is also the blackness in the blackness of *Porgy and Bess* that redeems it. It is possible to sing one's song in a strange land, in stranger languages, even songs written by someone else — simply because in doing it there is a transformation and a change of ownership. Perhaps that's why the opera didn't seem to bother my father. But "Ol' Man River" who "just keeps rollin' along," and showboats and tragic mulattos did; he saw no redemption. Maybe he disliked the pathetic fallacy. When I consider how long I've spent thinking about *Porgy and Bess*, *Show Boat*, and everything else, because of one night in front of a television set, I suspect my father of being the broker of the cultural exchange, a rare combination of Socrates and Sportin' Life.

Bernarda Alba's Picnic,
Or: The Myth of the
Eternal Return

I HAVE A black and white photograph taken in 1958 at a picnic somewhere outside of Kansas City. For a family of camera fanatics, it is surprising and distressing to discover the real dearth of group pictures of us. This photograph is an exception and someone outside of the family took it. In it my mother is standing next to a tree, her handbag slung over her left arm, her thin, summery skirt blowing slightly in the wind; she has one of her wry smiles on her face. At her feet, sitting on the ground, are my sister and I. We both have on sailor caps, but my sister has the thick brim of hers turned down; she is fifteen and cool. As usual, she is looking more or less directly at the camera. I am sitting next to her in a fairly graceless pose, looking chubby and gazing skeptically at my sister's manner, since this was of the time when I had to be on the lookout for guerrilla attacks from her. Over my shoulder, off to my left by several feet, is my father, sitting on a folding canvas stool. He has his old behemoth Graflex camera by his feet and he is hunched forward on the stool, his hands clasped together, a summer straw hat with a wide ribbon band planted solidly on his head. He is looking dead straight at the camera.

I don't remember who took the picture, but from the looks

of it I suspect it was taken with a Brownie, either my sister's or my own. But I like the picture because all four of us are in it and we reveal typical aspects of ourselves: my mother, always oblique, is looking away from the camera, content to have her eye focused somewhere else; my father and sister are relaxed looking at the camera; I am consciously turned away from the camera. All three of them are smiling; I look hesitant through glasses. As one might suspect, my father was photogenic, as is my sister, each of them rarely taking a bad picture. My mother and I hate photographs of ourselves; we would burn about eighty-five percent of them if we had our druthers.

Two memories stand out from that picnic: first, it was given by members of some lodge or organization my father belonged to, so the rest of us did not know anyone there. The second is of a man who came up to my father and greeted him warmly. It seemed obvious that they had not seen each other in many years. My father introduced his family. After the requisite "howdy-dos" the man turned toward my father and boomed, "What — no boys, Pem?" My father immediately answered, just as emphatically, "Hell, no! What would I want with boys?" We were a physically demonstrative family — many hugs over the years — but those were private expressions of love. So I suppressed my desire to run and grab my father in a bear-hug or jump solidly onto his ample belly. I wanted to thank him for defending the existences of his girl children, for loving us and wanting us, and for throwing what I saw as an egregious gaffe back into the man's face. I don't remember anything else about the afternoon; everything around me turned brown, as if filmed through a sepia-colored lens. I blotted everything out, and I have no idea what transpired in the rest of my father's conversation. Perhaps the man took the photograph and maybe that's why I'm looking so curiously at my sister.

It is true that my father was being gallant, but I also believe that he really did not want sons. I'm sure that my mother would have risen in Grandma's estimation had she produced one or two of them. And I quake at the thought of what an adored son might have done to the self-esteem of my sister and me. Perhaps my father did not want to cope with unadulterated adoration from the older generation while he attempted to instill his brand of reality in a son. Maybe he feared the competition psychologists tell us is at the core of the father-son relationship. Possibly he felt that he would never be able to make up for the disappointments a black son would have in this culture. Perhaps I'm all off track. Suffice it to say, on numerous occasions he would chuckle at the public behavior of some young men and boys, saying that if he'd had a son he would have murdered him before the poor boy grew very old. Maybe he would have; my father didn't seem the Laius type. The converse of this was his insistence that my sister and I become completely independent women; he said he never wanted to see us having to rely on a man for anything. He came very close, once or twice, to saying he thought men were bad for women.

My sister and I have talked about Daddy's quest for our independence many times. He was quite successful — in my sister's estimation, too successful. She says that what her eczema didn't do, Daddy did. He set up paternal roadblocks like, "Who are his parents? I don't know them. Forget it." And because the nature of his work brought potential beaus to his office looking for jobs, my sister says it was perceived by the whole lot of them that one did not want to get on the wrong side of Mr. P. So my sister spent a lot of time going out with the girls and every now and then watched the odd movie with Mother and me.

The ironic side to all of this is that Daddy also really wanted his daughters to marry. In self-contradiction and paradox, he believed we needed taking care of. And, although he did not like the man my sister married, he kept his criticism — that is, beyond what he told Mother and the occasional eye-roll and wink at me — to himself. His scenario was that his daughters would go from cloistered virginity to blissful marriage in one short step. This very Old World concept was consistent with his stated belief that moderation in all things is best and that one keeps one's nose solidly out of other people's business. But like Ben Franklin (when it came to absolute categories), what he said and did were two different things; he was a most immoderate eater and smoker. He died before my sister's divorce and we both think he would have had a very hard time accepting it, being unable to accept the realistic outcome of his pedagogy of polarities.

He was different with me, perhaps because the five years that separated my sister and me amounted to a small revolution in possibility. My relationship with him was more nonverbal than verbal, but we got our messages across to each other loud and clear. Occasionally we talked. He said he wanted me to go to a good school because I would have the opportunity to make "connections" that would last all my life. I have made connections, but I inappropriately befriended scions of middle-class families, where nothing in life was understood except that one found a trade and plied it. The influential and rich — the real "connections" — were different, and I didn't meet them. But he was proud of me, and even though he missed my college graduation and was dead before my Ph.D. he was happy when I got my M.A. I marched particularly to give him the show. I remember that we ran into a white man he knew from Kansas City at the ceremonies. The man was quite taken aback to see my father there and said so. Daddy put his arm around me and proudly introduced me to the bemused Kansas Citian. (This reminds me of the time my English friends Millie and Harry Park and my parents finally met, after more than ten years of hearing about each other. We were having lunch together in a restaurant in Boston when my father spotted a white Kansas City couple who were in the city for the same convention. They came over to the table and were introduced to us. The woman came as close to dropping natural teeth as humanly possible when she heard the Parks' accents. She froze, unable to carry out the formalities smoothly, astonished at how these black people knew royalty.)

Daddy also feared for me, though he would always take gracefully my plans to move, yet again, from one good job to another. He believed, as my friend Wallace does, that I am beset by the Furies of wanderlust, always packing up and moving toward I don't care what. He would look at me, his eyes saying, "I want you settled. Planted. Happy." And I would smile back, bite my lower lip, and make up some garbage about career paths and better outlooks for tenure.

When we were all together for the holidays my father never failed to pick on my sister and me. He was always dropping some of his favorite one-liners. One of these grew out of the complex intersection of the differences between his notion of reality and my sister's, and the subtle variations in each of their hopes for her life. Daddy believed that the only way a black woman could gain independence was through a good education and a teaching job. He probably would have steered a son to the Post Office. I remember a long and loud family argument at the dinner table when my sister, home from college, said she was taking secondary education courses. My father went berserk for some reason. He thought the constant demand for elementary school teachers guaranteed work for them only. He said she was crazy as my sister tried to tell him, calmly at first, that she was not the type to teach toddlers anything, least of all French. The shouting match then began, with my mother and me staying clear. I silently took notes and vowed never to be in her position. Daddy was a good teacher himself, so, resisting the implication that she needed a man to take care of her — in the guise of a father this time — she did what she intended anyway and became settled, teaching high school French. Probably with that argument still alive in his memory, Daddy would taunt her on long distance telephone calls, or when she arrived home for a visit with, "And how's my school-teaching daughter today?" demonically giggling at her. She would rise to the occasion and call him all sorts of endearing foul names.

He would pick me up at the train station and tell me that the other "crumb snatcher" was home for the holidays and that the clothes I was wearing were impeccably designed to force a father to take his daughter shopping immediately or hide her from public view. And as he ordered us to do various things in preparation for holiday meals — sitting back and laughing the whole time — he would tell us that parents were parents forever, and children, children. He said he couldn't wait to be an old, old man, watching his gray-haired, Afro-headed daughters scurrying around, taking orders like, "Daughter, fetch your pappy a cold glass of water!"

Over the years many of my female friends and I have talked about our relationships with our fathers. There have always been interesting resonances in our stories. It goes without saying that the cultural expectations of women and men are different and that this reflects itself in family behavior. I don't know how many times I've heard of parents, mainly fathers, signing up their sons to go to this or that college or military academy, having the "& Son" placard carved at the son's birth, spending what to me are outrageous sums on private athletic coaches and equipment that will somehow assure a lucrative professional sports career for a son. I know a few women, and have heard of far more, whose fathers refused to pay for their higher education, deeming it a waste of money and time for a being fit only for domestic life. These extremes illuminate just how easy it is for sons who resist programming to be disappointments, and how daughters can rise far beyond their parents' dreams. It takes a flexible form of mental and psychological gymnastics for a father to live through a daughter.

I've also known women whose fathers drove them mercilessly, never content with the quality of their acts, and sometimes sabotaging their triumphs with understated appreciation. But my father did not push my sister and me; he depended on osmosis to do his work. So lines like "I know what men are like" were sufficient to get us to strive for emotional, intellectual, and financial independence. Or if he told us that he'd heard a classmate of ours had to drop out of school to raise her newly born infant, he would just give the facts — no finger in our faces, no moralizing — and then he would go back to reading his paper. Without our having talked about it, short of agreeing that we would collaborate on his memoirs, I find myself doing what he said he always wanted to do himself — write. And many of my friends have the same story. The pressures were different and so were the expectations, but here we are in our forties, doing many things, among them trying to please our fathers.

These same friends of mine who have these subtly tortured relationships with their fathers also speak of having compensatory, wonderful, open and relaxed lives with their mothers. Much feminist writing concerns itself with the otherwise often neglected mother-daughter tie. The opportunities open to women born in the latter half of the twentieth century are greater than they were for our mothers. And I too look with awe on those women who smashed barriers and taboos to do whatever they wanted. Because her involvement with the world outside of the home was more limited and limiting, Mother has rarely argued with me about my choices. I'm sure that she has disagreed with some of them and that she, too, would love see me settled, planted, and happy. When I was in my twenties I wanted to ask her all kinds of questions — what she thought about me and the world and so forth. Much like Nana, I knew she would only give me an inscrutable smile; I had to say to myself, "Aw, leave her alone. You know quite a bit of it." After planting her "I'd rather see you dead than pregnant" line on us so early, she really had nothing to worry about apart from our health and my notorious-in-some-quarters inability to manage money very well. The one category that concerns her the most is loyalty. We've never let her down and she hasn't us.

My father came to visit me once when I was living in Manhattan. He walked into my apartment, spoke well of its order, liked what he called the "little greenery" that was here and there. He applauded my purchase of a serious easy chair, but told me it needed a hassock. He checked the kitchen, noting what I didn't have, and for months afterward, unprompted, would send me things like blenders, toasters, and extra, fancy pots and pans — "for the gourmet," he would say. We had never really had much time together before that; I was always too far away. My sister would see him more often.

We had a chance during that visit to talk about a few things, indirectly. He said he wanted to introduce me to some of his friends in Harlem who might function as social guides for me, who would introduce me to others my age and provide a social setting that might allow me to have fun. "Fun?" I asked. "Yeah." "I'm willing," I said. And we went to Harlem where I met some fascinating women with wonderful and tragic stories of the twenties, thirties, and forties. I was researching my first dissertation, and they spoke of going to parties with Langston Hughes, Countee Cullen, Chester Himes, and Zora Neale Hurston. They mentioned the achievements and exploits of many more whose names I did not recognize. I did go, once or twice, to meet some of the "younger set," but we didn't seem to hit it off. I was a bit older. I wasn't in a money-making profession and I didn't have high finance dreams as many of them did. My parents were, in effect, supplementing my low wages as a college teacher by sending me phone money and an occasional smoked ham from the Ozarks. More than that, I was an outlander and they were Harlem through and through. New York is a tough place to find a social world. It takes time. I would have preferred to hear more stories from the older women, but there wasn't enough of a context for that either, so I drifted back toward Morningside Heights and academia. Pretty soon after that Daddy was dead and I got no Christmas cards in exchange for the ones I sent the ladies.

The more I think about it, the more I am sure that my

father's intention was not primarily to find a social world for me, but rather to show me independent, successful black women who had survived much harder times than I had ever seen, who knew fun and joy along with the rest, who had husbands and children and grandchildren and careers, who owned homes and saw plays and read books and balanced their checkbooks. If I could get to know these women I might lose some of my social ineptitude and learn how to live with the independence he worked so hard to instill in me. The gravy would be a group of Harlemites as friends. There was something too solitary about the life I was leading and that bothered him. One night he trundled me into a taxi and we went to Manny Wolf's restaurant to talk. Daddy naturally gravitated toward solid American chop house food: red meat and potatoes. We sat down, he ordered a Gibson, I had a bourbon, and I told him some anecdotes of my professional life.

I told him I'd been on a roll for several years, from undergraduate through graduate school, when it seemed that nearly every white person I spoke to for more than four or five minutes felt compelled to tell me about his or her family racist — usually a parent or grandparent, or all of them. These confessions were spontaneous, umprompted by me; the conversation would always have originated with some innocent topic like the weather or where we had grown up. I was always baffled by these episodes and not a little annoyed. My experience, combined with elementary deductive logic and a knowledge of the cultural odds, made it likely that some members of their families were racists. Common sense dictated my silent response to their revelations: "Why the hell should I care?" What's more, these students seemed to be so pleased in the telling, as if they had crossed some tabooed line; in breathless whispers, like adolescents reading aloud their first paragraphs of pornography, they half-smiled, were half-disturbed. Usually these betrayals of "Daddy's" or

"Grandmother's" little secret, or proud assertion, were followed by the speaker, in exasperated tones, delivering his or her own impeccable liberal credentials: "I just can't understand it! Well I'm certainly not like that. S/he's really a good person except for that." In those days I would quietly disagree with those people and ask them if they had ever read the case study of the European inspector in Franz Fanon's *The Wretched of the Earth*, who became psychically disturbed when he found it impossible to torture Algerians in the day and love his family at night. That doing little to get my point across, I adjusted my tactics, and when I was a victim of such revelations — often from my own students — I would stare blankly back at them and say absolutely nothing.

I am an interested, and sometimes a depressed, observer of beginnings and opening lines between people. I used to ask myself why an appalling number of people I have chanced to meet have no options for opening a conversation apart from telling me that others, whom I have never seen nor met, who know nothing of or about me, hate me. These episodes highlight an ironic etiquette. These confessing people seek to reassure me — assuming I worry about it — that their own racial credentials are excellent, that I am "safe" with them. But what they actually reveal is a quality of objectifying me that is quite consistent with their upbringings. For the whole conversation is an effort, on their part, to handle their whiteness in the face of my blackness, and I am affronted. My presence puts the mirror in their hands and they attempt to describe to me what they see. I have absolutely nothing to do with their vision; I function as an image and concept that precipitates defective self-analysis. It's just another manifestation of my invisibility; part of the minority condition. I have talked to Jews who have had the same experiences. And I am reminded of a white girl who was in college with me. I didn't know her well at all, but we shared acquaintances, and once or twice I was in a small talk session when she was present. She was from Miami, Florida, and she was dating a Cuban. I recall her saying, with only slightly suppressed glee, that her father would kill her boyfriend if he found out his daughter's "little secret." She said she had no doubt about that. I wondered if her boyfriend was aware of the nature of the extra services he provided her through his invisibility.

Ultimately, it was not the family racism that troubled me. There was and is absolutely nothing I can do about that, even if I had the volition. Nor was it my passive complicity in the flawed self-portraiture of those confessing. What made me weary was the relentless irony of my position, of having to explain to these people, from behind the veil, the meanings, illusions, and rules of their own exclusive civilization. I was getting nothing — no tribute, no offerings — for being an oracle. There are several ways of seeing this irony. One is that it approximates Mammy in *Gone with the Wind* yelling to Miss Scarlett:

> "If you don't care what folks says about this family, I does. I have done tole you and tole you that you can always tell a lady by the way that she eats in front of folks like a bird. And I ain't aimin' for you to go to Mr. John Wilkerses and eat like a field-hand and gobble like a hog . . ."

Mammy is *maitresse* and perpetuator of an etiquette that denies her own human worth. I once had to explain to a class of mine, nearly half of whom consciously thought of themselves as Irish-American, what "lace curtain" and "shanty" meant in the story we were reading.

Another way of looking at the irony is as Richard Wright in *American Hunger* did, seeing it as filled with tragic dimensions:

> Perhaps it would be possible for the Negro to become reconciled to his plight if he could be made to believe that his sufferings were for some remote, high, sacrificial end; but sharing the culture that condemns him, and seeing that a lust for trash is what blinds the nation to his claims, is what sets storms to rolling in his soul.

And another is to see the whole mess as a joke, as illusory and absurd as it can be. The last time I was in a position to play mother confessor to a penitent I smiled demurely, and in broken English from the French, said I did not speak English very well and that I had to go about my beesnez.

My father smiled.

I told him about a picnic I had attended once, given by the senior members of my department for the junior staff. Paraphrasing Moses, the senior staff had said, "I hear murmurings of the children of the department, which they murmur against me." One of us had been heard murmuring, cursing our lot. Having been told we had no hope of tenure, to greater and lesser extents we felt devalued by the senior staff; here we were, a mass of youthful brilliance withering on the vine. The collective Moses sought to assuage our sorrow, which, of course, a picnic would do.

Naturally we all had to go. The double bind was on; staying away would have been stupid — enough about withering, if the vine is pruned the flower dies — as well as churlish. The day of the picnic was one of those Saturday spring mornings on the damp side, a little chilly and rather hazy; what some people call good weather for spring but that I find irritating.

I haven't been to a lot of picnics, but they have a special reserved, idealized place in my memory. Picnics are for summer, for windless hot days near lakes or rivers. They are for my mother's fried chicken, baked beans, potato salad, deviled eggs, and communally bought orange pop; for Neapolitan ice cream squares in white paper wrappers that stick to the magical dry ice in the cooler; for games of bid-whist and bridge, our minister in collar and jeans presiding; for the pious lady who sits in the first pew, weekly marching up and down the aisle for two round trips to the bathroom, now in a yellow caftan with matching bandanna, eating sweet potato pie and drinking something that looks like iced coffee but I bet isn't;

for standing in the outfield, the only girl, with about eight boys and men, hoping a ball will be hit to me; for dirty, nasty little boys finding snakes, worms, dead anythings, and something called "used condoms." But I knew from the outset that this one would be quite different; indeed all omens suggested a once-in-a-lifetime experience. So I gathered my less expensive, blue, Lou Brock autographed mitt, got in my car, and headed out. The buildings all along the drive out of the town looked indistinct and blurry. I anticipated high humidity and heat for the afternoon; I didn't know what else to expect.

Like any profession, the academic world has its proprieties, and English departments in particular are famous for theirs. Convention and ritual are extraordinarily important. There are many unstated dos and don'ts that are factored in with scholarly prowess and teaching skills when the elect review the credentials of the postulants for tenure. And the wisest know that a social misstep may be judged as great a heresy as publishing an article in which the department chairman and his literary methods are called old fartish. From my experience there are several givens: one, junior staffers are not required to reciprocate dinners they have attended at senior staffers' homes. The rationale for this is that even though it may look like a social function, it isn't. We're not talking about equals hooraying it up around the standing rib roast.

Two, any statements made, in formal or informal circumstances, can and will be used against underlings — or even for them — in closed and open departmental meetings. The wisest know that controlling the nature and range of their gossip is an effective way of keeping some control over their lives. I was once at a large faculty reception where a wife of one of the tenured professors had a mimeographed sheet with "data" on the newly hired. This crib sheet included information on the educational backgrounds, marital status, living arrangements, fields of expertise, sexual preferences, hobbies, and known shortcomings of the new crop of professors. The only rule that I know the wife broke was being careless with the data sheet so that one of the depicted saw it.

Three, if a senior member of a department congratulates a junior member on the high quality of his or her work, the recipient of the praise should rush for pen and paper and ask that it be put in writing. Failure to do this often results in confusion when the junior staffer is fired; he or she may rush to challenge with a "But you said . . ." only to receive a bland, "Yes. So?" as a response.

Fourth, but beyond the control of many, it is wise to avoid being female, Jewish, or black.

As far as I was concerned, I was going to the picnic in the name of solidarity with my fellow junior colleagues, one of whom had committed a don't by being heard complaining. I reasoned also that it might be worth it to see how the other half lived.

I arrived at the picnic, held on the grounds of a summer home belonging to one of the department's *éminences grises*. I was met by several wives, some of whom I had seen before: "So very, very happy to see you. We're so glad you could come." I found some of my colleagues — who had been greeted in exactly the same way — and we were given tours of the immediate area and house, served beer and wine from the kitchen, and sent to sit out on the lawn on chairs or blankets and enjoy the sun. Increasingly, as more people arrived, my friends and I began to notice how graciously we were being treated and served without the glint of sarcasm in a role-reversing scene that might well have been expected from a lawn full of Anglophiles.

Two things stand out from this picnic: the first is that I was sitting with friends eating and talking when the very accomplished wife of another senior member of the department joined us. The eating groups had formed themselves around power lines and this was obviously distressing to some of our hosts. So, they spread out. Our group had just finished eating when I winked at my best friend in the department, a European, who was sitting next to me, and asked her, in most sub-servient terms and accent dating from a darker hour in American history, whether I could take her plate to the trash basket. Winking back, she said curtly, in a British accent, "Of course; you're being slow today. And I need more celery." At which point I nodded and did the chore. The wife of the senior member was aghast; I found out later that she chastised my friend the following Monday for "treating" me so. My friend was furious but bit her tongue. I smiled, shook my head, and explained that in spite of the fact that I had initiated the whole thing and that the two of us were known as fast friends, there were layers of absurdity in American race relations that per-haps she didn't understand. I had been patronized before and I would be again. She knit her brow and softly asked me if it would have made any difference if she were American. I told her yes, and that her foreignness probably saved her from God knew what else.

The other thing I remember is a scene that was filled with so much ritual and drama that I have never been able to sepa-rate it from memories of Federico García Lorca's play, *The House of Bernarda Alba*, that solemn tragedy of repression and death. Earlier that spring the department had lost its premier *éminence grise* to the Great Leveler. Most of us at the picnic had not seen his widow since the memorial service weeks before. Slowly, in broken formation, alone or in twos and threes, we processed to another part of the grounds, over a short ridge to a meadow. There, on a white, wrought-iron bench placed under the trees and next to a brook, as if awaiting the arrival of the procession, sat the widow, in black widow's weeds, com-plete with mantilla over a large comb. I have not traveled widely, and I believe that if I had I might not have been so astonished by the sight before me. The only full widow's weeds I could recall having ever seen were in a poorly dubbed Spanish film I saw late one night on cable TV, though surely Maria Ouspenskaya wore them in something. And the only Roman Catholic mass I ever attended was in Denver, where

everyone was dressed in shorts and tennis shoes. It is important to note, too, that the illustrious departmental pair had
been neither Spanish nor Catholic.

It had become very hot. There was no breeze and although
it was bright, high clouds blocked the sun. The air was thick
and there was this peculiar silence as we all paid our respects
to la dueña and the softball game began. I think I lent my Lou
Brock special to the collective outfield and watched the game,
sipping a beer.

My father arched his right eyebrow and smiled.

The dessert menu came around and Daddy probably ate
something with chocolate in it. I passed; I'm not big on sweets.
We finished and left the restaurant. As the taxi bounced and
lurched on Seventy-ninth Street, cutting west across Central
Park, I asked him if he confronted the same sorts of things in
his work that I did in mine. He said the form was the same,
but that the circumstances were occasionally rawer and the
people less sophisticated. We bounced up Broadway in silence. He bit his lower lip and looked out the window and said
that he didn't know whether things would ever change; that
being black meant that one was both an individual and an
anonymous representative of the black group; that he felt the
real reason why black children, traditionally, were told they
had to be twice as good and work twice as hard as whites to
get anywhere was to make them create for themselves enough
space to be themselves.

"Do you know why I like holidays?" he asked me.

"Sure," I answered. "They provide a good excuse for you
to go out and buy presents that you can't afford."

"Humph," he said. "I like them because I can surprise your
mother and razz you kids to death and that makes up for the
rest. What do you have?" he asked me, his head bowed a bit.

"I don't know, Daddy," I said. I wanted to cry; I kept swallowing. "I have you all. I suppose I'm still looking for something else; I don't have the slightest idea what it is."

We got back to the apartment and switched on the lights, and he asked me how come I didn't have any roaches, like everybody else in New York? I said that after two months of concerted effort with boric acid the largest roach I'd ever seen came waltzing out, in broad daylight, onto the kitchen counter. With front legs akimbo this roach asked me what the hell I was trying to do. I told him I was just trying to create some place where I could live and that meant steeling myself from all sorts of things, like roaches. I vaporized him with a can of Raid.

Where I Lived, and
What I Lived For

WE DROVE WEST on Highway 40 in a 1958 powder-blue Buick Special two-door coupe, loaded to the fins with family and baggage. We were on our way to Kansas City from Dayton, moving away from Grandma's house toward independence. Our emotions were quite mixed. Daddy had been promoted, was going to head the Kansas City office; he knew the city, had worked there for two years when I was an infant; he had friends and contacts there. Doubtless he was sorry to be leaving his mother and sister behind, but the job dictates — that's the way the game is played in the United States. Mother was delighted to be getting out from under the glare and thumb of her mother-in-law to set up her own home once again.

My sister was devastated. She had always attended well integrated schools and was able to avoid most of the racial epithets and tensions of my grade school. She loved her high school, had won a trophy for being the best sophomore Spanish speaker, had traveled widely through the state with the chorus, had a boyfriend and many pals, loved the church choir and all the activities there for teenagers. We didn't bother each other in the back seat of the car for the whole trip; she rolled herself into a ball in the corner and when she was not sleeping she silently counted the miles, swallowing hard, her jaw tight.

I didn't know what to think. I was happy to be leaving our basement life in Grandma's house and the crude varieties of my experiences at school. I would miss the church, too, but there were far fewer children my age there; it didn't have the strong social pull for me. But I wasn't excited at all about moving to Missouri. If we had to go somewhere why wasn't it Los Angeles to be with Nana and Papa, or New York, or Philadelphia? I was a voracious map reader in those days and from what I could see, Missouri was smack dab in the middle of the country, but "slave state" and the Missouri Compromise kept ringing in my ear and I was terrified at the thought of moving to the South.

The trip took nearly a whole day. We quickly crossed the border into Indiana, a state my father was fond of saying was a geographical mutation, belonging in its sensibilities next to Mississippi, and not to the northern industrial sector. Traffic was fairly heavy on the two-lane highway and it was raining. Watching the road constantly, hanging over the front bench seat behind my mother, I would look for license plates I'd never seen before, and cringe when I saw Roadway and Campbell's "Humpin' to Please" trucks playing highway tag, dangerously passing each other with inches to spare and spraying our windshield with muddy water. Cars in those days didn't come equipped with sprayers. I couldn't sleep, didn't want to. I was too excited at the idea of being in motion; I wondered why Daddy would pull the car off the road every now and then and sleep for a couple of hours.

There were no places to stop for food, restaurants were segregated; we ate a picnic lunch on the fly, Daddy asking my sister to peel him a boiled egg or hand him a cheese sandwich. We drank Coke — the kind they really don't make anymore — from gas station vending machines, the heavy effervescence getting in my nose and always making me belch.

We approached the outskirts of Kansas City at dawn, the

sky coming alive in segments as if someone were turning on the switches to light up a vast stage. My sister was awake as we passed the city limits sign; sounding like a weary conductor calling the last stop, she announced "Kansas City. Kansas City." The sky was pink, turning blue, and streetlamps began popping off on the horizon as we drove down the last undulating hill into the city I would reluctantly call home.

We moved into the black section of town, where large homes, shaded by elms, had limestone foundations and frame tops. It was hilly and hot. I understood the need for the large porches that appeared to be on every house in the neighborhood. The pace of life was slower; it seemed to take an age for people to finish a sentence, but in church they appeared less relaxed than in Ohio. There was one black radio station that played rhythm and blues; the others, pop standards mixed with country and western music. If Missouri had been a border state in the Civil War, Kansas City appeared to me still to be a border town, caught somewhere between the West, the South, and the North, the rural and the urban, the sophisticated and the country.

The nights were eerie to me there. Like Huck a hundred years before, on the other side of the state, in another world, the wind "made the cold shivers run over me." I never got used to it. And I was terrified of the storms that would come in spring and summer, with warnings of severe weather and tornados and the peculiar stillness in the air just before all hell broke loose.

Over the years I made my peace with the city, relishing the barbecue from Gates and Bryant's, looking forward to the Christmas lights that glowed on the Country Club Plaza. I remember Daddy saying that in order to get Count Basie out of town he had to be drugged. That I couldn't understand, but I enjoyed my friends and school as the pace of life quickened and my expectations were ignited by the promises of the 1960s. There in the "Heart of America," as they called it, I advanced into puberty, and I dreamed of a future and a place where I would find contentment.

Thoreau wrote in the "Where I Lived, and What I Lived For" section of *Walden*:

> I went to the woods because I wished to live deliberately, to front only the essential facts of life, and see if I could not learn what it had to teach, and not, when I came to die, discover that I had not lived. I did not wish to live what was not life, living is so dear; nor did I wish to practise resignation, unless it was quite necessary. I wanted to live deep and suck out all the marrow of life, to live so sturdily and Spartan-like as to put to rout all that was not life, to cut a broad swath and shave close, to drive life into a corner, and reduce it to its lowest terms, and, if it proved to be mean, why then to get the whole and genuine meanness of it, and publish its meanness to the world; or if it were sublime, to know it by experience, and be able to give a true account of it in my next excursion.

My colleagues would blush for and at me, suspecting me of internalizing too pure a dose of Thoreau — one isn't supposed to get emotionally involved — but I don't mind. I had no carefully orchestrated two years at a Walden Pond, but there was plenty of nature in Kansas City. Like Langston Hughes with his "I like wild people much better than I do wild animals," I spent my time watching, studying the world around me, trying to capture the meaning of everything that went into my creation, hoping I'd be alert and alive to possibility wherever I saw it. As I grew older I realized there was a greater dimension to what I had to try to understand — that more than just scrutinizing things or people I needed to recognize the connections between them. Another Thoreauvian, Martin Luther King, Jr., wrote in his "Letter from Birmingham Jail": "We are caught in an inescapable network of mutuality, tied in a single garment of destiny. Whatever affects one directly affects all indirectly." As a black American it was so easy to see and feel the effects of acts done by others. From the perspective of my blackness the connections were so clear. Emmett Till tortured past recognition; Rosa Parks, exhausted, boarding a Montgomery bus; Orville Faubus, George Wallace calling out the Guard; a gunshot in Dallas, another in Jackson, another in New York City, another in Memphis, another in Los Angeles; *Sputnik* launched, *Challenger* exploding; a Bay of Pigs invasion, a storming of Grenada; *Brown v. Topeka* in 1954, a euphemism called "forced bussing" in the 1970s; a Watergate, a disinformation campaign; a life spent working for equal opportunity, three sheets of yellow legal paper enigmatically beginning a tale — I have seen and felt the ripples, the obvious race-linked ones, the others obvious because of "where" I lived. And I taught American literature emphasizing the connections. Sometimes it went well, sometimes it didn't, but I could never conceive of any other approach.

Montaigne, addressing the subject of his lifelong career, wrote:

> And if no one reads me, have I wasted my time, entertaining myself for so many idle hours with such useful and agreeable thoughts? In modelling this figure upon myself, I have had to fashion and compose myself so often to bring myself out, that the model itself has to some extent grown firm and taken shape. Painting myself for others, I have painted my inward self with colors clearer than my original ones. I have no more made my book than my book has made me — a book consubstantial with its author, concerned with my own self, an integral part of my life; not concerned with some third-hand, extraneous purpose, like all other books. Have I wasted my time by taking stock of myself so continually, so carefully? For those who go over themselves only in their minds and occasionally speech do not penetrate to essentials in their examinations as does a man who makes that his study, his work, and his trade, who binds himself to keep an enduring account, with all his faith, with all his strength.

Three already yellow sheets of paper were the only self-created record my father left. I don't know, given the radically different circumstances of his life, whether imitating Montaigne would have interested him very much. But given the clarity of his insight and the fine quality of his humor, I suspect he would have done a wonderful job of it — with a leaf of collard green.

What I learned through the years was that my father, my mother, my sister, my grandparents, all my family — the sinews that linked us, the paths and processes of our lives separately and together, and the illusions and absurdities of the world — became vivid for me when I read those sheets of paper. In my quest to know the difference between illusion and that loaded word, reality, I slowly came to realize that I could not exist, that I had no memory, no consciousness, no sight, no hearing, no touch, without the pure simplicity and utter intricacy of the fabric woven of my life and the lives of my family. My book is "consubstantial with its author*s*." Trying to understand their lives and mine became most assuredly what I lived for.

During that turbulent tenth year of my life I spent every night for about three weeks trying to get off to sleep, but I couldn't. I was plagued by thoughts of nothingness. It might have been an aftershock of the San Francisco earthquake. I would toss and turn and then look out the window of a door that led to the roof, directly across from my bed. Often I could get a glimpse of stars and sometimes the moon, still rising, as I gripped the sheets, my heart racing, my breathing irregular, perspiration forming at my temples. Looking out the window at the stars I was overwhelmed with my insignificance as a human being on the planet Earth. I was filled with cosmic dread at the thought that inevitably I would have no consciousness, no sight, no hearing, no touch. It was a profound and terrifying atheism no Christian eschatalogy could touch.

The anxiety would last for hours, broken only when I embarrassed myself by calling for my mother. I would not tell her what was troubling me — I didn't know how to say it — but I would moan that I did not feel well. She would feel my hot forehead, assume that I had one of my many childhood fevers, tuck me in, and tell me that I would be fine. After that I could manage to drift off to sleep.

After three weeks I made a pact with myself to concentrate on other thoughts when I went to bed. I would pull down the shade on the door window and put a little transistor radio next to my pillow, falling to sleep to country music on the only station I could get. Unfortunately for my mother, the days of checking on me were not over; the radio, turned off, would be sitting on the little desk next to my bed when I awoke.

It was not an immediate, conscious reaction, but gradually, after my three weeks of angst, I began to look harder at the world around me. It seemed to me that being alive meant one series of difficulties after another. I thought the lives of the adults around me were extremely complex. There was so much to know, and although many things came easily to me, I did not believe that I could possibly learn enough to survive. Contemplating nothingness left me with no alternative but to think harder about what I could see; everything else was beyond my control.

Elm trees that lined the streets were dying of disease and being cut down, leaving a new, too-bright light on the streets as I dragged school bag, gym bag, and violin case home from school. Television showed me pictures of racial violence, of Herculean struggle against perverse, state-sponsored terrorism as white America resisted school desegregation. Two teachers and five students — hysterical during a severe thunderstorm — froze on the stairwell as we were ordered to the basement while air raid sirens announced the sighting of a tornado in the area. Satellites were being launched into outer space. Educators told us we had to do better in math and science to catch up with the Russians. We drilled for air raids

259

and learned words like "thermonuclear war." And I would see my father at the breakfast table, up long before the rest of us, silently looking out the window, finishing his first pot of coffee, his head resting against his hand.

Notes

Antidisestablishmentarianism:

James Baldwin, *The Devil Finds Work* (New York: The Dial Press, 1976), 21.

Do He Have Your Number, Mr. Jeffrey?:

Michael Wood, *America in the Movies* (New York: Basic Books, Inc., 1975), 16.

On Andrew Wyeth, Checked Suits, Broken Hair, Busted Dreams, and Transcendence:

Roland Barthes, *La chambre claire* (Paris: Cahiers du Cinéma, Gallimard Seuil, 1980), 183–184.

Roland Barthes, *Camera Lucida*, transl. Richard Howard (New York: Hill and Wang, 1981), 119.

"All Glory, Laud, and Honor," *The Hymnal 1940*, no. 62 (New York: The Church Hymnal Corporation, 1940).

Barthes, *Camera Lucida* 106.

Barthes, *Camera Lucida* 118.

Alain Locke, ed., *The New Negro*, 1925. Reprint. (New York: Atheneum, 1968), 7.

Barthes, *Camera Lucida* 106.

Barthes, *Camera Lucida* 117.

Barthes, *Camera Lucida* 76.

Betsy Wyeth, quoted in the *New York Times*, 11 August 1986, Section III, 1.

"O Sacred head, sore wounded," *The Hymnal* 1940, no. 75.

On the Lower Frequencies:

"Brother, Can You Spare a Dime?" E. Y. Harburg, music and Jay Gorney, lyrics, New York: Harms Publishing Company, 1932.

F. Scott Fitzgerald, "The Ice Palace," in *Babylon Revisited and Other Stories* (New York: Charles Scribner's Sons, 1960), 9.

W. E. B. Du Bois, *The Souls of Black Folk* (Chicago: A. C. McClurg & Co., 1907), vii.

Du Bois, *Souls of Black Folk* 3-4.

W. E. B. Du Bois, *Dusk of Dawn*, 1940. Reprint. (New York: Schocken Books, 1968), 186.

Du Bois, *Dusk of Dawn* 173.

Booker T. Washington, "The Road to Negro Progress," reprinted in *The Annals of America*, Vol. 12, 1895-1904 (Chicago: Encyclopedia Britannica, 1968), 10.

Letter from W. E. B. Du Bois to Booker T. Washington, reprinted in *The Correspondence of W. E. B. Du Bois*, Vol. 1 (Amherst: University of Massachusetts Press, 1973), 39.

Letter from Garrett Distributing Co. to W. E. B. Dubois, in *Correspondence* 223.

Letter from W. E. B. Du Bois to Garrett Distributing Co., in *Correspondence* 223.

The Koan of Nana:

Phyllis Rose, *Writing of Women* (Middletown, Ct.: Wesleyan University Press, 1985), 135.

Gloria Naylor, "Hers" column, *New York Times*, 6 February 1986, Section C, 2.

Ralph Ellison, *Invisible Man* (New York: Random House, 1952), 13.

Ellison, *Invisible Man* 438.

W. E. B. Du Bois, "Social Evolution of the Black South," *American Negro Monographs, I*, March 1911. Reprinted in Elliott M. Rudwick, *W. E. B. Du Bois, Propagandist of the Negro Protest* (New York: Atheneum, 1968), 149.

Richard Wright, *Native Son* (New York: Harper & Row, 1940), 82.

Ellison, *Invisible Man* 395.

Toni Morrison, *Tar Baby* (New York: Alfred A. Knopf, 1981), 45–46.

Morrison, *Tar Baby* 113.

Morrison, *Tar Baby* 219.

Zora Neale Hurston, *Their Eyes Were Watching God* (Greenwich, Ct.: Fawcett Publications, 1965), 159.

Inner Lives:

Susan Sontag, *On Photography* (New York: Farrar, Straus and Giroux, 1978), 23.

I Light Out for the Territory:

Mackay-Radio News, U.S.A. Copyright Press New York, 12 August 1966, 13 August 1966.

Hart Crane, "Chaplinesque," in *The Complete Poems and Selected Letters and Prose of Hart Crane*, ed. Brom Weber (Garden City, NY: Anchor Books/Doubleday, 1966), 11.

Professor Dearest:

George Bernard Shaw, *Pygmalion*, in *Complete Plays with Prefaces*, Vol. I (New York: Dodd, Mead & Co., 1963), 270.

Simone de Beauvoir, *America Day by Day*, trans. Patrick Dudley (New York: Grove Press, 1953), 60.

The Zen of Bigger Thomas:

Marianne Moore, "Picking and Choosing," in *The Complete Poems of Marianne Moore* (New York: The Macmillan Co./The Viking Press, 1967), 45.

Ellison, *Invisible Man* 268.

Wright, *Native Son* 256.

Ellison, *Invisible Man* 437–438.

Wallace Stevens, "Sunday Morning," in *The Collected Poems of Wallace Stevens* (New York: Alfred A. Knopf, 1968), 67, 70.

Waiting for Godot on Jeffery Boulevard:

Benjamin J. Davis, "Why I Am a Communist," *Phylon* 8, no. 2 (Second Quarter 1947), 106–107.

Dorothy Butler Gilliam, *Paul Robeson, All American* (Washington, D.C.: The New Republic Book Co., Inc., 1976), 15.

T. S. Eliot, "The Hollow Men," in *The Complete Poems and Plays* (New York: Harcourt, Brace and World, 1971), 59.

Eliot, "Four Quartets," in *Complete Poems* 144.

Mary Maples Dunn, "A Letter from the President," in *The News-Smith* 2, no. 1, (Winter 1987), 2.

Alexis de Tocqueville, Author's Introduction to *Democracy in America*, in *Annals of America*, Vol. 6, Encyclopedia Britannica, 211.

Tom Stoppard, *Rosencrantz and Guildenstern Are Dead* (New York: Grove Press, Inc., 1968), 124.

Stoppard, *Rosencrantz* 125.

The Anglophile Moment, Or: You Came a Long Way from Saint Louis:

"Editorial," Macon, Georgia *Telegraph*, quoted in "The Looking Glass," *The Crisis* 1, no. 13 (November 1916), 22.

John Winthrop, "A Modell of Christian Charity," in *The American Puritans: Their Prose and Poetry*, ed. Perry Miller (New York: Columbia University Press, 1956), 82.

Winthrop, *American Puritans* 83.

Sacvan Bercovitch, *The Puritan Origins of the American Self* (New Haven: Yale University Press, 1975), 186.

Nathaniel Ward, *The Simple Cobbler of Aggawam*, in Miller, 98.

Henning, II, *Virginia State Laws*, "On the Killing of Slaves (October 1669), in *Annals of America*, Vol. 1, Encyclopedia Britannica, p. 226.

Thomas Jefferson, *Notes on the State of Virginia* (New York: Norton, 1982, Copyright 1954 by the University of North Carolina Press, 142, 163.

Saunders Redding, "The Negro Writer and American Literature," in *Anger and Beyond*, ed. Herbert Hill (New York: Harper & Row, 1966), 16.

Hurston, *Watching God* 120.

W. E. B. Du Bois, "Social Evolution of the Black South," *American Negro Monographs, I*, March 1911, Reprinted in Elliott M. Rudwick, *W. E. B. Du Bois, Propagandist of the Negro Protest* (New York: Atheneum, 1968), 149.

O Porgy! O Bess!:

William Dean Howells, "Introduction," in Paul Laurence Dunbar, *Lyrics of Lowly Life* (New York: Dodd, Mead and Co., 1899), xviii.

Howells, *Lyrics of Lowly Life* xiv.

Jefferson, *Notes on the State* 140.

Paul Laurence Dunbar, "Unpublished Letters of Paul Laurence Dunbar to a Friend," *The Crisis* 20, no. 2 (April 1920), 73.

Dunbar, *Lyrics of Lowly Life* 110–111.

Toni Morrison, *Sula* (London: Allen Lane, 1974), 4.

Dunbar, *Lyrics of Lowly Life* 30–32.

Howells, *Lyrics of Lowly Life* xix.

Dunbar, *Lyrics of Lowly Life* 6.

Dunbar, *Lyrics of Lowly Life* 167.

Great Scenes from Gershwin's Porgy and Bess (New York: RCA Victor LSC-2679, 1963).

Serge Koussevitzky quoted in the *New York Times*, Vol. 85, no. 28, 1 October 1935, 27.

H. L. Mencken, "Editorial," *American Mercury* 12, no. 48 (October 1927), 159.

Du Bois, *The Souls of Black Folk* 5.

George and Ira Gershwin, "Summertime" (New York: Gershwin Publishing Corp., 1935).

Eudora Welty, "Why I Live at the P.O.," in *A Curtain of Green and Other Stories* (New York: Harcourt Brace Jovanovich, 1979), 109.

Eudora Welty, "Why I Live at the P.O.," in *The Collected Stories of Eudora Welty* (New York: Harcourt Brace Jovanovich, 1980), 56.

Porgy and Bess, music by George Gershwin, libretto by Du Bose Heyward, lyrics by Du Bose Heyward and Ira Gershwin (New York: Gershwin Publishing Corp.,1935), 311.

Porgy and Bess 316–318.

Joseph Lelyveld, "Britons Stirred by New 'Porgy' at Glyndebourne," *New York Times*, 8 July 1986, 15.

Langston Hughes, *The Panther and the Lash* (New York: Alfred A. Knopf, 1967), 81–83.

Oscar Hammerstein II, lyrics, Jerome Kern, music, "Ol' Man River" (New York: T. B. Harms Company, 1927).

Bernarda Alba's Picnic, Or: The Myth of the Eternal Return:

Gone with the Wind, David O. Selznick, producer, MGM, 1939.

Richard Wright, *American Hunger* (New York: Harper & Row, 1977), 14.

Where I Lived, and What I Lived For:

Henry David Thoreau, *Walden and Civil Disobedience* (New York: W. W. Norton, 1966), 61.

Milton Meltzer, *Langston Hughes: A Biography*, 1963. Reprint. (New York: Crowell), 1972, 252.

Martin Luther King, Jr., "Letter from Birmingham Jail," in *Annals of America*, Vol. 18, Encyclopedia Britannica, Chicago 1968, 144.

"Of Giving the Lie," in *The Complete Essays of Montaigne*, transl. Donald M. Frame (Stanford: Stanford University Press, 1971), 504.

1984

Photo by Katharine Stall

Gayle Pemberton was born in St. Paul, Minnesota. She has a B.A. in English from the University of Michigan and a Ph.D. in English and American Literature from Harvard University. She has taught at Smith College, Columbia University, Middlebury College, Northwestern University, Reed College, and Bowdoin College. She was associate director of African American Studies at Princeton before joining Wesleyan in 1994 as Chair of the African American Studies Program and William R. Kenan Professor of the Humanities in the English Department. She currently is under contract with W. W. Norton for a book entitled *And the Colored Girls Go . . . : Black Women and American Cinema.*

University Press of New England

publishes books under its own imprint and is the publisher for Brandeis University Press, Dartmouth College, Middlebury College Press, University of New Hampshire, Tufts University, and Wesleyan University Press.

LIBRARY OF CONGRESS CATALOGING-IN-PUBLICATION DATA

Pemberton, Gayle.
  The hottest water in Chicago : notes of a native daughter / Gayle Pemberton
        p.   cm.
  Includes bibliographical references (p.).
  ISBN 0–8195–6337–4 (pa : alk. paper)
    1. Afro-Americans—Social conditions.   2. United States—Race relations
  3. Pemberton, Gayle.   4. Pemberton family.
  5. Afro-American college teachers—biography.   I. Title.
  [E185.86P46 1998]
  305.896'073—dc21   97–42988